Marianne MacKinnon is a qualified translator and State Registered Nurse. She has taught German and English, worked as a court interpreter in the Far East, and travelled widely. She came to England in 1948 to work and study English. She married a Scotsman and has three sons. Marianne MacKinnon now lives near Glasgow. A prize-winning author of short stories and poetry, she is now working on a sequel to The Naked Years.

'A remarkable human and social document . . . the author resists the temptation to look back with hindsight. The result is a fresh and vivid book' – *The List*

'For the first time the shadowy, faceless enemy of our wartime years becomes flesh and blood. The cardboard cut-out Germans of film and fiction topple before this very real and moving picture of ordinary Germans at war . . . a most remarkable book' – Magnus Magnusson

THE NAKED YEARS

MARIANNE MACKINNON

Das ist der Weisheit letzter Schluss:
Nur der verdient sich Freiheit wie das Leben,
Der täglich sie erobern muss.

Goethe, *Faust*, II

CORGI BOOKS

For my sons

THE NAKED YEARS

A CORGI BOOK 0 552 99326 3

Originally published in Great Britain by Chatto & Windus

PRINTING HISTORY
Chatto & Windus edition published 1987
Corgi edition published 1989

The characters portrayed in this book are real and the events described took place, but fictional names have been used in parts to protect the privacy of those referred to.

This book is set in 10/11 Sabon

Corgi Books are published by Transworld Publishers Ltd., 61–63 Uxbridge Road, Ealing, London W5 5SA, in Australia by Transworld Publishers (Australia) Pty. Ltd., 15–23 Helles Avenue, Moorebank, NSW 2170, and in New Zealand by Transworld Publishers (N.Z.) Ltd., Cnr. Moselle and Waipareira Avenues, Henderson, Auckland.

Made and printed in Great Britain by
The Guernsey Press Co. Ltd., Guernsey, Channel Islands

Contents

List of Illustrations

The author at her school desk
The author at the age of five
On the steps of the primary school
The study in the author's grandparents' house
The salon
The opening ceremony of the Berlin Olympics
The flagged Unter den Linden
Potsdam before the Allied air raid
Potsdam before the air raid, with the dome of the
Nikolaikirche in the background
The Home
The author at the age of ten
The author's secondary school in Potsdam
The author at the age of fourteen
The baron's villa in Potsdam
The lake and the Marmorpalais in Potsdam
The author competing in Potsdam stadium
The author being interviewed by a sports reporter
Running a rural Kindergarten
Cocoa time
Playing games
The council chamber at Tangermünde
Tante Bertha's house
The author shortly before leaving for England
The author's mother in 1950
The author's father

PROLOGUE

A Midwinter Adventure

Germany, 1946: British Zone of Occupation

'Remember, once we're there, it's every man for himself. We'll make the border just before dawn, that's when they're changing over. It's the best time. One lot is waiting to turn in, the other hasn't quite sobered up yet. They drink vodka like water, I hear. But make no mistake: when they come on duty, they don't fall over their own feet, and they're always quick on their triggers. Be ready at four o'clock sharp. The going will be slow once we reach the woods. Keep close to each other, and no talking! On a night like this you can hear voices for miles.'

The guide's instructions had been explicit.

The forest is dense and dark, the narrow footpath barely visible in the pale light of the sky, against which the jagged ridges of conifer tops stand out as dim silhouettes. We are walking in single file, stealthily, like deerstalkers, a silent procession resenting each crackle of dead branches underfoot and the sound of shoulders brushing against the undergrowth. There are no lanterns, no torches, no lights to give away our presence, for not even the guide knows the exact point where the strip of no-man's-land begins, nor how far Soviet border patrols might venture into the British Zone at night. A sense of danger is tangible, is growing more acute with every step that brings us closer to the border and with every hoot owls are sending out into the night like warning calls. I am trying to keep close to the man in front, now and then touching the hard, bulging mass of his rucksack, so as not to loosen my link of the human chain. And, as my eyes are straining to pick up any grain of light, my ears any sound that might threaten our clandestine track, the main obstacle still waiting ahead looms in my mind like a wall spiked with broken glass.

It is bitterly cold. The frost of the small hours is clawing at my face, and soon it no longer respects the threadbare fabric of my gloves and socks, nor is it deterred by the thin barrier of my coat which has seen many wartime winters.

I remember *Herr* Schuster mapping out my route to Berlin, from the small West German town in the British Occupation Zone to the border village in the Harz Mountains where, with some luck, he reckoned, I might slip across the new arbitrary frontier into the Russian Zone.

'Of course, as long as the border is closed and there are no travel permits for German civilians, you'll be taking a risk, just like the others. But once you're on the other side and have put a few kilometres between yourself and the Russian border guards, you ought to be safe. Try and skirt the first village and on no account use the main road!'

Surely, I thought, *Herr* Schuster, the sly fox and inscrutable postwar operator, ought to know.

The war has been over for eighteen months, yet here we are trying to steal across the border like smugglers, escaped prisoners or a wartime reconnaissance patrol – just one batch out of thousands of German civilians bent on reaching East or West under cover of darkness. For a few hours, for the final critical minutes, I am one of them, one of that desperate throng of people driven by the human need for love and roots, by an urgency which does not recognise a drawing-board divide, being stronger than the fear of capture by Russian border guards and, with six days to go before Christmas, more frantic and poignant than ever.

I do not know the names of the men and women I had joined at nightfall. In the dim light of the barn, where we were to await the arrival of a guide, my own anxiety had barely allowed me to register their faces, though I had sensed around me that unmistakable air of urgency and intensity of purpose which, like fear, pungently clings to a person.

Before retreating into a waiting silence, or to the hayloft for a few hours' sleep, many of them had explained their motivation in cryptic sentences as if to justify, before their would-be companions of the night, the risk they were about to take.

'I've been trying to track down my children since the end of the war. They were evacuated from Upper Silesia . . .'

'I've been discharged from a British POW camp. Family lives on the other side . . .'

'I'm hoping to join my husband. I've just had word. He's back from Siberia . . . been working in a mine for four years . . . says his lungs are in a mess . . .'

'He's lucky to have made it at all! I'm still searching for mine. Called up last month of the war he was . . . *Volkssturm* . . . on his sixtieth birthday! I hear there is a place . . .'

'I've got a new lead on my son . . . someone thinks he's seen him in a hospital near Küstrin . . .'

'I'm hoping to visit my mother in Berlin,' I had chipped in. 'I haven't seen her for almost two years.'

Some had remained silent, perhaps suspiciously so. But no one had felt inclined, or had been inquisitive enough, to ask questions. But then it was common knowledge that not only desperate souls were attempting to sneak across, East or West, and that not everybody was hoping to return to a place which had once been home, or which might provide new roots, just as not every man smuggling himself into the Western Zones was escaping from a communist system and Soviet *Komendaturas*. Indeed, even the papers were spelling it out now, loud and clear, claiming that many a *Grenzgänger*,[1] his conscience full of Nazi or SS crimes, was 'trying to shake off the bloodhounds by seeking a new identity on the other side of the fence'.

One by one we emerge from the forest, and I make out acres of flat ground ahead – white fields over which the moon has thinned the night, and which will not afford cover. How many steps, how many anxious metres to the invisible border? Fifty? A hundred?

'This is it!' the guide whispers. 'This is as far as I'm taking you. You're on your own now. Good luck!'

I am making a dash for it, keeping low, crawling along a frozen furrow or crouching, motionless, whenever I hear voices in the distance. Progress, dictated by fear and caution, is slow.

Suddenly, shots are ripping across the field, are slashing at the fringe of dawn which is beginning to mark the horizon. I throw myself on the ground, my heart pounding furiously, my body edging forwards, moulding itself into a shallow trench.

[1] Person crossing a frontier.

11

'*Russen!*' a man hisses not far from me. His voice is faceless, his body a mere rise in the ground.

There is no telling how close the Russians are, and whether they have been strafing the field with intent to kill or merely firing rounds into the air to keep their prey pinned down. Pressed against a pincushion of frozen, stubbly soil, I feel the frost rushing into my bones, numbing toes and fingers. Infinitesimal shifts of position do not afford much relief. Shall I take a chance and run? Where are the others? Have they made it? How alien, how hostile the ground feels on this side of the border! Yet this too is Germany, and the war has long been over . . .

Shouts in Russian, rough soldiers' voices, a barrage of commands. They are closing in on us. Perhaps there is still time to run? If only I had the courage! But then, perhaps it takes more courage to stay put and live?

The fear of rape hits my empty stomach like a boxer's fist; it is pressing my thighs together. What would rape be like? Would it make me die slowly inside, and afterwards torment me forever with a sense of defilement, a disgust for my body? Was there not ample evidence for such humiliations in recent history? I remember zonal newspapers confirming personal and eye-witness accounts, recording, making official, what one columnist had termed 'the sexual abuse of the German woman in the final drama of the war'. And I can still hear refugees in shop queues and in the market square narrating the harrowing experiences of women brutally raped by Russian soldiers during their advance on Berlin and in the course of their protracted victory celebrations.

'It didn't matter how old a woman was, what she looked like or to what class she belonged.'

'To *Iwan*,[2] a skirt was a skirt!'

'It was the second wave, the rough lot, the pock-marked or slit-eyed bastards, those who came up behind their élite troops!'

Others were more blunt.

'A quick lay in a barn, in a cellar, in some ruins, while their comrades were queuing up.'

'In our village – one soldier after the other – the whole night. It was awful. Two women, neighbours of mine, hanged themselves, another bled to death. O God! I can still hear them scream.'

[2] Russky (colloquial).

And among the ghastly echoes of the past, I thought, weren't there accounts of how even a nun's air of prayer and charity, her cross and the sexlessness of her habit had failed to protect her from violation?

Heavy footsteps are crunching nearer. The seconds are drumming away as they had done in the cellar of the Berlin tenement, the night the whistling of the *Luftmine*[3] overhead had suddenly, and all too ominously, stopped. My mind creates split-second images – a cornfield, yellow and undulating, speckled with poppies.

'*Vstani!*'[4]

I stare at a human shape which has emerged from the paling greyness, at straddling, tough-booted legs, at a gun barrel, at metal which is gleaming faintly in the dawn.

Rifle butts are shoving us into line and prod us forward like cattle. Like cattle we walk, mutely, our heads lowered. In the rising sun, bulky shapes are growing into grey-coated figures, and voices take form. I feel the hard, urging push of a rifle in my side and look up into the slanting eyes of a mounted Mongolian soldier, into a face which rouses instant memories of history classes and coloured illustrations: Genghis Khan and his rampant Asian hordes riding away from pillage, conflagration and massacre . . .

I draw closer to the man in front, using his back as a shield against the soldier's sly and glowering look.

A farmhouse, barns, stables, blots of habitation set into the seeming vastness of wintry fields which, in the east and northeast, are bounded by the higher ranges of the Harz Mountains. Soviet army jeeps; a brightly-lit farmyard; a sign in cyrillic lettering; the smell of horses, petrol and cabbage.

Commands and hard metal are pushing us into the house like sheep through a stile. We cross a low-ceilinged guardroom crammed with maps, wooden tables and field telephones, yet still hinting – with its tiled stove, a heavily fringed lampshade and an Alpine picture on the wall – at former Sunday parlour *gemütlichkeit*.

[3] Huge parachuted bomb ('blockbuster').
[4] 'Get up!'

13

Another room. Flaking wallpaper, cyrillic graffiti, a littered table. The male prisoners are sidling, the women tiptoeing, past a row of camp beds and stocky, square-shouldered men. I duck under the leering eyes of peasants who are fingering their crotches or ponderously stroking their chins at the sight of female prisoners. An effluvium of massed, ill-constrained virility fills the room. Tentacles seem to reach out, groping under the women's skirts and slipping up their rough-stockinged legs . . .

Pulling my coat tighter around me, I stumble up a narrow staircase with the rest of the group, noting with relief that the clatter of our wooden soles is drowning the soldiers' catcalls.

Our prison, an empty room, is dark, except for fractured light which threads through the cracks of boarded-up windows. A key turns in the lock, heavy boots retreat down the staircase, the room grows quiet. And now, time seems to drip through the hourglass like treacle.

It was a strange fellowship in which, through Russian whim or policy, men and women suddenly found themselves. Sitting on the naked floorboards, with not an inch to spare between the bodies of strangers, no one appeared to mind an enforced propinquity which afforded warmth and support. Someone opened the door to an adjoining room, and quickly shut it again. The overpowering stench of human excrement left no doubt about the customs of our captors.

During the day, yet more prisoners were crammed into the room, until the solid human mass would give no further. As the hours passed and discomfort began to spread, requests to shift a foot or lift the weight off a shoulder often evoked the kind of wry, humorous comment which tries to make light of a desperate situation. Physical relief was, however, possible only in the revolting room next door, which, in the dark, felt underfoot like the forecourt to hell, and access to which called for a major shifting operation. Matches from smokers, lit in turn whenever the occasion demanded, provided a flickering, ghostly light, only to deepen the darkness once they had gone out.

We knew night had come when the husky voices downstairs grew louder, the laughter higher-pitched. There came the sound of breaking glass, and as deft fingers began to play the accordion, the scene downstairs exploded with boisterous singing and the rhythmical stamping of boots. It was not long before the door was unlocked and a torch tossed its naked light on the nearest woman prisoner.

'*Frau komm!*' a rasping voice commanded. More boots pounded up the stairs, torches penetrated deeper into the room, resting on each individual face.

'Put your hair up, girl!' a man next to me whispered. 'Here, let me help you.' A peaked cap was pulled over my head, a cold pipe found its way into my mouth and the collar of my coat was clumsily raised. 'Don't hide your face, pretend indifference!'

When the light reached my face, it seemed to hesitate, to linger in indecision on a young man's complexion, on shapely lips which sucked an empty pipe with the devotion of a life-long smoker – seconds only, but long enough to feel my feet slipping over the edge of a precipice. Slowly the beam crawled on and found what it was looking for. Now, not waiting for acquiescence, eager arms dragged or carried their screaming booty downstairs, leaving behind a male silence heavy with apologies – a silence which seemed to imply that a lost war does not produce gallant knights, nor the stuff of which heroes are made, but aspirations, germinating into an obsession, to see the day when the quality of life would no longer be measured by degrees of hunger and cold, happiness by the length of an English or American cigarette.

'Thank you,' I said to my neighbour when the room had grown quiet again.

'*Ach*, it was nothing,' he said, 'I was thinking of my daughter. Now let's try and get a wink of sleep. The *Scheisskerle* won't be back tonight, I'm sure.'

His arm went round me, and in reply to his paternal, protective gesture, I rested my head against his shoulder. His coat smelled of tobacco and mothballs, but at this moment I couldn't think of any more homely and comforting smell.

Around midnight, when even the locked door could no longer keep out the victims' screams downstairs, a tenor suddenly filled the room with an old German folk song, '*Ich weiss nicht, was soll es bedeuten, dass ich so traurig bin . . .*' One after another we joined in, humming, steadily raising our voices, then striking up other folk songs and popular tunes, until the first postwar hit – a sentimental chant full of Italian sunset, love and *Lebensfreude* – finally grew into a defiant chorus which shut out the hell below.

I wake to the roar of engines warming up and revving, to snow crunching under footsteps, to the early hustle of a guardroom and to a host of other unidentifiable sounds. My limbs feel cold and stiff, my stomach no longer remembers the last passage of food, for when sleep had finally come towards morning, it had been of the guarded, ear-pricking kind which does not leave the sleeper refreshed, but more acutely aware of physical discomfort. And now heavy boots are clumping up the stairs, the door is unlocked and our sad heap of humanity is ordered to line up in the yard.

On the way out we have to pass through the soldiers' quarters again – a room thick with the smell of stale pub air, urine and fornication, with a floor fouled by ash, empty bottles and broken glass, a table littered with empty sardine tins and the remnants of food.

Dazed, with the distress of the night still weighing heavily on mind and body, we stumble into the yard, and for the first time I get a good look at my companions' faces which mirror my own fatigue and apprehension. Here and there, among the women, red or cast-down eyes, a blotched face or a clumsy gait betray those who after their ordeal had returned to the room upstairs in the early hours. I feel for them, and I am grateful to have been spared.

Leaning against the doorframe, and rolling a cigarette, a tall, flaxen-haired officer with gold-braided shoulder straps and medal ribbons is giving orders. Another party of prisoners, many women among them, is joining us from the barn. A small platoon stands to attention, receives instructions and, using rifle barrels, proceeds to shove us into a treble column. Bovine faces, eyes narrowed in vigilance or still clouded with vodka, rekindle my fear. But, I remind myself, fear can read fearsome things even into the most banal and innocent, and I am willing to believe that behind their uniforms and their barbaric behaviour, peasants are pining to be back home in their villages and with their womenfolk, worlds and cultures away from this foreign, burnt-out land which has soaked up so much of their comrades' blood.

Heavily guarded, the trek starts moving in a northeasterly direction towards the hills and into picture-book scenery. The snow is cracking under our feet, our breath is freezing, curling like smoke the moment it meets the icy air. In the east, the sun is rising like a fireball, dressing the white sheets of fields and the distant rounded hilltops in a pink light.

It promises to be a long march. My feet are moving automatically – left, right, left, right. My mind stops racing, is trying to keep time with my steps, only to stumble into flight now and again.

I am twenty-one, and since my tenth birthday I have not known a time when some form of coercion or other has not been exercised over my life, nor when uniforms have not demonstrated unity, or power, or both. For many years, and like most of my generation, I have not been allowed to cultivate happy, carefree thoughts, nor to shape my own future. From childhood I was pushed straight into adulthood; from dolls and teddy bears, by a short cut, into duties and obedience; from the coloured pictures of my *laterna magica* to the sight of burning houses and close-ups of mangled bodies; from proper home-cooked meals to institutional semolina puddings and watery cocoa, from the thin, meatless cabbage soups of the last war years to the hunger rations of postwar Germany.

I'm not harbouring feelings of self-pity: survivors have no right to glance back and moan. To have stayed alive is what counts, to be able to pick up one's life again, or to build it up, brick by brick. I know it is the monotony of heading towards an unknown destination and an uncertain fate which makes me ask a question to which I have no answer: when will the day come when peace will be synonymous with freedom and warmth and a full stomach, when – to modify a German proverb – people will allow God to make room in heaven again?

The air seemed spiked with ice crystals. For hours we had been walking without rest, food or drink, prodded on by fists and rifle butts. An elderly man slumped down at the roadside. The column jammed to a halt. There were shouts. A soldier, coming up from behind, kicked the man, who had folded his hands as if in prayer; another, finding no resistance, calmly removed his watch. A single shot rang out. Immediately, the column started moving again.

Minutes later, the trek left the road and entered a denser part of the hills where firs, the size of large Christmas trees, pressed close to each other, their branches interlocking to form a tight, coniferous web and an effective cover.

'*Stoi, stoi!*' the guards shouted, groping for prisoners' wrists and removing watches. Enraptured, they held them up to their ears, like children listening to their ticking magic for the first time, like men who had never owned a modern timepiece before.

It was the moment a young man chose to fling himself across a snow-filled trench towards the safety of the forest.

He never had a chance.

With the vigilance and split-second reaction of one trained in ambush warfare, a soldier calmly dropped his spoils and fired a round from his machine-pistol.

'*Mörder!*' a man cried. And now others did not hold back with anger-fired sarcasm.

'The war has been over for them too long!'

'. . . or they were too late for it, and this gives them a share of the action!'

'News travels slowly, man! After all, they're thousands of miles from Moscow!'

'*Scheisse!*' my neighbour exclaimed between clenched teeth as we passed the spot where the young man had collapsed so agonisingly close to freedom, and where, beside his mouth, the snow was no longer white.

The sun had reached its zenith for late December when the trek stopped at a *Gasthaus* which had once catered for hill-walkers, skiers and day-trippers. Most of its windows were shuttered up, yet on its outside wall, and prominently nailed against a tree trunk, weathered metal signs still pointed to a *Kaffeegarten* and skittle alley, or praised the inn's home-made *Apfelkuchen* and its draught beer.

A soldier hammered with his fist against the door and, without waiting, kicked it open. The wood splintered. An old man in slippers, followed by two plump women, made a timid appearance.

'*Schnaps, Kaffee!*' The order slapped the startled faces.

'*Jawohl, jawohl!*' the man replied, offering a leathery smile and instant servility. '*Kommen Sie!*'

One by one, we are being packed into the former restaurant – a cold dimly lit room which, with its dust-covered tables and upturned chairs, its stale air of sour beer, tobacco and fried onions, rejects any notion of hospitality. In the adjoining taproom, drinking *schnaps* straight from the bottle, our guards are amusing themselves, playing with syphons and tossing beer

18

mats around. Behind the bar, his sangfroid visibly returned, the old man is polishing glasses as if his life depended on their sparkle.

But now the sight of buckets containing steaming ersatz coffee, and of trayloads of earthenware cups, brings movement into our shivering bodies. The brew, though thin and tasting of tree bark, instantly revives our circulations, while a voice from within our slurping ranks echoes my own thoughts: 'I bet even cream and sugar wouldn't make this muck more palatable.'

Our respite was short and hours later our sluggish column was still heading in a northeasterly direction and deeper into the mountains. Exhaustion began to take its toll. Some prisoners were limping, others falling back, never to regain their places. There were shots, but no one protested, no one looked back any more. As my own movements grew laboured, I found myself thinking every thought twice, until finally each kept revolving around the same question: how much longer?

'How are you doing, girl?'

I recognised the voice of the man who had helped me into male disguise.

'Still managing,' I replied. 'Any idea where they're taking us?'

I did not hear the man's answer as a guard bellowed something in Russian which sounded like an order to shut up.

Dusk came early that afternoon. One moment there was a white, wintry forest, with branches bending deep under the weight of snow, and sunlight trapped in snow crystals and in fir cones turned to icicles, then the light went. Within minutes, the bluish shadows had merged and the darkness was closing in – a darkness which lured with its promise of freedom, yet at the same time discouraged one with its threat of unknown danger. The frost sharpened. As the guards switched on their torches and flashed them over the crawling trek in a criss-cross pattern, while themselves remaining hidden behind the beams, and no doubt covering the triggers of their guns, only a fool would have tried to break out from under the netting of light.

Another hour or two had passed when the path ran into a forestry road on which frozen tyre-tracks made the going difficult. Soon, however, the walls of pines receded and opened out on to a plateau. A full moon was rising in a sky which would have made romantic poets put pen to paper, and which reminded me of tales I had read, of seafarers, travellers on

19

camelback and eastern explorers gazing enthralled into wide, resplendent skies. Making out the Great Bear, my favourite constellation, I remembered the night my memory was born: my mother picking me up from my cot, drying tears and, having returned darkness to the room, opening curtains and window wide, to allow the magic of a moonlit night to flood the nursery. Other nights forced themselves into my mind, nights in which a full moon had shone upon a pitiful refugee trek or stood harshly over the scenes of bomb terror, often creating, in the skeleton of a house, the mound of rubble and the silhouette of an amputated tree, contours evocative of a Caspar David Friedrich painting. And there had been others, scary, lonesome or hauntingly beautiful nights in which I had reached out for the God to whom I prayed in the way my eyes reached for the stars.

Level ground, feet welcoming a smooth tarmac road. Ahead, the outlines of several large buildings. Barbed-wire secured walls, search lights, sentries. The massive iron gate is shut.

'Stoi!'

Shouts and clipped commands pierce the night. Someone at my elbow claims to recognise the place.

'It used to be a convent and boarding-school before the war. Looks like the buggers have turned it into a barracks. God help us!'

The fist is back, using my stomach as a punch-bag. I mustn't be afraid, I tell myself, clinging to the words my father had entrusted to me on his deathbed, 'Fear not, for I am with you.'

The heavy gate creaks open.

Inside the compound armed guards go about separating the women prisoners from the men, but massive bodily resistance and loud cries of protest, provoking a warning shot and a torrid exchange of arguments between the guards, ensure that we are all herded together into a former gymnasium.

'Here, stay close to me, girl! Take my hand. What's your name?'

'Marianne.'

It is the familiar voice again, but now the face of a middle-aged man has attached itself to it.

'My name is Busse. I have a daughter of your age. I'm looking for her, and for her mother. They were refugees. We're from Silesia. Come on, let's find a sheltered corner in this mausoleum.'

Through the tall, broken windows the moon suffuses the hall with light and the cold finds easy access. One by one we slump down on the linoleum floor between vaulting horses and parallel bars. The door bangs shut.

Herr Busse is taking out his pipe. 'Where are you heading for, Marianne?'

'Berlin, American Sector. My mother lives there. I was hoping to spend Christmas with her. Most of my family is dead or missing.'

'I'm sorry. Well, perhaps they'll let us go in the morning. I certainly hope so – I still have a lot of ground to cover.'

From *Herr* Busse's pipe comes the smell of burning garden refuse.

'What would be the worst?' I ask.

'Forced labour.'

'Oh my God!'

'Don't worry, girl, let's try and get some sleep.'

I am searching my knapsack for some elusive crust of bread, conscious of the cramps in my empty stomach, but also of something less tangible – a foreboding that the nightmare is only just beginning. 'I am hungry.'

But *Herr* Busse no longer hears me.

Sometime after midnight, the door opens and drunken soldiers call for female 'volunteers' to clean barrack rooms and offices, an appeal which, leaving no doubt as to the true nature of the chores involved, elicits no response. Guffawing, and all too visible in the path of torchlight, they begin to loosen their belts and unbutton flies. And now naked, lusting flesh shocks us into a rigid silence. There is a quality of animalism about the vulgar spectacle, a boldness that suggests that the soldiers have been given carte blanche for the night.

'*Dawai!*'[5] The call is growing more impatient, more commanding, then its tune changes. One soldier promises soup and bread, others follow suit.

'*Frau komm! Frau schön essen und trinken. Frau schön warm.*'[6]

Now there is movement on the floor. Here and there, a woman rises and goes forward, and her eagerness, her air of dejection or vague apologetic gesture reflects the despair of one who is prepared to offer her body as a bartering object, choosing

[5] 'Come!'
[6] 'Woman nice eat and drink. Woman nice warm.'

21

perhaps what she feels to be the lesser of two evils.

'Whores! Bitches!' Cries from male prisoners brand the women as they follow the soldiers outside.

As soon as they are gone, I experience an inordinate, a shameless sense of relief – a feeling which is to remain short-lived, for soon there are more soldiers, and this time they do not ask for volunteers, or make promises. In search of females they lift gym mats and peep into vaulting boxes, and the beams of their torches scan every face.

Herr Busse, awake by now, resumes the role of protector, quickly helping me back into male disguise.

Leaning against the wall, my hair squeezed tightly under my cap, my arms crossed nonchalantly over my chest and *Herr* Busse's empty pipe stuck in the corner of my mouth, I desperately try to exhibit an attitude of weariness and male unconcern. A torch reaches my face, loiters on it for quivering seconds before passing on and, once again, ignoring the young man with his strange partiality for a pipe, probably a rare sight even among Russian youths.

The door closes behind the last soldier and his human booty. The night seems to stand still, while cold, hunger and anxiety erode sleep and morale.

The women return at dawn, some walking as on stilts, some stealing back to their places, marble-faced or sobbing, while others, smelling of vodka and *makhorka*, look no more seedy than they would after a roaring all-night party, no less high-spirited than after a lusty tumble in the hay. And everybody knows that their bodies are warm and their stomachs full.

I woke to the sun streaming through the broken windows. My limbs felt stiff, my tongue dry, my stomach as if it had given up caring. Like the rest of my companions I was conscious of the need to relieve myself. A guard, summoned by those already crowding the entrance, gestured, 'Outside! Line up!' I assessed my chances of successfully posing as a young man in broad daylight and remembered the woollen dress in my rucksack, my Sunday best, complete with pleats and carefully ironed collar. Stuffing it under my coat it made for a nicely rounded belly, and with my hair let down I now looked like a young mother in her last month of pregnancy.

'I'm going to join the queue,' I explained to *Herr* Busse, who had been watching me, and who was quick to draw from his reserve of wry humour.

22

'I bet you're going to have twins.'

The gymnasium opened on to a concrete yard of parade-ground size. It was alive with platoons engaged in marching drill and maintenance teams busying themselves on heavy vehicles. Nearby, a group of soldiers stood idle, watching prisoners perform on a mound of rubble and slack which had been delegated as a latrine, and cracking the kind of jokes which needed no translation. Totally devoid of privacy, men and women stood or crouched on an open-air stage, providing amusement for a grinning and obscenely gesticulating audience.

My turn came, and I was alone with my outraged sense of modesty. Applause greeted me as I stepped down, carefully navigating my way past excrement, broken glass and lengths of piping, my hands folded over my abdomen as if protecting the unborn life in my womb.

'*Dawei, Frau komm!*' a voice called out to me from the doorway of a nearby building.

There it was again, the call which German women had come to fear, and which, abetted by a rifle or sheer muscle-power, left no option but to obey. Like a slave, like a scolded child, I walked towards the figure, about which everything seemed to be square, remembering in good time to adopt the waddling gait of a pregnant woman.

'Follow me!' His hands translated the command.

The whitewashed corridors looked like hundred-metre tracks. Cyrillic letters screamed names, directions, orders at me in code. Here and there, a black forgotten cross was hugging a niche. With a strange detachment I registered the sound of boots beating the naked stone floors, of doors opening and closing, of husky Russian voices desecrating the demure stairways and venerable corridors – sounds which seemed to symbolise the power to which, presently, I would have to submit.

This is it then, your turn has come, my mind stated flatly, while my body was praying for a miracle.

The white-tiled basement resounded with the clatter of pots and pans. There was a smell of cabbage, and steam escaped from a huge vessel which reminded me of washday in the cellar of my grandmother's house, of boiler, tubs and washing board. I realised I had been taken to the cookhouse.

The soldier donned an apron and poured me a mug of tea.

23

'Here, drink, *matka*,[7] good for you!' His impish smile suggested he had just parted with a surprise gift.

The steaming liquid warmed and relaxed me. I drank hastily and asked for a refill.

'You good man,' I said, pointing first at him, then at my heart. He understood and looked pleased, and his German came falteringly, delivered with the deliberation of a toddler building a tower of bricks.

'You, young *matka*. Baby soon?'

I nodded.

'I, Sergje, Ukrainian . . . young *matka* in Russia . . . baby come one month . . . good *matka*.' A hand went to his heart.

I smiled and made cradling movements.

'Baby,' the cook said, growing suddenly taller in anticipation of fatherhood. Then I was free to go and take a bucket of tea back to my fellow prisoners.

I thanked my benefactor and returned his broad smile. I was conscious of an immense sense of relief and, on my way back to the gym hall, mused how one gesture of kindness had been able to break down − if only for minutes − the apparently insurmountable barrier between two enemies.

The morning light cruelly exposed human wretchedness and turned into something distinctly Hadean a scene in which people stood shivering, leaning against walls or vaulting boxes, lying on the floor in the foetal position or pressing close to each other in the freezing draught. No sooner had I put down the bucket of tea than the motionless came to life, crowding around the hot liquid, pushing and jostling each other in their desperate bid for the 'life saver' that was robbing them of their dignity and their earlier spirit of comradeship. Now only the power of elbows and the instinct of survival triumphed, turning men and women into animals, the strongest of whom secured and defended their places at the bucket as at a trough.

What had happened to the man who with his singing had raised morale only two nights ago, I asked myself? And why did self-discipline disintegrate so quickly? But then, back at the cookhouse only minutes ago, had I not been drinking greedily myself, without sparing a thought for my companions? Was life perhaps teaching me another lesson in human nature − how far

[7] Mother.

24

man can be stretched before he gives up, or joins the fight for the survival of the fittest?

Herr Busse looked at me anxiously.

'Are you all right, girl? The others told me. What did he do with you, the swine? *Komm Frau!* That's the only German they know!'

I calmly removed my padding.

'I'm fine,' I said. 'All he wanted was to give me something hot to drink, and to bring a bucket of tea back.'

'What?' *Herr* Busse cried, 'a philanthropist among all those savages? He must have been an eccentric, your *Iwan*! What are you smiling about?'

'*Ach*, he was rather nice. He must have felt sorry for me . . . you know, sorry for the expectant mother.'

'Sorry?' *Herr* Busse queried, shaking his head in disbelief at my naivety or at the existence of a 'nice' Russian.

The hours passed at a snail's pace. There was no food, and the sunshine did little to take the splinters out of the air. Leaning against *Herr* Busse's back, arms folded around my knees, I wondered how long man can survive on an empty stomach and how long it takes to freeze to death.

It was noon when the door opened and an interpreter translated instructions into German. Prisoners resident in the British or American Zone were to line up on the left, those living in the Russian Zone, or in Berlin, on the right. Segregation, however, posed a new problem. Which side was one to choose, in order to end up where one wanted to be? Which side promised freedom, which further punitive measures? One might as well throw a coin for heads or tails.

'I'll pretend I live in the Russian Zone,' said *Herr* Busse. 'With luck they'll let us go and I won't have to cross the border again. What about you?'

'I'll take a chance and go for the left one,' I said. 'Perhaps they'll send us back across the border, which would be fine with me. I've had enough!' I pressed his hand. 'Thank you again for your help, and I hope you'll find your family.'

Herr Busse patted my cheek. '*Ach, Mädchen*, every father would have done the same for his daughter. Take care!'

We are herded into open trucks like sheep packed off to the slaughterhouse. Engines roar, vehicles clear the compound and, once on the main road, quickly gather speed.

The icy wind is wrapping itself around my head and shoulders, numbing, making my eyes water, which forms crystals on the lower lids. Yet, jammed right in the middle of our human consignment, I feel privileged compared with those standing on the outside and taking the full brunt of the arctic airstream.

Inexorably my own physical discomfort evokes awkward questions which I had never asked myself before, because they had simply not come to mind, or which, caught up in the war years and with my own bid for survival, I had not allowed to surface: was this perhaps the way Jews had been crammed into trucks and rail waggons in wintertime, stripped of freedom and dignity, starving, freezing, and in their misery praying to a God who seemed to be deaf. Yet something inside me is crying out to the same God.

There came a point during the journey when my mind refused to acknowledge the protests of my body, and merely registered the rattling of the truck, a widening road, deciduous trees forming lone colonies amid the coniferous forest and naked tree-felling sites hewn into the wooded slopes. In the distance, teasing the eye: hamlets no larger than specks on a white blanket, church steeples no taller than pencil stubs.

A sudden turning focused my attention on a smooth tarmac road leading to a complex of single-storeyed buildings. I noticed a high wall, a barrier, Russian sentries fingering machine-pistols and a concrete yard where, keenly watched by two Russian officers, members of the newly formed *Volkspolizei*[8] were in evidence.

Armed, standing jackboots astride and hands on hips, our new stone-faced guards set about demonstrating the same eagerness to please their masters as Hitler's storm-troopers had one morning in 1938.

'*Juden raus!*' Germans had then screamed at Germans.

'*Runter, los!*'[9] Germans now yelled at Germans.

The same metallic voices. Swastika minds attuned to red star, hammer and sickle. A force said to have been recruited from communist ranks and from those quick enough to trim their political sails to the wind. But whether they were opportunists,

[8] East German People's Police.
[9] 'Down with you, on the double!'

men greedy for power, covetous of a uniform or trying to disown a disgraced past, it was obvious that they had changed their loyalties as effortlessly as the colour of their shirts and breeches.

A Russian officer approached.

'*Mensch, beeilt euch!*'[10] the *Volkspolizisten* shouted and, in the manhandling of some of the prisoners, proved their new allegiance with the zeal of religious converts. I knew no help would be forthcoming from countrymen who as POW or concentration camp guards would have shown the same unconcern for human misery.

It took time to unload us, stiff-limbed and frozen as we were. With knees sagging once their support had gone and legs numbed into uncoordinated movements, we gingerly stalked or hobbled towards our new prison. Behind us, a red sun was about to set in the west, while an outsized moon, still pale in the spectrum of parting daylight, stood high above the skyline.

Whitewashed barrack-style rooms on the first floor. Bunk beds with straw-filled mattresses and horse blankets. Naked light bulbs. Windows, glazed and without bars, overlooking the yard of the compound. On the corridor, German guards, armed, stern-faced and uncommunicative.

In a top bunk, coiled up under a blanket, I felt the blood rush back into my limbs and my body relax. My mind refused to receive any more messages and surrendered to sleep as swiftly as if I'd been anaesthetised.

The light had come on, when voices and a scuffle catapulted me back into consciousness, and made me join the ration queue in the corridor. Like my ravenous companions, and in less time than it takes to say grace, I wolfed down two thin slices of black bread with a dot of margarine and jam, and a cup of ersatz coffee.

I should have known better. Hadn't I practised the lesson for years? Chew every bite slowly! Fool your tummy and yourself! Now, back in my bunk in an embryonic position, familiar fantasies returned with a vengeance, not of the staple postwar diet of doughy bread and cabbage soup graced by grease spots and pieces of gristle, but of crisp, buttered ham and *Leberwurst* rolls, chestnut-stuffed roast goose, juicy meat roasts with flour dumplings and rich gravies, apple cake dusted with cinnamon and speared with almonds, strawberries and cream . . .

[10] 'Hurry up!'

'*Alle wiederanstellen!*'[11] a guard barked down the corridor. The room woke slowly and resentfully to the order to queue up again. It was dark outside. My head felt like lead, my limbs were aching, and I had to make a giant effort to climb down from my bunk.

Two slices of bread and jam.

'They're feeding us up,' someone scoffed.

The elderly kitchen hand looked over his shoulder and whispered, 'It's tomorrow's provisions. They're taking you to a labour camp in the morning, early, in railway waggons, some sixty-odd people.'

A guard approached.

Someone at the head of the queue cursed and furtively relayed the message to the person behind who, in turn, passed on the grim news like a brick in a human chain. There came feeble cries of protest and anguish, while one man, dipping deep into his courage, shouted, '*Diese Schweinehunde!*'

The guard's hand moved to his holster.

Suddenly, my craving for food was gone and all I wanted was to slump back on my mattress. But first I had a job to do. The window of the lavatory across the corridor faced the forest and the path beyond the nearby stone wall, along which, on arrival, I had seen peasants passing with handcarts. I fetched pen and paper from my rucksack and wrote down a message for my mother, and in another asked the finder to send a telegram to Berlin. These I wrapped around a five-Reichsmark piece.

I felt dizzy as I crossed the corridor, but the lavatory window opened easily and, although the rush of cold air momentarily stunned my hot skin, I had a lucky throw, landing the weighted missive right in the middle of the moonlit path.

I was not to know for some weeks that my childlike trust in man's basic goodness was to be rewarded.

Everything was quiet in the room. The light had been turned off, and only the creaking of the bunks betrayed the restlessness of those from whom anxiety was withholding sleep. And sleep, instantaneous though it had been the moment I had first hit the bunk, eluded me now. My head felt as if it was storing the heat of a midsummer day and fits of shivering made my teeth chatter like loose casement hinges in the wind. I watched pale shafts of

[11] 'Everybody line up again!'

moonlight slanting into the curtainless room, shifting and gaining in luminosity as time passed. After a while the shivering stopped, the clamp around my head slackened off and my body surrendered languidly to the build-up of temperature – but not so my thoughts, which kept jumping and zigzagging on their feverish course.

I thought of my mother. This would have been our first Christmas together since the end of the war, which we had witnessed hundreds of kilometres apart. We had both lived through cold and hunger and bombing, often cheating death, and learning in the process how to cope with the repeated loss of personal possessions. By applying the same stubborn determination to our day-to-day lives, wherever we found ourselves, by not allowing the war to drain our spiritual resources, we had both discovered, like an untold number of our sex, that when the need arises woman can grow physically as strong as a man, and in willpower taller than her own shadow. We had been fortunate, we had survived. We had come out as winners in the lottery of war or – as I preferred to think – because it had been so written in the Book of Providence.

I tossed and turned. A man's snore was trying to saw the room in half. An engine spluttered in the courtyard.

'Are you awake?' The voice was close to my ear.

I turned my head. Moonlight, floodlighting the room, revealed the features of a man in his twenties.

'I am,' I said.

'What's your name?'

'Marianne.'

'My name is Rolf. Where's your home?'

'My home?' I asked, and my mind started wandering again. Did I have a proper home? The memory of the one I had had for the first ten years of my life had long faded, and I had not had another since, not really, not if home was a place with roots, in which happy memories are born, and where even the air one breathes smells of 'homeness'. But perhaps even the plainest of rented rooms might deserve such a proud definition if sleep came easy in it at night. Indeed, wasn't I lucky to have a furnished room of my own, however shabby, at a time when millions of homeless people were still living in hovels, in the cellars of ruins or in Nissen huts?

'My home?' I repeated.

The voice at my ear tried another approach. 'Where do you come from, Marianne?'

'Berlin . . . Potsdam . . . Gandersheim, British Zone.'

'This is Ilse.' The young man pointed to a tall girl into whose fair hair the moon had put silvery streaks. She smiled and shook my hand.

'It looks as if they were waiting for more people to make up a transport,' Rolf explained. 'We got here early this morning . . . got caught not far from here. We're pretty close to the border – no more than two hours on foot, I daresay.'

I stayed silent.

'Ilse and I come from Göttingen, we were hoping to make it home for Christmas, and perhaps go back to university once they open up again. We are medical students. Look, we've had enough of this, we're not going to that bloody slave-camp tomorrow.' His voice was a mere whisper. 'Want to join us? We thought we'd jump from the lavatory window shortly after midnight, when things should be quiet around here, and head straight for the woods. I reckon we have a good chance.'

I ached with the heat in my body.

'I'd like nothing better,' I said, 'but I'm running a high temperature.'

Instantly, the young man turned professional. He felt my forehead, took my pulse and went to fetch some pills from his bag.

'Quinine,' he said. 'Here, take two with plenty of water. It'll make the fever go down. I'll give you some more later. And now try and get some sleep. We'll wake you in about an hour.'

Ilse's voice said, 'I'll go and get some water.'

Rolf patted my hand. 'Don't worry, you'll be all right. *Onkel Doktor* is looking after you!'

I felt as if they had only just left me when Rolf woke me from a shallow drifting sleep. With shaking legs, and with a degree of reluctance, I followed my new friends across the dimly lit corridor at the far end of which four uniformed men were playing cards. Rolf opened the lavatory window, and, as freezing air rushed into the cubicle, I was tempted to stay behind and yield passively to fever and fate in my bunk. But suddenly, there was the inner voice again, that same voice which for years had been both whip and gentle guide. 'Come on, Marianne,' it said, 'you know you can do it!'

The window was an ideal exit for our escape, for at this hour the high roof of the building prevented the moon from illuminating the strip of ground which extended from the back of the house to the stone wall – three metres of darkness, not too impenetrable to jump into, yet solid enough to provide effective cover.

Using their bundles as cushions, Rolf and Ilse jumped first and landed safely, while with one leg I slipped awkwardly off my rucksack onto the frozen ground. I tried not to cry out as pain seared through my ankle; there was no time for groans, no time for an assessment of the new situation. Limping towards the wall, I lumbered across it, helped by four strong arms and Rolf's coolheaded instructions.

As I hobbled across the lane before plunging into the woods as fast as my strength and my injured ankle would allow, I saw my coin-weighted message still lying in its place.

The years have not blurred the memory of that night; I can still smell the keen scent of pine, feel the cold on my burning cheeks and see the forest closing up around us.

The track was narrow, our movements cautious, and I kept looking over my shoulder, expecting bloodhounds on our scent and ready to strike any moment.

We had not covered much ground before we reached a clearing and the unflappable Rolf pointed to a tree stump.

'Sit down, Marianne. Let's do something about that ankle of yours.'

Ilse produced a spare stocking and Rolf expertly bandaged my ankle.

'Now all you need is a walking stick,' he said, breaking off a dead branch and coiling a handkerchief around its upper end. 'There you are, complete with knob. It'll take the weight off your foot. How are you feeling otherwise?'

'Not too bad. I hope I won't be slowing you two down too much. If it wasn't for me you'd be . . .'

'Rubbish!' Rolf snapped, helping me up again and patting my back. 'We're in this together! Mind you, the cold will keep down the swelling as well as your temperature! And now *allons-nous, mes enfants!*'

Ilse mocked a strapping military salute. '*Jawohl, Herr General!*'

For the first time that night, we laughed.

Rolf took the lead again, keeping hard to a path where fractured moonlight made walking easier. Presently, however, shouts and whistles from the direction of the compound forced us off the beaten track and deeper into the forest, where darkness swallowed us up and we needed both arms to machete our way through the invisible latticework of undergrowth.

Branches whipped and grazed my face, serrated edges and spiked shoots threatened like primeval weapons. I slipped and stumbled over tree trunks, and once fell soundlessly into a snow-filled hole, for moments welcoming the snow like the softness of an eiderdown.

For what seemed like hours, and long after the whistling and shouting had stopped, we groped along like blind people in what we hoped was a westerly direction. As we toiled with the obstacles I began to 'see' in the dark. The pitch-black, amorphous, yet all too tangible world around me slowly revealed various degrees of density, and as shapes assumed outlines, and a sense of location returned, I was no longer scared by the hooting of owls. Indeed, in my feverish mind, the birds of the night were sylvan scouts trying to guide us safely through their forest. Childhood stories forced themselves back into my memory, tales of magical woods featuring goblins and gentle beasts which spoke in the tongues of men – fantasies which, with their hallucinatory effect, managed to take the edge off the cold and pain.

Gradually, the forest thinned out, allowing moonlight to steal through the treetops. Rolf took our bearings.

'If we go by the position of the moon, we're still moving west – right on course.'

'Thank God for that!' Ilse exclaimed. 'I should hate the thought of having walked in circles.'

'Rather a sound bit of orienteering, I'd say,' Rolf joked. 'Proper Hitler Youth stuff, this. I remember some of the weekend camps, we boys loved them. Night-time scouting games, mock reconnaissance patrols, learning how to take one's position without a compass. I had no idea then those skills would come in handy one night. Christ, it is cold! Are you still with us, Marianne? Won't be long now.'

'She's doing fine,' said Ilse.

I snapped out of my woodland fantasia and tried – despite the growing reluctance of my ankle and every muscle in my body to walk any further – not to fall behind on the rising terrain.

A strong smell of resin. A forestry road. Throwing all caution aside, we followed it to the edge of a large clearing in which timber lay neatly stacked. On its far side, a room-sized log cabin leaned against a wall of pines. Light was struggling through a small window.

'Woodcutters,' Rolf whispered, 'but we can't be sure.'

We approached the cabin with the stealth of burglars, but with boldness returning at the sound of male voices arguing in German or exploding with laughter, and of cards being slammed hard on a table. Like Peeping Toms we stood and stared through the sweating window at the four men playing cards in the light of a petrol lamp, smoking and now and then drinking from a bottle. One man heaved himself up and went to poke the fire in an iron stove.

Rolf knocked at the door. Inside, a chair was pushed aside and the door creaked open. The men's weatherbeaten faces registered little surprise.

'Come in,' they said, 'warm yourselves up. It's a hell of a night to be out.'

While Ilse and I steered straight towards the stove, Rolf gave a brief account of our capture and escape, interspersed by the men's hoarse-voiced expletives. Gratefully, we sank our teeth into rough, brown bread thickly spread with dripping, and took a swig from a bottle of *korn*. I winced as the spirit scorched my throat like liquid fire. The men laughed and offered me coffee from their thermos flask to wash down another quinine pill. Finally, giving in to a sudden, irresistible longing to lie down, I veered towards one of the camp beds.

'Sorry, *Mädchen*,' one of the woodcutters said, not unkindly, scratching himself behind the ear, 'you mustn't stay here. It isn't safe. We're only two kilometres from the border, and the patrol, which passes here at least once a night, hasn't been yet. The Russkies come up the forestry road and always check in here for a bit of booze and a warm-up if we're in. Bring their own vodka, they do. We'll give them another ten minutes, then hit the sack.'

The other men did not hold back with their comments.

'If you stayed, you could get us into trouble.'

'You should be across in an hour or so, if you're careful. Follow the path right down into the valley, and try and keep out of sight, especially the last hundred metres. There's good ground cover.'

One man looked cautiously outside. 'The coast is clear. Off you go then. Good luck!'

Calloused hands accepted our thanks.

As we slipped back into the brushwood jungle, our instincts immediately reverted to those of the hunted who with every step are trying to match their wits against an invisible enemy.

Were the minutes ticking away at double their speed? Had the hands of time stopped moving? I could no longer tell. Once, when we heard voices ahead, and footsteps crunching nearer, when suddenly metal gleamed in the moonlight and flashlights combed the undergrowth at no greater distance than the leap of a hare, we froze into crouching, hunched-up positions, hoping that our dark-clad bodies and posture, if spotted from the path, would look like tree trunks. The patrol had been gone a minute or two when Rolf stepped out on to the path.

'Let's chance it,' he said, 'I don't suppose they're likely to come back this way tonight.'

By now I was limping heavily, and every time I put weight on my ankle I felt like crying out. I was also desperately thirsty and my whole body was aching for a bed and the abandonment that comes with it. All of a sudden, my legs seemed to be made of plasticine, the sky's fun-fair illumination to be dimming and the Chinese-lantern moon to drop out of the sky.

Rolf caught me and pulled me back into the woods.

'Let's rest awhile,' he said, letting me down on a bed of snow-covered moss and dead branches. 'Just a minute or two, mind you — we'll freeze to death if we stay longer.'

'I don't think I can go on much longer myself,' Ilse moaned, vigorously rubbing her calf muscles and kneading her fingers in an attempt to restore circulation.

'Now, rule number one,' Rolf continued, 'is to preserve body heat. Let's cuddle as close to each other as we can. Yes, that's it! *Mensch*, how I would enjoy this under normal circumstances!'

Arms around each other, thighs glued together and breath mixing with breath, our inert bodies seemed to grow into one, and as the cold of the small hours descended upon us with a vengeance, my mind started shifting between a state of semi-consciousness and moments of clear-headedness.

'It's no good!' Rolf said after a few minutes, shaking Ilse and

34

me by the shoulder, 'if we go to sleep, we won't wake up again! Resist the temptation, girls. Come, let's get up! Can you make it to the valley, Marianne? It'll be dawn soon.'

'I'll try,' I said, feebly; and now there was Aurora to look out for, the pink-fingered goddess of the rising sun, the symbol of hope and of brighter things to come. Anchoring my arm under Rolf's, and resting my full weight upon the walking stick, I hobbled towards the valley with renewed spirits.

'Look!' Ilse cried when we had reached the edge of the forest and the point where the hills dipped into a moon-flooded valley. 'I've never seen anything like it!'

From where we stood, the valley seemed to merge seamlessly with the sky. A small town, nestling at the bottom of the white valley, looked fast asleep: no solitary light marked a window, and with its streets unlit and no lights showing, it would have remained undetected on a moonless night.

'Reminds me of some nights in Poland in forty-five . . .' Rolf said.

'Yes, I know,' I said, not allowing my mind to dwell on the horrors of a refugee trek, but marvelling at the church steeple gleaming like a silver cone, and at a scene which reminded me of a miniature iced-cake village created by a Berlin *Meisterkonditor* for a Christmas fair before the war.

Rolf woke us from our reveries.

'I thought we were desperate for shelter. Let's move on! Do you see the farm on the right? A warm barn would suit us fine, wouldn't it?'

No dog barked, no life stirred in what, on closer inspection, turned out to be a derelict property. Windows were broken, gates and shutters torn from their hinges, part of the roof was missing.

'Shall we try here?' Rolf asked, and without waiting for an answer he prised open the rusty lock. Seconds later I collapsed on the remnants of hay and swiftly fell asleep.

When I woke my head felt clearer, if still feverish. There was a pain in my chest and back, and freezing sweat made me feel like a bather who had stepped out of the warm waters of an August lake into the fury of a November gale.

Half an hour later we were on our way again, having first removed from each other's hair and coats webs of hay, pine needles and other prickly reminders of the night's ordeal.

For the last time Rolf assumed command.

'Now, first things first. Let's find out whether we are on the right side of the border, eh? Then we'll head for the station and for something to eat.'

An old man, muffled up to the nose, and pulling a rickety handcart containing empty milk-cans, provided us with information.

'Yes, you're in the British Zone all right.' His eyes narrowed. 'You folks come from across? Hm, you look as if you had. I can tell. You were lucky, you know. A few nights ago we heard shots. A British patrol found her. Young woman. The bastards had shot her not far from where they say is the border. And only yesterday they brought down a man, frozen solid he was. Glad you made it!' His cough exploded into the quiet valley.

'Are there any trains out of here?' Ilse asked. I was wondering how much longer my legs would support me.

'There are a few, but no one knows when they're running. It's all a question of waiting again . . . like in forty-five. But then waiting is something we've learnt all right.' As the ghostlike philosopher shuffled away, his bronchitic cough mingled with the clatter of his cans.

'God bless him!' Ilse cried. 'Now come on you two!'

In the crowded, unheated waiting-room of the small railway station grey-faced people were dozing beside rucksacks and battered suitcases. The air was thick with the smell of unwashed humanity and home-grown tobacco; a buffet counter served a coffee-coloured liquid and sandwiches made with an ominous-looking paste. As we waited on our hard chairs for trains to take us in different directions, for the inevitable moment when we would have to part company, conversation dried up between us.

The train for Göttingen arrived first, and now all that was left were parting words and hugs that were both impulsive and embarrassed, before a last clasping of hands sealed and broke a one-night friendship.

I stood, waving, long after the train had left the platform, and I suddenly realised that I did not even know the surnames of my two good Samaritans. But then, this was Year Two, the second postwar year. Too many people were still on the move, and there was no telling how many, passing each other like trains in the night, had become friends, or even lovers, until dawn, after

which they had continued their journeys in different directions.
   A symptom of the time, they said.

The mist around me is lifting. Rudely, magnificently, the bells of
the nearby minster are demanding my attention. I am lying in
bed, in my own bed, in my room at the inn, which in all its
dreariness has been doubling up as home for over a year now. I
am tucked up with blankets to the chin. The room is dark and
cold, but through the open curtain I can see a square metre of
starlit sky which sends my thoughts wandering back to the hills
and to the moment when, stumbling off the train, I had seen the
platform coming closer and closer . . .
   I remember the feel of strong arms, and in my ears the chaotic
sounds of an orchestra running amok, with the drum beating
like a heavy-artillery barrage, the strings screeching and the
flautist playing his piccolo as if blowing glass.
   Gradually a voice had come through to me, pulling me back
whenever I was tempted to sink back into that lovely, beckoning
void; and, penetrating my blurred vision, the face of my friend
Ruth had attached itself to the voice, and I realised that she had
been urging me to drink and be 'a good girl'.
   A knock. Ruth elbowed her way through the door, carrying in
one hand a pine bough with a burning candle and balancing in
the other a tray with a glass of milk, rusks and an apple. Her foot
kicked the door shut.
   I smiled at her. I felt like jumping and somersaulting.
   Ruth's face lit up. 'See who's smiling as if she's won first prize
in a lottery!' she said, putting the tray down at my bedside. A
smell of pine, candle wax and apple harvest filled the room.
'Thank God you've come round. You really had us worried!'
   'The bells,' I said. 'What day is it? How long . . .?'
   'It's *Heilig Abend*.[12] You've been quite ill for three days, you
know. There were moments when the doctor thought . . . They
couldn't get you into hospital, absolutely packed it was, patients
lying in corridors and bathrooms. Dr Brandt, the old dear, and I
looked after you. He said he wished he had penicillin – that's the
name of the new wonder-drug. But there's not much about yet,
they say, at least not for us Germans. So in the end it was all up to
the doctor's magic and grandmother's good old home remedies.'

[12]Christmas Eve.

'It seems to have worked,' I said.

'Ah, but then you owe much to your horselike constitution, and there's quite a bit of fighting spirit in you!'

I pressed my friend's hand. 'Thank you.'

Ruth noisily blew her nose. '*Ach*, just get better quickly, eh? And now, how about a wash and giving your pillow a shake-up? But first let me help you drink the milk while it's still warm.'

'Where did you get it from?'

'Your innkeeper's wife – the one with the pinched lips.'

'You're joking! Did you have to go down on your bended knees for it?'

'Not at all. She seemed to be in a Christmas spirit. You know, silent night, holy night, bells ringing and all that. Soft as candle wax she was!'

'Her good deed for the year!'

Ruth clapped her hands in mock applause. 'Bravo! I see my patient has got her sense of humour back. Now let me make you comfortable, and if you feel well enough, perhaps you'd like to tell me what happened out there. We're all dying to know! And just you wait until I tell you the latest gossip!'

Long after Ruth was gone I gazed into the light of the candle, the glow of which seemed somehow to soften the shabbiness of the room and to give it an illusion of warmth. I put my hand in front of the flickering light, moving my fingers and playing with the bizarre shadow-pictures they produced on the whitewashed walls. Soon, the candle would burn itself out and the long hours of the night were already waiting in the wings. But I did not mind, for could I not see the stars from my bed, and was it not great to be alive and safe?

My prayer, when it came, had no element of self-pity. Instead it was full of gratitude, and jubilant in the hope and light of Christmas.

PART ONE

CHAPTER 1

The Ark

In the summer of 1936 my parents' marriage began to break up. As a ten-year-old, I was too young to realise what was happening, or to work out the repercussions on my own life. All I knew was that I was increasingly driven into a peripheral position, becoming an observer, and questioning with a sudden perspicuity the child's godlike image of its parents.

It was indeed a baffling experience to stand watching and listening. However, when my mother finally allowed her tears, and my father his verbal abuse, to spill over into the living room, when even the dinner table or my bedroom were no longer safe from their marital wrath, I took refuge in my world of play and make-believe, embarking on voyages to happier lands. I covered an upturned table with an old blanket, took a zoo of stuffed animals aboard for company, and an apple and my sugar-coated afternoon bun for provisions. Looking out 'to sea' through moth-eaten portholes, and setting course for some beautiful island, I felt safe in my ark from the rising waters of a domestic deluge.

My ark, however, did not sail on nocturnal seas, and I found myself all too often at the mercy of nightmares in which sinister shapes, half-human, half-animal, pursued me with an armoury of elephantine hands, pincers and claws, while my feet, seemingly shod with hundredweight irons, were unable to move an inch. I would wake up, screaming, and not go back to sleep until my mother had stroked away the terror of the dream.

One day the open hostilities between my parents came to an end – not through an armistice or through peaceful negotiations, but more as though constant warfare had exhausted them. And where before rooms had been vibrant with tearful, angry or argumentative voices, they were now filled with a heavy silence which scared me as much as my nightmares.

As the weeks went by, I began to neglect my piano practice, and fingered the keys listlessly during lessons. *Fräulein* Petri, the grey-haired piano teacher, raised her voice one afternoon.

'Stop, child! How long will you be playing Schubert like a barrel organ? Put your heart into it!'

But how could I put my heart into something on which I could not fix my mind?

My growing sense of insecurity found a welcome and effective distraction in external events, which soon monopolised my attention: Berlin was preparing for the Olympic Games.

The Führer had been in power for three years, and for three years our *Volksempfänger*[1] had been carrying his voice into our living room, sending little shivers down my spine and making me bite my nails, even though half the time I had no idea what the man was talking about. Addressing the nation in special broadcasts, his voice in turn preached, commanded, bellowed or trembled with grand-sounding words. Sometimes it would belong to a schoolmaster, sometimes to a father-figure or, as my imagination would have it, to an angry prophet. Thus, for me, Adolf Hitler came to be synonymous with the Voice.

One evening Uncle Ludwig, a former concert pianist who was thoroughly at home in the world of modulation and tempi, articulated my impressions more eloquently, calling the Führer a 'master of the rhetorical nuance', and describing his voice as a music critic might review an artist's range of expression.

'In the development of his themes,' he explained over his second helping of roast pork and sauerkraut, 'the man modulates his voice very cleverly, like a virtuoso. Just listen to the way he moves from an *adagio* to a *crescendo* or drives home a point *sforzato* or in a *tempo maestoso*! Just like you, Marianne, at the piano, if you pay heed to modulation,' he added, on seeing my blank face rise behind my polished plate.

My idea of the Führer became more specific once I had seen him staring at me from posters or the front page of newspapers; the Voice was no longer anonymous but belonged to a man with a Charlie Chaplin moustache who never smiled unless he was posing with children or dignitaries. There came the day when,

[1] People's radio (utility 2-station receiver.)

straddling my father's shoulders and seething with excitement, I watched him passing through our street in an open car, dressed in a mustard-coloured uniform and holding his right arm at a right angle to his body, palm downwards, more in a gesture of benediction than a salute. Roadside crowds were cheering, and small children, waving paper swastika flags distributed by storm-troopers, looked as bewildered or frightened as if they were watching Punch and Judy falling under the witch's spell.

I often did not know what to make of people's descriptions of the Führer, and whether these were meant to be complimentary or disparaging. Once, hearing a political broadcaster refer to the leader of the nation as 'the Messiah of Germany', I asked my father to explain the meaning of the word 'Messiah', and he translated it into the language of ten-year-olds as 'Someone who has come to liberate his people and his country'. I forgot to ask from what Germany and its people needed liberating.

Similarly, *Frau* Klein, the janitor's wife, who, according to my father, had her ears too close to the tenants' doors, often spoke of the Führer as a 'godsend', and there was no doubt as to the views of *Herr* Kahl, the baker, who, in a cross-counter argument with a customer, had called Hitler 'the right man who had come at the right time'. Several people, on the other hand, had used the term 'dictator' in conversation, and perhaps, I thought, it was no coincidence that they had all lowered their voices, or had looked over their shoulders at the time. And then there was the old actor from the third floor. Playing ball in the back yard one day, I had heard him label the Führer 'a Mephisto in uniform' during a heated discussion with a neighbour, whereupon he had emptied his rubbish pail into the communal bin with theatrical aplomb.

But there were more interesting things to occupy my mind: games of marbles with Eduard, the boy from next door; the weekly visit of Aunt Martha, when there would be chocolate éclairs and iced nut-cakes; the *laterna magica*, my birthday present; and, in my room, the ark of which I was captain.

There had been a lot of changes in school, too. Some had been barely noticed, others had been introduced as though with drums and trumpets. None of my neatly dressed, well-behaved primary-school mates questioned the new books, the new songs, the new syllabus, the new rules or the new standard script, and when – in line with national-socialist educational policies – the number of PT periods was increased at the expense of religious

43

instruction or other classes, and competitive field-events added to the curriculum, the less studious and the fast-legged among us were positively delighted.

The rector spelled it out for us. 'Physical fitness is everything! It is what the Führer wants for you. It is what you want in order to grow strong and healthy!'

In class, *Frau* Bienert, our form teacher, explained why a healthy mind could only be found in a healthy body, and – instead of two PT periods a week – the revised time-table featured a daily class and a compulsory weekly games afternoon. Running, jumping, throwing balls, climbing ropes, swinging on the bars or doing rhythmic exercises to music, we fitted smoothly into the new pattern of things, into a scheme which, for most of us, appeared to be an attractive feature of national socialism, for an hour spent in the gym or on the sports pitch seemed infinitely preferable to sweating over arithmetic or German grammar.

I loved the new physical-fitness programme, but not the loud, aggressive songs we had to learn, the texts of which our music teacher would rattle off in a funereal voice. But then, *Fräulein* Kanitzki had been born in the Cameroons and suffered from bouts of malaria, which, in our eyes, entitled her to some form of eccentricity. And it was no secret that she never raised her arm in the 'Heil Hitler!' salute at the beginning of class or in the school corridors, forever hugging sheets of music or books under her right arm, which prevented her from performing the prescribed motion. The new greeting was, after all, a bore. Arm up, arm down. Up, down. But it was the formal salute in Germany now, and everyone did as they were told, including my father.

Dr Isaac Frankenstein, on the other hand, didn't. He had certainly not done so during a recent march-past of storm-troopers and Hitler Youths, when, at the crucial moment, he had kept his eyes screwed to the ground as if, poor-sighted, he were afraid of stumbling over some obstacle.

'Dr Frankenstein is a good man,' my mother had stated more than once, and my father would add, 'A fine physician!' Many a time he had been called out in the middle of the night without grumbling, and once he had spent half the night at my bedside, applying compresses to my chest. Yet he had not been asked to attend me the last time I was ill. Another doctor had been summoned, one whose hands were cold and whose breath smelled of tobacco.

44

'Dr Frankenstein doesn't come any more.' There had been an embarrassed finality in my father's voice, and he had looked the other way. But then I remembered that he, too, was now a member of the Party, and that a brand-new uniform was hanging in his wardrobe in between a fine worsted suit and a dinner jacket.

Returning late from work one evening, he had flashed the news across the dinner table.

'They've blackmailed me into joining the Party!'

My mother, putting down her knife and fork, uttered a single word of disbelief: 'No!'

'I've been offered a directorship if I join,' my father said. 'Hammacher pointed out – very politely and with a bottle of 1929 Moselle between us – that he was only obeying orders, and that my refusal would certainly mean the end of my executive career. He even quoted from one of the Führer's speeches – "All decent Germans are national socialists, but only the best of them are members of the Party!"' Pushing his untouched plate away, he went on: 'You'd think that after ten years with the company they wouldn't resort to this kind of blackmail! I like to make up my own mind about things. There's the Röhm affair . . . the Party programme . . .' He looked at me. 'Marianne, have you finished? Go and play in your room until bedtime! There's a good girl!'

'But Vati, I haven't finished my cocoa!' I protested, skilfully delaying my departure from the table by taking well-measured sips from my cup. Disregarding my lame excuse, my father continued:

'Hammacher spoke of being under pressure, of having to think of the firm's "political" image, of our order books, in short of the future of all staff in top-level and middle management. He might be right, of course, after all he's the boss, but damn it I'm no martyr! Shall I have myself demoted to a sales clerk?'

Spitting out the last words like food which had offended his taste buds, he stormed out of the room into his study where, long after I had left the table, the noisy opening and shutting of drawers suggested both anger and conflict unresolved.

In the end he had taken the oath, and now he obediently raised his arm for the salute, pinned the badge on the lapel of his suit and wore his uniform for rallies or when attending *Ortsgruppenabende* – the compulsory weekly meetings which, as he once confided to my mother over the *Abendbrot* table, reeked of beer, perspiration and the indoctrination efforts of halfwits and megalomaniacs who would be incapable of holding down a job in his company for a week.

My father seemed to like his job and to be good at it. Always immaculately dressed in a tailored suit, a white handkerchief folded in his breast pocket, he certainly looked the part as the company's sales director. He was a member of the best club on Unter den Linden and a frequent diner at the Adlon or at Horcher's, the expensive restaurant where he used to take important clients. At the age of ten, I realised that he had saved his career at a price, but not until I was very much older would I understand that by doing so he had become just another puppet in Hitler's political theatre.

CHAPTER 2

The Berlin Olympics

I looked forward to the Olympic Games with all the excitement and the innocence of my age. My class was among those chosen from Berlin schools to take part in the Youth Pageant in which the opening festivities were to culminate. There had been practice sessions on the *Maifeld* for weeks, whole days of warm summer sunshine, music, packed sandwiches and – what bliss! – days without homework.

One day we were ready. Every step, every manoeuvre of the intricate mass display blended with the organisers' concept. The city was ready, too. In appearance alone, it seemed to click its heels and salute its guests. Streets were lavishly flagged, and in Unter den Linden and on the Siegesallee, which had been termed by journalists the 'Via Triumphalis', huge flagpoles had been erected to form a fleet of banners in which swastikas, Olympic rings and the emblems of the fifty participating nations merged effortlessly.

Happy crowds sauntered along the broad boulevards where generous flower displays lent grey, stuccoed façades and mon- umental Third Reich edifices a cheerful touch. There was a holiday atmosphere about the city, a festive mood which not even the sight of massed uniforms could dispel.

Competitors and visitors from all over the world injected more colour into the street scene. Their sight thrilled me, for never before, except in picture books, had I seen people with black or yellow skin, or slit eyes, women in kimonos, men in skirts or turbans.

For two weeks, the world had come to Berlin; for two weeks, the world seemed to have shrunk to a few square kilometres.

'Don't stare, child,' my father would say more than once, pulling me forward through the throng of people and a medley of foreign languages, of which some – while asserting themselves

47

against the powerful Berlin patois – made me think of roller coasters, piano quavers, African savages or my father's Gigli records.

Before school broke up for the Games, the headmaster, at a special assembly, stressed once more the importance of the Games for Germany, as well as the role each of us had to play:

'Today, no other city is so filled with the Olympic spirit as the capital of the Reich. Berlin and its people are not only waiting to show off their accomplishments, but to demonstrate to the world that Germany has left the Treaty of Versailles behind, and with it its national inferiority. And now, girls, off you go. Let the world see what happy, healthy maidens you are! Heil Hitler!'

A fine evening descended over Berlin. Earlier rain clouds had dispersed and, following the day's grand opening ceremony, special church services, band concerts and rallies, a perfect scene was set for the evening's Youth Pageant in the Olympic Stadium.

Heralded by fanfares, cheered by over 100,000 spectators, the Führer and his entourage take their seats in the grandstand. The churning mass on the terraces quietens down. The show begins.

When our time comes, we take up our positions on the lush green stage over which floodlights have spun a friendly web.

The first bars of music burst forth. Dressed in white, and carrying boughs entwined with white crepe paper, hundreds of schoolgirls begin to dance sequences combining grace and harmony. Our bodies are moving back and forth like pendulums, heads and shoulders are swaying like tulips in a breeze. Arms bend or stretch to the command of the music, feet are moving nimbly over the grass floor. In the centre of the white rectangular tableau schoolboys dressed in coloured tunics and linking arms are forming the five Olympic rings. The audience is gasping, and more than once my eyes stray over to the grandstand where I know the Führer is watching – is watching me!

An enraptured crowd finally rewards us with enthusiastic applause, and we leave the Stadium past the Olympic fire as light-footed as we had entered it.

On the neighbouring *Maifeld*, still in formation and each of us at her own threshold of enchantment, we listen to the jubilant strains of Beethoven's Ninth Symphony in the evening's finale, '*Freude, schöner Götterfunken*', Schiller's 'Ode to Joy' set to music, while spears of light are arching high above the Stadium bowl to form an impressive silver dome.

The national anthem follows, '*Deutschland, Deutschland über alles.*' A mighty chorus surges across the Stadium walls, and explodes into an unending roar.

Over the next two weeks I was introduced to competitive sports at their best. My father had organised tickets for the main athletic events and I was privileged to watch Jesse Owens set new world records, a Japanese come first in the marathon and Finnish runners triumph over the long distances. I set my teeth every time a high-jump favourite attempted to beat a new height and trembled with the three pole-vault finalists who, in a five-hour battle, would not concede victory, not until, under searchlights and amid the bated breath of the spectators, a last supreme effort secured for one contestant the gold medal. As I watched the athletes, and shared the champions' euphoria and the losers' disappointment, I bit my nails, cheered, applauded or sighed in chorus with the crowd.

There were many hilarious moments when laughter dispelled the tension; there was drama, when a member of the German women's relay team dropped her baton only seconds away from victory. But then, I was beginning to realise, it was all part of the Games, and my father explained that it was the sort of thing which made them human.

But the athletes' fighting spirit impressed me most, their battle for centimetres or tenths of seconds, for which they had to tap their last physical reserves, and which struck a waiting chord inside me.

For two weeks my father and I talked like experts about track records and the placing of individual competitors; we bent over our programmes and counted team points; we chewed an endless number of *Bockwürste* splashed with mustard and sandwiched in crisp rolls. I was happy. I had my father to myself, the sun was shining, and wasn't life wonderful?

But one day, the wonder and excitement of the Games came to an end; the Olympic flame was extinguished and the flags hauled down. Reluctantly, I settled back into school life, more aware than ever of the strong undercurrents at home. Afternoon street-games now no longer held any attraction, and even my 'ark' would lie at anchor for days. Instead, I regressed to a toddler's stage, clinging to my mother's apron strings and my father's coat sleeve, perhaps suspecting that the time for play had run out, and that the flood which was raging towards me was unstoppable and inescapable.

In the afternoons, I often accompanied my mother into the park where I collected horse chestnuts which, on our return, she patiently helped me to carve into baskets and fill with heather. In the evening, my father might take out the cards and play rummy with me, a pfennig a point. For these hours, the world would seem outwardly in order – a world in which I stood otherwise watching, listening and waiting.

But not for long. A straight-faced man with a bulging briefcase kept coming, and my parents made sure that the door was firmly shut behind them and their visitor, and that I was out of earshot. My mother mystified me as well, spending hours teaching herself shorthand and typing, a form of self-inflicted torture which made no sense to me. For wasn't she married and a mother, and didn't she run a household and hold coffee parties and play the piano and have regular appointments with the hairdresser and dressmaker? And why, in a sudden show of indulgence, could I have chocolate pudding and vanilla sauce for dessert as often as I liked? Why was my bedtime extended and I allowed to see two Shirley Temple films in one week? Even more ominous were the compassionate glances from Erna, our maid, and the fact that the toffees in the red kitchen tin, normally reserved for easing the misery of cuts and bruises, were now there for the taking.

In bed I hugged my teddy bear and sucked my thumb, dreading the dark and the waiting nightmares, while in school I was increasingly reprimanded for sloppy homework and lack of concentration.

One day, after breakfast, and in no more than a dozen words, my parents confronted me with facts the implications of which required the rational approach of an adult, if not the objectivity of a stranger. At ten, I was capable of neither.

My father put his arm around me, summoning up the courage to speak, while my mother, not wanting to be excluded, clung stubbornly to my arm, dabbing her tear-swollen eyes with a dainty handkerchief.

Explanations and regrets followed, expressed in halting, choking voices. This then is the deluge, I thought. My parents are to be divorced later this afternoon. My mother will be taking me to Potsdam where I am to board in a girls' home catering for orphans and daughters from broken marriages. (Why can't I live with my mother?) I am to attend a local *Oberschule für Mädchen*.[1] My father is going to foot all the bills. He will not be required to pay alimony. (What is alimony?) My mother will have to get a job. (What job? Surely she hasn't learnt anything at her ladies' finishing school that can be turned into money?) They will both be pleading 'guilty' in court. (Guilty of what? And why then are they constantly putting the blame on each other?)

As I try to understand the implications of the changes ahead, I feel like going down on my knees, begging, 'Please, don't give me away!' But my tongue feels dry, my throat tight. Silently, I start screaming . . .

Visiting arrangements are made. Still I cannot cry, but something inside me is growing rigid and very cold. Questions no longer demand an answer.

Somewhere I hear a key turning in a lock.

Aunt Katja, mother's sister, a Valkyrie type with the gentlest of voice and manners, accompanied us to Potsdam for moral support.

'It's a lovely place, Marianne, you're going to like it,' she said, fidgeting on the wooden seat of the suburban train. But her well-meaning words merely brushed my ears. An elderly couple in the opposite seat, seeing my mother's tear-stained face, and her hand which held mine as if manacled to it, offered silent sympathy to what must have looked like mourners returning from a family funeral.

From my window seat I watched trees, houses, gardens in their late summer bloom flitting past. I was afraid of the open space that lay before me, afraid of the unknown beyond the threshold which I would have to cross in forty minutes, in thirty, in twenty . . .

[1] Fee-paying girls' secondary school.

CHAPTER 3

Home is a Horsehair Pillow

A substantial villa in several acres of garden, with a view of a nearby lake, the Home occupied a corner site in a quiet, select suburb of the former Prussian capital. Old trees added to the character of the building, which on one side was heavily shaded by a majestic horse-chestnut tree.

I squinted at the polished windows in which, from where I was standing, the light of the midday sun was glaringly reflected. I submitted passively to my mother's farewell hug, unable to respond to her tears in the sudden no-man's-land I had entered, with the images of the home I had left barely two hours ago already dimming in my mind and my new home, though only a few steps away, as yet barred by a heavy iron gate.

My mother rang the bell.

A minute later the gate opened and closed again behind me, leaving my mother in that grey territory in which arms can reach no longer, and as I looked back at her through wrought-iron curls and spirals the gate seemed to symbolise our severance.

'*Guten Tag!* I am *Schwester* Erna.'

The grey-haired woman who greeted me and took me by the hand wore a starched cap and an equally crisp white apron over a grey calico dress. Pointing to the recently scrubbed stone steps, and examining my shoes for evidence of dirt, she escorted me into the building, where I floated across mirrorlike parquet floors and up gleaming linoleum-covered stairs into a dormitory.

Here, rows of white iron beds and bedside tables stood against bare, bright green walls like soldiers on parade, the beds in their creaseless, spotless uniformity not tolerating any nonsense like teddy bears or dolls, and the table tops no childish trinkets.

'This is your bed, Marianne,' the sister said, putting my suitcase down, 'and this is where you keep your things.' She pointed to a locker-type wardrobe. 'You'll find two dresses in there. The one with the white collar is for Sundays. Now, unpack and change quickly! It'll be lunch soon. Leave the room tidy, and wash your hands before you come down. The wash-room is down the corridor. You'll find everything a bit strange to begin with, but you'll soon settle down. Matron will see you after lunch. I hope you'll be happy with us. We're all one big family.' She smiled, but her smile had hardly time to touch me before the door closed behind her.

A smell of cabbage rose from downstairs. I hate cabbage, I thought, and did as I was told.

The gong was calling for lunch. The sound of scrambling feet and children's voices drifted into the dormitory. In the full path of the sun, the room was aching with brightness. Wearing a cotton dress, which felt at least one size too large and scratched under the armpits, I sat motionless on the edge of my bed, shivering in my sudden nakedness.

In the coming weeks I found that I was adaptable – a quality which enabled me to fit into the communal life of the Home without sustaining too many mental bruises. In this I was fortunate, for having grown up without brothers or sisters I might easily have withdrawn into a corner or, in the cruel fashion of children, been rejected and driven into a new kind of isolation. Perhaps it was instinct, rather than a ten-year-old's callow reasoning, which told me that, in order to function as one big family, the Home would not, and could not, afford to suffer loners and self-absorbed members in its midst. Like my father, I had no alternative but to conform.

Conformity began in the dormitory locker. In winter it contained two grey knitted jumper-dresses which – despite their fortnightly airing and annual dry-cleaning – seemed to retain the underarm odour of a generation of previous wearers; in summer, two cotton frocks which lacked seasonal gaiety; while all year round aprons were worn indoors and in the garden. Conformity also came in the form of brooms, floor polishers, brushes, leather cloths, potato peelers and garden tools. It challenged us at bedtime, at table and on duty rosters, and it seemed to work through the single common denominator of obedience and discipline.

It was not long before I was another cog in the Home's

53

machine. I took my turn sweeping dormitories and polishing linoleum floors; I cleaned windows, helped to peel potatoes and, as part of my weekend duties, raked or weeded my allotted garden patch. I learned to mend the holes in my stockings, to say grace at table and the Lord's Prayer in church. And as bathtime on Fridays, pre-dinner shoe-cleaning sessions and supervised homework became part of a set routine, so too did woodwork, needlework and choir practice during the weeks of Advent. Yet there was always time to dawdle home from school, to play games or to be alone with my thoughts in some niche of the house or a corner of the garden.

Tucked away in such a corner behind old trees, and little favoured by the younger girls on account of its seclusion, a swing afforded me the privacy I often desperately sought during the first months at the Home; and from here, pushing myself into the gentlest of pendulum motions, I watched the glorious Indian summer turn into autumn: colours waning, changing or intensifying, oak leaves gliding through the air like tired kites and blackbirds stalking through the crinkled litter. Around me, horse chestnuts were dropping with the sound of muffled gun-shots, but I no longer picked them up to fondle their smooth skin or to carve them into baskets.

One day a bicycle offered a new freedom and fresh horizons, by bringing parks, lakes and the riverside within easy reach. And suddenly, cabbage and turnips seemed to taste less crude, the symbolism of the iron gate to be less severe, the prospect of peeling a bucket of potatoes to be less daunting.

I also found ways to assert myself, for in our domestic community, where a girl's age determined her place at table, her bedtime and even the fabric of her stockings, it was not her accomplishment at the piano, her dexterity at woodwork or needlecraft, which assured her status beyond her own dormitory, but her adroitness in turning chores into fun, her prodigious tales of 'true-life' experiences and her physical prowess.

My chances to boost my ego and consolidate my prestige came twice a year. In winter, once the lake had frozen into an ice rink, I basked in the admiring glances of the young spectators as I skated fearlessly, drawing figures and venturing dashing pirouettes; and in September Matron would ask me, as the most athletic, to climb the plum tree and pick the soft fruit for jam-making.

No one else dared to climb this tower of a tree, which required not only courage but the agility of a squirrel and a head for heights. For an hour or two the stage was all mine.

'*Marianne geht auf den Pflaumenbaum!*' the cry went up, and the younger girls scrambled round the tree to watch me scale the ladder and work my way up branch by branch as if no special effort were involved. Once at the top I always took my time. I enjoyed the views, looked down smugly into anxious faces and savoured every minute of my exalted position, before filling basket after basket with plums and lowering them down by means of a makeshift rope-pulley. And I never forgot to take my own fill of the purplish fruit, nor my dormitory's traditional midnight feast.

'It's strange,' the matron declared during lunch one day in September, looking disapprovingly at several untouched plates, 'that some of you always suffer from a lack of appetite, and look positively ghastly, the day after plum-picking!' She tried hard to suppress a smile as she tucked into her marinated herring, and as one girl after another from my dormitory asked urgent permission to leave the table.

I shared my dormitory with five other girls. Faded green curtains provided the only colour, and its hygienic, functional appearance often reminded me of the hospital ward where, frightened by its clinical whiteness and the smell of ether, I had once become tongue-tied at my mother's bedside. At first the dormitory had struck me as a room which would not encourage or tolerate happy thoughts, nor soothe the souls of its occupants. But then I did not know about the magical qualities of habit, about the collective power of homeless ten- and eleven-year-olds which can transform any room into a place of giggles and excitement.

Perhaps the dormitory's bareness and cool detachment excited our imaginations, so that the most hair-raising stories made the rounds after lights out – stories which enlarged, if only temporarily, our small world and provided colour, excitement and a blueprint of love.

When Manuela, the daughter of a divorced actress, joined the dormitory, her alleged insight into the world of the theatre soon added a new dimension and a certain piquancy to storytime. Her gaudy tales about Bohemian life held us spellbound and gave her an air of authority and worldliness which conferred instant status on her. Her 'true' stories were adorned by rich fantasy, and it was often hard to tell where truth ended and fiction began. One night, allegedly drawing on her own summer holiday experiences, and supporting her claims with a host of strange anatomical details, Manuela lectured us on the 'facts of life'. Not a single mattress-spring could be heard creaking.

'What was it like?' one girl finally asked.

'Tell us more!' begged another.

'Quiet!' the sister commanded from the door. 'Or do you want your weekend leave cancelled?'

Under my bedclothes, the monstrosity of Manuela's revelations touched my breasts, touched the soft down between my legs, until sleep eventually erased images of Manuela and two boys playing at 'babymaking' in a cornfield, and of babies born through terrifyingly small orifices.

Reading adventure stories by the light of a torch provided blood-curdling thrills, all too often at the expense of run-down batteries and bleary morning eyes. Later, adventure was replaced by the world of romance. Ten-pfennig novels, obtainable at every news-stand, and forbidden by the matron as unsuitable reading material, would pass from bed to bed, holding us enthralled with the sweet excesses of the heart, and making us chew on our handkerchiefs over an ill-starred courtship or a seemingly insoluble triangular situation, before the inevitable happy ending sent the avid reader to sleep with a sigh.

One bedtime in August held thrills of a different kind. For the third successive day, an unrelenting heatwave had closed schools early and thronged open-air swimming baths and ice cream parlours. At the Home, Matron and Sister were sweating freely, waving their handkerchiefs like flags. Windows and doors were left wide open to create a cooling draught, and for *Abendessen* cook served her own *pièce de résistance* in the form of a chilled blueberry soup. Dusk, however, did not bring the much hoped-for breeze to cool brows and rooms.

'You may sleep on the terrace tonight, children,' the matron said, rewarding my dormitory for scoring the week's highest marks. 'Take your mattresses out and make sure there is no nonsense!'

I am lying spellbound, with eyes wide open and sleep at bay. A full yellow moon is rising over the treetops and, in the sultry air, the sweet scents of the garden merge with its instrumental score. The scenario for the night is set. Whispers.

'I can see the man in the moon.'

'Just look at the Milky Way.'

'Isn't it romantic?'

Anita starts humming the first bars and, *pianissimo*, the rest of us join in the evening song which we have learned as small children, just as our parents and grandparents did before us:

> *Der Mond ist aufgegangen,*
> *Die gold'nen Sternlein prangen*
> *Am Himmel hell und klar . . .*

A tram is rattling in the distance – a single wave, swelling, breaking, ebbing away. A clock strikes. Lone footsteps on the pavement die away. The night has sucked up all human and mechanical sound, and I am alone with my stargazing until sleep comes like a shooting star.

I tried not to think too much of my parents, preoccupied as they were with the demands of their own lives – my father, the busy sales director of one of the country's leading steel companies, my mother now earning her living as a secretary at Luftwaffe headquarters.

Gradually, separated from them not only by time and distance, but by the sum of new experiences, the echo of happier childhood days grew weaker, while my love for the two former mainstays in my life resembled the tides, with the waters of the heart rising on visiting weekends and during holidays, and falling again once I was back among the Home's familiar smells of kitchen, laundry room and polished floors.

Subject to the availability of parents, relatives or guardians, the fortnightly or monthly weekend leave arranged for boarders proved a welcome change from communal life. Under the provisions of my parents' divorce settlement, my visits were to alternate, while Christmas and summer holidays were to be split between my father's comfortable rented rooms in the city centre and my grandmother's luxurious flat in suburban Zehlendorf, where my mother had come to live.

Weekend visits demanded a different kind of adaptability from me. Although I recognised the need to divide my loyalties equally between each parent, and in doing so, to reorientate myself emotionally each time I passed from one to the other, I was not prepared for the refined tug of war which ensued between them for my affection.

No doubt visiting two separate households brought me distinctive material advantages. Everything doubled up: gifts, praise, Christmas trees and birthday parties, but nothing could blunt the sense of commuting, of passing timetabled leisure under the watchful eye of a loud, ticking clock, and cramming weeks of living into parolelike hours which created no more than a temporary illusion of being 'at home'.

Intent on compensating me for the traumatic end to a happy childhood, and perhaps lost in the emotional maze of their sporadic parenthood, my parents reacted the only way they seemed able to – my mother by showering me with demonstrations of love and fussing solicitude, my father by taking me out to expensive restaurants, to the boulevards and into the show-world of the city.

On arrival, an initial feeling of strangeness would be quickly overcome by the exchange of news and by activities which seemed to race against time. Often enough, however, I might have to wait until my beloved hosts had detached themselves from their preoccupations or from some task in hand. And always there loomed the grey moment of departure when, looking at my watch like a visitor afraid to be late for another appointment, I got ready to return to Potsdam and to the Home which was not a home proper. My bag might be stuffed with chocolate and cake, but my mind would still be teeming with unvoiced or unanswered questions, and my heart often feel as naked as before.

Weekend visits always followed a set routine. Once I had completed my Saturday morning chores, and these had withstood close scrutiny by the matron, I went first to visit my father. In summer, we might go for a walk in the Tiergarten or visit the zoo, in winter we might stroll through a museum or attend a matinee. I remember long afternoons in his flat in the cool leather armchair, with books and magazines on my knees, and my father busy behind his desk, writing or bending over company papers – only a glance away, yet unreachable behind the wall of concentration. He would look up and say:

58

'I won't be long now, *Kind*, we'll soon have coffee and cake.'
The clock was ticking away . . .

Later we might have dinner at some expensive restaurant or at an exclusive Hungarian eating-place where the band, on seeing my father, would break off in the middle of a tune, to strike up his favourite *Csárdás*.

Friends and acquaintances. Introductions *en passant*.

'This is my daughter. Say "*Guten Abend*" to *Herr* Krause!'

'What a pretty daughter you have, *Herr* Gärtner!'

Strangers' hands, strangers' smiles. Quick curtsies between *à la carte* dishes with French names – gorgeous food which filled a ravenous stomach and lingered on the palate.

So many questions hovered on my lips while waiting for my father's glass to be refilled with wine. Tell me about life. Tell me about growing up. Tell me that you love me . . .

'*Vati* . . .?'

'Yes, child? What would you like for dessert?'

Racing thoughts during the *crème d'orange* or the *Fürst Pückler*. What time is it? I shall have to leave soon. Next stop Zehlendorf. Grandmother's house.

An unguarded moment at the station. Sadness flickering across my father's face while the automatic doors are closing.

'*Auf Wiedersehen, Kind!*'

Sundays spent with my mother and grandmother. Home-cooked meals. Cake fresh from the oven. My mother over-wrought, nervous and tired. A walk along the Schlachtensee. I am feeling rebellious and resentful, and don't know why. Even more disturbingly, I am avoiding physical contact, rejecting any mother-daughter intimacy while something inside me is crying out to be touched.

Again, questions on my lips. Tell me about life. Tell me about growing up. Tell me that you love me . . .

'*Mutti?*'

'*Ja, mein Kind?* Come, let's walk back. Time for lunch. What would you like for dessert? Watch your right foot! Is that a hole in your glove? I'll mend it later. There's *Herr* Kieper. Smile! *Guten Tag, Herr Kieper!* What did you say, Mariannchen?'

In contrast, there were Sundays and short holidays spent alone with my grandmother in a cosy, relaxed atmosphere in which, rummaging through an old chest or leafing through the magnificently illustrated pages of a priceless, gilt-edged Bible the width and length of my arm, I could easily forget about my mother being at work or in a sanatorium. There might be a cooking lesson, complete with pots and pans, wooden spoon and apron.

'Now, child, today I'm going to show you how to make a *sauce béchamel* without lumps.'

Visits to Philharmonic concerts.

'That's Furtwängler, the famous conductor. And now, listen to Beethoven, Marianne, the second movement . . .'

Walks beside the Schlachtensee.

'When I met your grandfather . . .' A journey back in time, which never failed to lighten up my grandmother's face and gave breadth to my own perception of the past.

But then there were summer and winter school holidays to redress my emotional imbalance – weeks spent with my father in the Silesian Riesengebirge or with my mother in the Harz Mountains, during which to my delight the solitude of pine forests, the grandeur of peaks or the charm of a brookside scene proved conducive to intimate dialogue and to forming a new, if temporary, parent-daughter relationship.

My school stood on the northern outskirts of Potsdam in a quiet residential street lined by lime trees and low-storied houses. Here and there, a shop hid behind an ornamental façade, neat and tidy in appearance, displaying in its narrow windows a minimum of goods as if to retain the genteel character of the street.

Except during the winter months, I cycled to school every morning, in summer often pushing my bike through the park and dallying down by the lake whose unspoilt beauty held a strange fascination for me – so much so that on many a fine, calm morning when its surface resembled a mirror that had been breathed upon, I would forget the time and only a desperate race through the streets, cutting corners and mounting pavements, would get me to school before the ring of the bell.

In my second year at school it became evident that I was good at sports. I was not only leaving my mark in the gym hall but on the sports field, where I ran faster, jumped further or higher, and managed to put more power behind the ball than anyone else.

It was an exhilarating experience to be good at something, and to feel superior to the rest of the class for at least an hour a day, for socially, in my drab, institutional dress, I found myself miles apart from the daughters of titled parents, high-ranking officers and government officials. Bringing the ghost of an orphanage into the classroom, it did not surprise me that I was never asked home for a birthday party, a meal or even to play for an hour. Perhaps status-conscious parents thought of me as an abandoned child growing up without social graces, and without the pink-cheeked look of their offspring. The assumption that my presence might tarnish their coat of arms or the family silver did not, at the time, appear altogether absurd.

Despite their parents' prejudice and my segregating clothes, most of my classmates treated me as their social equal, but the moment they unpacked their dainty *Wurst* sandwiches during the main break, or nibbled at a slice of home-baked cake, my own modest *Pausenbrot*[1] would all too clearly remind them of that invisible barrier which not even my new bicycle, my tales of weekend adventures in Berlin or my description of my grandmother's elegant drawing room could break down.

Membership of the Hitler Youth, however, soon brought a measure of social equality which I did not find in school.

[1] Sandwich taken to school.

CHAPTER 4

'I promise to do my duty . . .'

In the spring of 1937, the Home – self-sufficient as it was, and sheltered against the outside world not only by its iron railings but by the refusal of the matron to allow the disturbing news of political developments and the obtrusive messages of national socialism to invade the premises – was still clinging stubbornly, and demonstratively, to its own values and way of life. Here, no radio blared march music, no speeches by the Führer stirred its domestic peace, no picture of the great leader adorned the walls. Instead, firm rules left enough room for traditional after-school activities, and these were never more popular than during the weeks of Advent when hands got busy with wood, cardboard, glue, paint and needle, making tree decorations and presents for parents or guardians, while in stairways and corridors the smell of candle wax and pine wreaths mingled freely with the scent of Christmas cookies.

By spring 1938, however, even the Home had become politically permeable, and with due pressure exerted by school and Party authorities, even the matron, the gentle matriarch, had to submit to the dictates of the time, by allowing her young wards to join the *Hitlerjugend*.

One day, fittingly enough on Hitler's birthday, my age group was called up and I took the oath: '*Ich verspreche in der Hitlerjugend allzeit meine Pflicht zu tun, in Liebe und Treue zum Führer.*'[1] Service in the Hitler Youth, we were told, was an honourable service to the German people. I was, however, not thinking of the Führer, nor of serving the German people, when I raised my right hand, but of the attractive prospect of

---

[1] 'I promise always to do my duty in the Hitler Youth, in love and loyalty to the Führer.'

participating in games, sports, hiking, singing, camping and other exciting activities away from school and the Home. A uniform, a badge, an oath, a salute. There seemed to be nothing to it. Not really. Thus, unquestioningly, and as smoothly as one day slips into another, I acquired membership, and forthwith attended meetings, joined ball games and competitions, and took part in weekend hikes; and I thought that whether we were sitting in a circle around a camp fire or just rambling through the countryside, the old German folk songs and *Wanderlieder*, with which generations before us had celebrated the beauty of the country, had never sounded so good:

> *Kein schöner Land in dieser Zeit,*
> *als wie das uns're weit und breit . . .*[2]

It was not long, however, before plain-faced leaders taught us marching drill and marching songs:

> *Singend marschieren wir,*
> *Adolf Hitler soll uns führen*
> *in die neue Zeit,*
> *wir sind stets bereit . . .*[3]

I hated marching. For me, the column was no more than a powerful yelling body in which the marchers lost their identity and the sound of their own voices, and which, whether they wanted to or not, kept them rigorously in step.

There were now lectures on national socialism, stories about modern heroes and about Hitler, the political fighter, while extracts from *Mein Kampf* were used to expound the new racial doctrines. And there was nothing equivocal about the mother-role the Führer expected German women to play.

At one meeting, while addressing us on the desirability of large, healthy families, the team leader raised her voice:

'There is no greater honour for a German woman than to bear children for the Führer and for the Fatherland! The Führer has ruled that no family will be complete without at least four children,

[2] There is no fairer land around than ours . . .
[3] We sing while we're marching. Adolf Hitler shall lead us into a new era. We shall be ready at all times . . .

and that every year, on his mother's birthday, all mothers with more than four children will be awarded the *Mutterkreuz*.'[4]

Make-up and smoking emerged as cardinal sins.

'A German woman does not use make-up! Only Negroes and savages paint themselves! A German woman does not smoke! She has a duty to her people to keep fit and healthy! Any questions?'

'Why isn't the Führer married and a father himself?' The question was out before I had time to check myself. It was an innocent question, devoid of any pert insinuation that the Führer ought to practise what he preached. Silence filled the whitewashed room, but the team leader offered neither answer nor reproved the question. She strafed me with a murderous look, then called for attention.

'Now, I want you all to learn the *Horst Wessel Lied* by next Wednesday. All three verses. And don't forget the rally on Saturday! Make sure your blouses are clean, your shoes polished, your cheeks rosy and your voices bright! Heil Hitler! Dismissed!'

Perhaps not surprisingly, by the time I celebrated my thirteenth birthday, my initial *Wanderlied* and camping euphoria had gone flat and I felt bored with a movement which not only did not tolerate individualists but expected its members to venerate a flag as if it were God Almighty, and which made me march or stand en bloc for hours, listen to tiresome or inflammatory speeches, sing songs not composed for happy hours or shout '*Führer, befiehl, wir folgen!*',[5] one of the many slogans which, somehow, went into one ear and out the other.

But being old enough to realise that absenteeism from group and mass meetings, or a negative response to the demands of the movement, would be treated as political maladjustment, I thought it wise not to step out of line. '*Denke daran, dass du eine Deutsche bist!*'[6] they said, and that there was only '*Ein Reich, ein Volk, ein Führer*',[7] a motto which, like others, if trumpeted loud and long enough, would often come dangerously close to a Bible truth.

In my third year at the *Oberschule*, a minor classroom incident cruelly brought home to me how much my institutional label,

---

[4] Decoration similar in design to the Iron Cross (came in bronze, silver or gold, depending on number of children).

[5] 'Führer, let's have your orders, we are following you!'

[6] 'Remember that you are a German!'

[7] 'One Reich, one people, one Führer!'

and the wearing of the same dress for days or weeks, had made me a social outcast. This discovery happened to precede events which were to go down in the black chapters of German history.

Most of my classmates had received invitations to a birthday party. There were cries of delight, faces flushed with anticipation. Carola, one of the lucky ones, came up to me, clutching her invitation card like a winning ticket. Perhaps she could not help her smug expression.

'Hurrah! I've been invited to Biene's birthday party!' she cried. 'You know her mother always produces the most gorgeous cakes. And they have super prizes . . . and a magician . . .'

'Why don't I ever get an invitation?' I asked.

Raising her eyebrows as if she was surprised at the audacity of my question, Carola had her answer ready.

'Why, er . . . I suppose . . . it's because you live in a Home! Anyway your dress . . . it . . . it always smells!' She turned and skipped back to her friends in their fine woollen clothes and white knee socks.

Embarrassed, I fingered my hated winter dress and looked at my long, woollen hose. But then, I remembered, there was a PT period to come. Long-jump practice. I would show them how to fly five metres through the air! I would make them green with envy!

One day in November 1938 I woke to a clear, sunny morning, the kind which startles the early riser not only with its absence of clouds, but with a crisp, bracing air that holds a touch of frost and often portends an early winter. With time to spare before my first class, I cycled leisurely into town, unprepared for the sight that awaited me.

Along the main street the windows of Jewish shops and department stores have been smashed, their contents looted, torn, broken up and scattered. Shop signs, carrying Jewish names, are being hauled down, books are burning outside a bookshop and anti-Jewish slogans are screaming from walls and hoardings next to giant swastikas. All too visibly, storm-troopers are in command of the street, and still more are arriving in open trucks, sitting straight as boards, with tight lips and arms crossed in front of their chests. Here, jackboots are kicking in yet another window; there, a uniformed looter is helping himself to shirts and trousers. There are shouts of '*Juden raus!*' And now, hatred is spreading, is

65

moving into side streets, is sweeping my bike and me aside.

'Out of the way!' a trooper warns me, getting ready to hurl a brick into a first-floor window. '*Jude verrecke!*'[8] he shouts, and glass breaks.

The sun is streaming into gaping shops, flashing on glass splinters, highlighting the yellow Jewish stars smeared on doors like the sign of the plague. Frightened by the display of violence, by feelings which – as one trooper remarks – reflect those of every decent German, I turn to an elderly man who is watching from a doorway.

'Excuse me, why are they doing all this?'

'It's the Jews they're after.'

'Why, what have they done?'

The man looks at me as if I were trying to tease him with my question.

'Nothing, really,' he says at length. 'They're different, they know how to make money, they . . . don't they drum the lesson into your heads at school and in the Hitler Youth?'

I stay silent, wondering whether I have been wearing blinkers or earplugs lately. Look here, I should like to say in my defence, in the past I have seen anti-Jewish feeling expressed only in its nonviolent form: the sudden rejection of Dr Frankenstein, the family physician; a sign over a shop, '*Juden unerwünscht!*';[9] vulgar slogans in the street; Sarah, brunette and pretty, suddenly staying away from school, and no one has seen or heard from her since; the Aryan passport which, complete with family tree and evidence of at least two pure Aryan generations, identifies the holder as a 'first-class' citizen. Perhaps I have been trying too hard for too long to find my own feet, perhaps I have been too busy spinning a cocoon around myself.

The man noisily blows his nose.

'They took a lot of them away last night . . . burnt down their synagogue . . . and now all this! Poor devils!'

He shuffles away and I ride off to school without looking back, aching with what I have seen and heard and don't quite understand; conscious, too, of a strange affinity with people who are classed racially as inferior, just as – to all appearances – I am, socially, by my classmates and their parents.

[8] 'Death to the Jew!'
[9] 'No Jews!'

PART TWO

CHAPTER 5

A War Like Any Other?

Early in September 1939 I was playing in the garden after lunch, bouncing a ball against a brick wall and trying to catch it on the rebound. I was good at it, and in the process often threw myself sideways like a goalkeeper. I was in high spirits. The sun was shining, and for lunch there had been a bumper portion of chocolate pudding, which had caused the lower table to express mock concern for cook's eyesight. School had been good, too. My French essay had scored an acceptable mark, and in the high jump I had cleared 1.25 metres for the first time – the school record, as a delighted *Fräulein* Kaberski noted, congratulating me in front of the class.

And there was the garden. In its autumn colours, and with dahlias in their buoyant reds and pinks forming a striking contrast to the sated green of the lawn, it seemed to add substance to my own mood.

Suddenly, aggressive march music exploded from the open window of a neighbouring villa, drowning the beat of the ball. I missed and the ball shot into the shrubbery. I was about to extricate it when the brass cacophony was cut off in midair and fanfares prepared the listeners for a *Sondermeldung*.[1]

Motionless, not unlike a fly caught in a spider's web, I listened to the special announcement. The German *Wehrmacht* was advancing fast into Poland . . . Britain and France had declared war on Germany . . .

The Second World War had broken out.

I inched myself out of the shrubbery and resumed my game, not experiencing any particular emotion. Were my history books not full of wars and boring battle dates which we had to learn by

[1] Special announcement.

heart? War, as I pictured it as a thirteen-year-old, and as it had been captured in paintings, photographs and sculptures, was wounds and dead bodies and wooden crosses; it was galloping horses, flying banners and gleaming swords, guns, battleships and fighter planes. It was also soldiers' faces marked by battle fatigue or defeat, jubilant in victory or startled in death. But on this beautiful, untroubled afternoon, the very idea of Germany at war seemed to me as inconceivable as snow falling over Potsdam in July. Wasn't the sun shining, my bike waiting in the shed? And there would be fresh ham rolls for *Abendbrot*. Anyway, who was afraid of a fire-spitting dragon whose path one had never crossed?

In a series of staccato bounces my ball beat the wall like a drum.

Potsdam reacted to the declaration of war with the equanimity of an historic garrison town. Despite an increased military presence, and barracks swallowing through their gates pink-faced recruits like insatiable monsters, despite special front-line trains steaming out of Potsdam with the slogan '*Räder rollen für den Sieg*'[2] painted on their coaches, the town, with its baroque grace, still managed to evade internal mobilisation by refusing to abandon its serenity and its leisurely pace every time a special news-bulletin about blitz offensives invited public euphoria.

The weather played along as well and did not help to confront residents with the realities of war through an abrupt change of season. Instead, autumn descended gently upon Potsdam, keeping rain and winds for the time at bay.

The transition when it came was gradual. Perhaps it was occasioned by the sight of hundreds of Hitler Youths collecting for the national Winter Aid programme, their furiously shaken tin cans reminding Saturday shopping crowds that their country was at war.

Participation in street collection was compulsory, but despite the bonus of a school-free morning, most of my schoolmates seemed to see the scheme as a waste of good playing, swimming or skating time. Even so, a day on the streets could always be turned into a bit of good fun, by making bets as to who would have her can filled first, and to this end I subjected every

[2] 'Wheels must turn for victory.'

passer-by to my hitherto untested charms and powers of persuasion.

During the door-to-door collections of bones, rags, scrap metal and waste paper, we would sing ditties and, after ringing front-door bells with youthful persistence, grind our appeal for donations into the householder's face like a barrel organ:

> Lumpen, Kochen, Eisen und Papier,
> selbst ausgekämmte Haare sammeln wir . . .[3]

Whatever Hitler Youth and Party leaders wanted us to collect we collected, and we did so without questioning and without offering excuses. It was no time for questioning orders, for pleading fatigue or lack of enthusiasm, nor for explaining away one's absence on collection days with a visit to the dentist or an ailing aunt.

In the second year of the war *Eintopf* replaced the traditional family Sunday lunch, and the nominal amount of fifty pfennig – assumed to have been saved by cooking a hotpot of meat, vegetables and potatoes – was donated by each household to the Winter Aid scheme. Later, during the meatless years when seldom anything but potatoes, cabbage or turnip simmered in most urban cooking pots, and the Party's slogan 'Guns before butter!' tried to justify the spartan diet, the scheme was abandoned.

Appeals to school classes to assist the war economy never remained unanswered. In spring and summer we were sent afield to pick medicinal herbs, in autumn to collect acorns and horse chestnuts, in winter silver foil. In June, we were whisked off to farms to pick strawberries, in September to help with the potato harvest.

Over the years, the class's increasing extra-school activities inevitably upset the curriculum and made us limp or skip through our studies. Yet while the headmaster, a golden-badge Party member, zealously bowed to the exigencies of the time, many dedicated teachers boldly confessed displeasure at having to sacrifice academic standards on the altar of the war.

During the first years of the war our modest individual efforts

[3] Rags, bones and paper we collect,/even combed-out hair . . .

made good sense to me. The fatherland not only sent its sons to the front, I reasoned, but united in support of the common cause towards which end even schoolchildren had to play a role. However, one type of financial contribution I could not fit into the framework of worthy state charities and war funds – the monthly sum of fifty pfennig collected in school in aid of the countless countrymen and women abroad reported to be suffering from homesickness and yearning to return to the Reich in its great hour of destiny.

I would never have queried the truth of this statement had it not been for a letter from an aunt early in 1941, which my mother had given me to read. *Tante* Hilde lived in São Paolo, but far from wanting to return to the homeland, she had actually expressed her sympathy with my mother for having to live in Deutschland, war or not. Oh yes, she had not forgotten Berlin with its Havel lakes, nor that cute café on the Kurfürstendamm, or their favourite gallery on the corner of you know where – but were they not a small price to pay for freedom . . .?

The letter, which my mother had shredded afterwards, opened the door to a lot of questions. Were we not constantly reminded how fortunate we were to be living in the Reich under the leadership of Adolf Hitler, at a time of German offensives and massive victories? And now that German troops were reported poised to strike at Moscow, and swastika flags were flying over half Europe, wasn't the Führer being compared with Napoleon?

The Home had its own way of demonstrating its willingness to support the war effort. With an eye to its municipal accountants, it introduced new measures to save energy and running costs. Cabbage and turnips appeared more frequently on the table, butter was spread thinner, the amount of *Wurst* on each supper roll was halved. No food was to be wasted, and once I had to stay behind at table until I had finished my spinach.

Toilet tissue disappeared. Instead, the *Völkische Beobachter* – the official Party newspaper – was cut up into neat squares and threaded on a string. 'No more than two at a time, girls!' the sister screeched.

Great savings were hoped to be achieved during bathtime by having two girls share one bath. However, the novelty soon proved to be hilarious fun and, judging by the amount of water cascading onto the bathroom floor, to be something more in the way of playtime than a cleansing operation. Soap would fly around and ticklish soles shriek under nail brushes, while the tantalising sounds of splashing water and seaside merriment were spilling through the door, behind which the next pair of half-naked girls were waiting their turn.

It did, therefore, not surprise anyone when the original bathtime arrangements were resumed and the amount of water restricted to the height of a girl's navel.

'There's a war on,' Matron explained, 'even small sacrifices have a way of adding up to something in the end.'

A Sunday in March. My turn to share kitchen duties. A bucket of potatoes and a tub of water between us, my fellow peelers and I went about our business with as much enthusiasm as if we were doing arithmetic or weeding a flower bed. Desperate for fun, we dropped each peeled potato into the tub like a bomb. Water slopped around, cries of mock indignation ensued from those who got wet. Excited by our tomfoolery, we changed tactics, hurling each missile at a calculated angle.

'Stop it, girls!' the cook cried. 'This is not a bathroom! And if I don't put the potatoes on soon, you'll have half-cooked ones for lunch.'

A voice from upstairs. 'Marianne, your father is here.'

We went out into the garden.

'I'm afraid,' my father began, 'you can't stay on here after the summer holidays. Fifteen is the age limit. But I have found you another place, near Sans Souci Park – a room in the home of a titled family. One of their daughters, Reni . . .'

'She's in my class!'

'It appears she is struggling with French and English, and her parents hope that by doing your homework together she might improve her marks.'

'She's a genius in maths!'

'There you are! You could benefit from each other. And I don't have to remind you of your own maths marks, eh?' He took my arm. 'I met the baron and his family. He's running a boarding house for the sons of aristocrats, landowners and the like. A very high-class establishment. You'll have your own room, and will take your meals with the baroness, her daughters and the boarders. Otherwise, mind you, you'll remain strictly segregated from the boys . . . separate entrance and stairway, no communication except the odd word at table. It was a condition, a very sensible one, I'd say. What do you think?'

I watched my foot sink deeply into the slush. There was a similar sinking feeling inside me.

'I suppose it'll be all right,' I said, slowly lifting my foot. I still had three months at the Home left, a whole summer, a long time . . .

'. . . and for the summer holidays I'm taking you to the Riesengebirge for three weeks!' my father added, as if to sweeten the news. 'How about that?'

I saw peaks and pine-clad hills, crystal-clear water flowing over smooth stone like liquid silver and forming sleepy ponds between rocks; water crashing, leaping and foaming down the hillside with an unceasing roar, and millions of drops of water saturating the air around until it glistened and formed rainbow colours in the sunshine; I saw cosy *Bauden*[4] serving the famous Silesian *Streusselkuchen*, zither players providing *Stimmung* under the eyes of the *Schneekoppe*, steep and lonely paths haunted, no, watched over by Rübezahl, the wise, benevolent mountain spirit . . .

'I'd love it,' I replied and hugged my father's arm, hoping at the same time that the girls would have finished the potatoes by the time I returned to the kitchen.

[4] Mountain huts.

CHAPTER 6

Nothing but a Commoner

I clutched my father's arm. My feet dragged as if I were facing a session with the dentist.

Well away from the quiet residential street, and commanding a view over Sans Souci Park, imposing villas breathing wealth and class stood aloof behind iron railings and smooth lawns. I felt a strong surge of unrest and change in me, heightened by the sight of grey clouds racing in the sky and gusts of wind fitfully scooping up dried leaves from the gutter.

'There it is!" My father pointed to the house which was to be my new home.

Combining the ostentatious features of affluence with the nineteenth-century solidity of turrets and heavy stucco-work, the building suggested an authority which even its bay windows and alcoves were unable to soften.

I lingered at the bottom of the drive. As the wind whipped the trees around me, and the haughty house failed to extend a welcome, I ached with something akin to homesickness.

Five years at the Home had been a long time. I had pushed the heartbreak of the first weeks into a recess of my mind – the tears under my bedclothes, the pain of finding familiar faces and familiar views gone. Over the years, I had come to know every nook of the house and garden. 'Home' had been smells and sounds, the feel of my horsehair pillow. I had accepted rules and allowed adaptation to grow into strength. Now, with the sensitivity of a wind harp, I knew that I was not going to be happy here.

'Come, *Kind*,' my father said, easing me gently forward to the massive front door and ringing a polished brass bell.

A drawing-room. The regal figure of the baroness. An out-stretched hand waiting to be kissed. A condescending smile. An exchange of civilities followed by polite conversation about the weather and my school marks. My eyes seeking my father's, pleading, 'Don't leave me here, please!' Instead, a hug, a kiss. A maid showing my father out. A door closing . . .

When I saw my room my heart sank still further. Although pleasantly furnished, it was small and gloomy, and its view through the barred window and across the drive was bricked off by a stone wall. Left alone, I shot to the window and opened it wide, to let in the familiar bouquet of autumn – the musty smell of dying vegetation and the spicy scent of chrysanthemums, which reminded me of visits to my grandfather's grave, home-made kites rearing to fly and horse chestnuts, collected, carved and filled with heather.

When the gong called for lunch I still had not unpacked. An impatient knock at the door, and Reni stood on the threshold, smiling, her white-blonde hair, pale complexion and imposing height giving her, in my eyes, a very Nordic, very Aryan and very aristocratic appearance.

'*Tag*, Marianne! Fancy having you with us now! I hear you met my mother . . . hope you didn't find her too overbearing. Come on, I'll show you the dining room. You must meet the boys!'

In the oak-panelled dining hall, the baroness took her seat at the head of the long table, flanked by her three daughters. She briefly introduced me to the boarders and indicated a chair next to Reni.

'The boys are seated according to their age,' she explained, 'the younger ones at our end. The most senior boys have their own table over there.' She flashed a smile in the direction of an alcove where five young men were unfolding their linen napkins as if they were made of Brussels lace. 'All quiet now for grace!'

During the plain meal, which was served with the decorum of a gala dinner, I felt the eyes of fifteen boys upon me. A big lump in my throat made swallowing difficult.

'Eat up, Marianne!' the baroness commanded. 'Food is getting scarce these days.'

Between the main course and the dessert I watched the baroness celebrate her table rites. Ruffling her matronly feathers, fanning matriarchal authority like a peacock's tail, her cold, blue eyes roved over the diners and their plates. Her smiles and reprimands were graded, and while no more than the raising of an eyelid might indicate displeasure, her most affable smile seemed strictly reserved for her daughters, the youngest boarder and the senior table.

In between mouthfuls, and using her mother's temporary preoccupation with some domestic matter, Reni whispered the name of each boarder into my ear, complete with title, lineage and father's position; and if she wanted to impress me, she certainly succeeded. For me, history seemed to come to life at the mention of names intimately connected with the country's past, with political excellence or daring military leadership. Yet here, members of such noble families, the sons of diplomats, high-ranking officers or large-estate owners were polishing off their dessert as insatiably as any other schoolboys, although with impeccable table manners!

I felt reduced to the size of a dwarf and the status of a kitchen maid. But not for long, and at the end of the meal I walked out of the dining hall like a proper *Hansguckindieluft*.[1]

In the months to come I noted — not without a sense of satisfaction — that the boys' aristocratic hands could get just as dirty, and their knees just as chapped, as my own — not to mention their jokes which, once they thought they were out of earshot of the baron or baroness, were no different from those of commoners in their skittishness or in the forced crudity of adolescence. Discipline, however, strict as it was, seemed to come naturally to them, and, apart from clandestine backstairs meetings, to which Reni and I might venture after dinner for a mild flirtation or a verbal romp, the boarders always seemed to be conscious of their coats of arms and the precept that nobility comes with obligations.

It did not take me long to familiarise myself with the rooms to which I was confined, or in which my presence was restricted to a nightly ritual simulating court drill.

The ground floor was taken up by the family's drawing room and an adjoining conservatory, a marble-floored entrance hall, a wood-panelled library and my own room, which had easy access to a spacious cloakroom graced by a marble wash-hand basin and a WC of equal marble splendour. In an architectural grand slam, this complex of rooms encircled a mahogany-panelled reception room in which crystal chandeliers, wall candelabras, gilded

---

[1] Johnny-head-in-the-air.

mirrors and a mosaic parquet floor created the atmosphere of a royal antechamber.

The first floor contained the family's private apartments which, like the boarders' second-floor dormitories and studies, were out of bounds to me.

After dinner, the family would gather in the drawing room, to converse and cultivate each other's company in the fashion of large, aristocratic households. Here, the gloominess of my own room repeated itself, albeit with a difference, in that wealth was made to look unobtrusive, yet, paradoxically, was heightened by underlighting and dark, plushy colours. Velvet, brocade, silk and petit-point competed with lacquered tables, paintings in hushed Rembrandt tones with priceless bric-à-brac. Light oozed through heavily curtained windows, and in the adjoining conservatory, tropical flowers and trailing plants prospered around a small water-fountain.

Every evening, against this background, I made my nine o'clock appearance as instructed, to bid the family goodnight in a one-minute ceremony which, more than anything else, reminded me that I was not only an outsider but a commoner.

Wishing I could float across the Persian carpets, I curtsied and kissed the baroness's hand, then moved on to the baron, accepting a strangely limp hand and a magnanimous smile from the depth of his armchair, while Reni's sisters, whom I met only at mealtimes, brushed a 'good night' at me like a piece of fluff. Reni, my daytime friend, chained as she was to the drawing room in this sacred hour of family communion, and seemingly as distant and as unapproachable as her mother, would fidget in her chair, the expression on her face making it clear that she would like nothing better than to leave the room and end the day with some girlish prank or chatter. At such moments I felt the sense of nakedness return.

I did not see a single picture of Adolf Hitler about the house, and in rooms in which portraits of the Kaiser, Bismarck and famous soldiers adorned the walls it did not take me long to discern a hushed atmosphere of political dissent. Uniformed visitors, bulging briefcases, whispers – facts which on their own did not feed the imagination, nor give rise to suspicions, but which, once linked with a careless word dropped here and there, with snippets of conversation picked up through a door left ajar, gradually shook my prescribed notions of the Third Reich and planted something as yet too big, too crazy, too improbable to grasp. Only one thing I knew: the baron, his family and his wards formed a tight community, the ideas and aspirations of which did not seem to fit into the concept of 'Ein Reich, ein Volk, ein Führer', nor to complement the national socialist doctrines under which I was growing up.

My ideological confusion was thus complete.

The lady of the house reigned supreme. In this she was helped by a tendency to thrust out her formidable chest whenever the occasion demanded. And in an attempt to add height to her shortish figure, she used to sit or walk with a stuck-up chin and nose, which made her look terrifyingly aloof and superior.

In comparison, the eagle-eyed baron possessed the classical physical architecture of the professional soldier. His figure had retained some of the crispness and parade-ground agility of a cadet, while his bearing reflected the authority of his rank, his domestic decisions the maturity of a man who looks back on years of self-discipline and strict attention to moral and military codes. As an aristocrat he seemed to combine successfully a reverence for old military values with the tradition of his class.

His position as patriarch and out-of-school educator was never questioned, but I soon noticed that laughter did not come easily to him, which I attributed to the demands made on him as a man of his rank and station.

A lieutenant colonel and a staff officer, he was picked up every morning by a chauffeur-driven car long before Reni and I set off for school, and I would often watch him passing my window, immaculate in his uniform, a briefcase in his hand. Sometimes he carried a second one, which suggested that he was indeed a very busy man. (Much later I learned that the baron was a member of the Stauffenberg Group, the 'inner circle' of officers plotting to assassinate Hitler. The second briefcase contained the crucial plans that were to be put into effect should such an attempt be successful. It is believed that at times he also carried the bomb in it.)

Before he had his dinner served in his private apartments, and before changing into his mufti role as father, husband and the boys' tutor, he used to make a brief appearance in the dining hall – a grande entrée cleverly timed to coincide with the clearing of the dinner plates. Taking up a strategic position on a dais, not far from a portrait of Bismarck, his *Pour-le-Mérite*[2] and his monocle commanded instant respect, while his casual '*Guten Abend*' put the boys and me at ease. For some minutes, while we were tucking into our desserts, the hall resembled an operations room. The latest news from the fronts. Tutorial arrangements. Instructions to senior boys. A joke. A smile. Then his gleaming jackboots strode majestically out of the hall.

I quickly absorbed the new rules and learned to bow to a different etiquette. Yet, despite my willingness to conform, the lady of the house did not take kindly to me, frequently making me a target for humiliation and ridicule during mealtimes, in a voice loud enough to be heard at the senior table.

My latest flop in maths. My untidy room. Would I leave some potatoes for the others?

No surreptitious glances thrown in the direction of the older boys had a chance to go unnoticed: 'Keep your eyes on your plate, Marianne.'

Her sight, her hearing, her apparent omnipresence was truly remarkable: 'What business did you have on the boys' staircase last night?'

It took me some months to decide that if at least one country squire had featured in my family tree, or if my looks had been plainer, I might have found favour with the baroness.

Reni, I was quick to note, seemed to see in me more than a homework companion. Cheerful and easy-going by nature, she was always itching to have some fun and take off her domestic strait-jacket. And fun we had. Wasn't there the cinema and the ice-cream parlour? And what was wrong with clowning around a bit? Any excuse would do to explain our absence from the house on afternoons, and we could always pretend to have been at a school's choir practice or a games meeting.

We shamelessly copied each other's homework – English and French translations in exchange for square roots and the differential calculus.

When summer came, and with it a string of hot, cloudless days, we often took our books into Sans Souci Park. Seated on the steps of Frederick the Great's summer palace, it was not long before the scent from hundreds of flower beds, the procession of

[2] Highest Prussian military decoration, first awarded by Frederick the Great.

sightseers crunching their way over white gravel paths and the sweeping view of vine terraces in the afternoon haze instilled a delicious languor. Books would drop to the ground.

'I can't concentrate.'

'Neither can I.'

At other times such afternoons could be full of exuberance, with our noses pressed against the French windows of the chateau, or our eyes trained on visitors waddling in outsize slippers through the royal chambers like land-bound ducks. In the maze of secluded, shady paths, where formal hedges stood like brick walls and white marble busts on pedestals looked too solemn for respect, any trifling incident might trigger off giggles. Yet behind our fooling there seemed to lie a deeper need – laughter as therapy, bantering and teasing as a means of escape.

During the winter of 1941–2, the baron, giving his daily *Lagebericht*[3] in the dining hall, spoke of tactical withdrawals on the Eastern front. And he did not have to stress that the Russian winter had seriously weakened the combat ability of German army units. Somehow everybody seemed to know about the blinding snow-storms, about a ground too frozen to dig in for shelter, arctic temperatures freezing up guns, engines and mud-caked wheels and, worst of all, soldiers fighting without proper winter clothing. Those who came back from the front, wounded or with frost-bitten limbs amputated, knew best.

'The Russian winter is our worst enemy!' they said.

'Just wait until spring!' replied the armchair strategists; perhaps it was no coincidence that many of them wore the Party badge.

In school, we were knitting for the snow- and ice-bound infantry, but even someone as awkward with figures as myself could work out that by the time our woollen scarves and socks were finished and had reached the troops, spring would have arrived even on those distant Russian plains. And had we not been told that the war would be over by the summer?

Out in the streets, where recent snowfall had done little to assuage the sharp cold, I pulled my cap further over my face and flashed all my sympathy to the men on the Eastern front.

[3] Situation report.

81

With the late arrival of spring, trees had burst into leaf, and tulips and daffodils taken over the parks and garden, almost overnight. In the same spirit, summer did not bother with preliminaries but went into full swing.

At the baron's house, the date for the senior boys' June Ball was set.

The guest list was impressive, including many former boarders and parents. For two weeks, a nervous, expectant atmosphere hung about the house, dominated by the smell of wax, silver and brass polish.

A dressmaker had taken over the sewing room. Gradually, activities shifted to the kitchen; the baron's mid-*Abendbrot* appearances assumed a less formal note, while the baroness was too preoccupied with giving instructions to the cook, the maids and the colonel's batman to shoot verbal darts at me.

No one asked me whether I had a suitable dress to wear. In fact, no one asked me whether I would like to attend the dance, or at least watch it from the wings, just as if I had temporarily ceased to exist as a member of the household.

On the night of the ball, seated on my windowsill, I watched the guests arrive in their splendid robes or smart uniforms, and as soon as the dancing started, I sneaked into the library where a table lamp was spreading a slender light. The heavy oak door which buffeted the music of the band and separated me from the dance floor was locked, but the keyhole provided a tantalising view of the spectacle: smiling faces, swirling silk and taffeta, waltzing uniforms of grey and sober black, pearls, jewels and decorations, all forming fractured, fast-changing images, yet interlocking to become a dazzling whole. There was Reni in sky blue, her sisters in creamy white, the baroness in a robe befitting a duchess. Then darkness as someone stood with his back close to the keyhole. A voice behind me.

'Now, what have we got here? A *Schlüssellochgucker*?'[4]

Startled, I turned around. A young lieutenant was towering over me.

'My name is Klaus. I used to be a boarder. And you must be Marianne. I've heard of you. I thought you might be in there, all dressed up in white or pink or blue . . . I would have asked you for a dance. Can you dance?'

---

[4] Someone peeping through a keyhole.

I straightened up, still feeling tongue-tied and self-conscious. My eyes focussed on an Iron Cross.

'Yes, I can dance,' I replied at last. 'I had dancing lessons last winter. I love dancing!'

The young officer put a hand on my shoulder.

'Look, don't be sad! It's not all that much fun in there, anyway!'

'I'm not!' I burst out, hoping I could keep back my tears. 'I've got books to read . . . an essay to write . . .'

My new acquaintance reached tentatively for a strand of my hair and played with it. I held my breath.

'You know, we were never allowed in here,' he said, looking around the library. 'Splendid room!'

'How did you . . .?'

'I saw a light through the door . . . thought I'd have a look at what we used to call "Woodworm's Haven".'

I laughed. 'Reni and I do our homework in here.'

Klaus looked at me as if he was about to make a life-or-death decision, and when he spoke again, he did so hastily and with urgency in his voice.

'Look, I'm afraid I'll have to leave soon. I want to catch the last train to Berlin and the first one home tomorrow morning to our estate in East Pomerania. I'm on leave from the front.'

He took my hand, and wrestled every sentence from his lips. 'Do you think . . . would you . . . I know I'm rushing this . . . it's not the proper way to go about it, I know . . . it's this blasted war . . . what I mean is . . . would you like to visit us next weekend? I'd get my mother to send you a personal invitation. I'm sure my parents would love to meet you, and I . . . I'd love to see you again. Please say you'll come!'

I stared at him, speechless, wondering what a book on etiquette would decree for a situation like this. How was I supposed to respond to an impulsive invitation from a man I had only just met?

'. . . you could take the two o'clock train, and I'll pick you up,' he added as if to hurry my decision.

'She'll never let me!' I said, pointing my thumb in the direction of the dance floor in what I recognised too late as a gesture hardly befitting a young lady.

'Can't you ask your father for permission?'

'I'll try.'

'Please do! I'm off to the front again in ten days' time.' He kissed my hand and was gone.

I beamed. I felt no longer islanded in my nonbelonging.

'Who's Klaus, the lieutenant?' I asked Reni next morning on our way to school.

'Hardly saw him last night,' she said. 'He's awfully nice. Old family and all that. Loads of money, large estate. I wouldn't be surprised if my mother had plans for him and me. But then, mothers always want to marry you off to best advantage, don't they?' She grinned.

'I wouldn't know.'

'I say, Marianne, dear friend in need, may I copy your English translation before class?'

CHAPTER 7

'The countess requests the pleasure . . .'

The weekend invitation came on notepaper engraved with a count's crest. I felt as if I had won a hundred-metre sprint without really trying, and told the baroness of my intention to visit my father at the weekend. I was conscious of telling a lie – well, a small one, if lies came by size, one perhaps justified this once, and may the good Lord forgive me!

I rang my father from the station, and he voiced no objections. On the contrary, he seemed delighted and reminded me to take along some flowers for the countess, and not to bite my nails.

Klaus picked me up at the small rural station in a gig, and it struck me that he had taken off that magical cloak of manliness which comes with a smart uniform, particularly one boasting the Iron Cross, and which seems to make its wearer – be he the plainest of men – attractive to women. In his country clothes Klaus now looked no more than a Pomeranian *Junker*, a country squire born with horses, tenants and hunting rifles, as well as a title to land whose total acreage the naked eye could not survey.

A tentative June day was rising over the lime-green fields and the lush drills of potato and beet crops. The tall poplar trees at the roadside, which had grown with a bow to western skies, were, however, still small in leaf and mean with shadow.

'Summer is always late out here,' Klaus said. 'It's the winds – they find little resistance in the flat countryside. Mind you, we're not all fields, two kilometres up north we have some wooded land, our own hunting preserve . . . plenty of game. Would you like to go to one of the hides tomorrow?'

A gravelled drive led up to the manor house which, with its classic ochre-coloured façade, its white windowframes and sparsely-stuccoed cornices, looked like a chateau built to impress with unsmiling lines of sobriety and neatness.

Inside, thrilled but not overcome by the sumptuousness of the hall and reception rooms, I slipped easily into a role which I had seen others perform to perfection. I curtsied before the countess, and shook hands with the count. I remembered I had left the flowers behind on the train.

In the drawing room in which the family silver dazzled in the afternoon sun, the countess poured coffee into fragile-looking cups. A maidservant in a black dress, white, lace-edged cap and apron, served fresh strawberry cake.

'I hope you like strawberries, Marianne,' the countess said. 'They're the first from the greenhouse. You don't get them in town much, I hear.'

'I love them,' I replied, and accepted a large slice of cake.

Klaus handed me the whipped cream. 'We're pretty self-sufficient out here, anything from . . .'

'Damn well have to be,' the count cut in, 'the way that idiot . . .'

The countess shot a warning glance at her husband who checked himself and turned to his son.

'. . . I mean the way things are going. Fancy, a front line from Norway to Africa! Sheer madness! And in Russia . . . the man's objective is of course the Caucasus and Stalingrad, then strike at Moscow. He's gone mad, stark raving mad!'

The countess looked anxiously over her shoulder, but the maid had left the room to fetch fresh coffee.

'I'm afraid you may be right.'

'I tell you, the summer front won't hold,' the count continued, 'and the Sixth Army won't ride out another disastrous winter. And I am not playing Cassandra!'

Klaus, with a nod of his head, confirmed his father's view. The count speared a strawberry and looked around for support.

'Now, take Napoleon. He made the same mistake. I bet some generals last winter were haunted by the ghosts of his *Grande Armée*. Yes, Russia's winter is her strongest defence . . . and her most powerful weapon. Why doesn't he realise that?'

'Perhaps we ought to change the subject, father,' Klaus suggested.

'*Ja, ja*, there's nothing we can do anyway! Still, I wish they wouldn't post you back out east again, son!'

For a moment it was quiet in the room, then the count faced me.

86

'Forgive me, *Fräulein* Marianne, I got carried away. What a poor host I am! I ought to ask you about life in Potsdam and about all the things young ladies dream about. But first, tell me, what are they drumming into your heads in the Hitler Youth nowadays?'

'I . . . we . . .'

The countess rushed to my assistance. 'Would you like another piece of cake, Marianne? And you, son, what plans have you for the rest of the afternoon?'

'Have you been on a horse before?' Klaus asked me.

'Yes, a couple of times. I've had a few riding lessons with Reni at the Hippodrome in Potsdam.'

I was wondering whether good manners would allow me to accept a third slice of cake.

'Well, then we'll go for a gentle ride later, shall we? We keep an assortment of riding gear for visitors.'

I came marvellously alive in the saddle. We rode through the fields at a slow trot, not wasting any words. My eyes were greedily storing all the sights of the emerging Pomeranian summer, not missing a wayside cornflower nor a rabbit in flight, so that I could take a composite picture back to Potsdam and into the confinement of my barred and viewless room.

A few friends had been invited for dinner which was served in the banqueting-room by an elderly manservant whom I thought I had seen earlier performing duties as butler, gardener and groom. The white table-linen and the abundance of crystal and silverware on the table added a festive note to a strangely plain menu. During the meal I felt many eyes upon me, scrutinising the table manners of the young lady whom the heir to the estate had brought home for a weekend. Anxious to pass my test, and to show off my refinement, I did not load my plate, handled the heavy silver as if I were born to it and held the stem of my glass – to toast Klaus's safe return from the war and hopes for a good harvest – as I would hold a single rose.

After dinner we took our seats in the great hall around a blazing log fire and Klaus wound up the gramophone. During the light conversation which followed, which held no traps for me, the countess kept watching me with the kind of detachment with which a mother might assess the potential of a prospective daughter-in-law, and she did so discreetly and under a cultured smile. The count, less inhibited in sounding me out, asked bold questions about my family, while his sombre-faced ancestors stared down at me from the walls. The wine was heavy, and so was Klaus' hand on my waist as we danced to the music of the Twenties and Thirties.

Long before the ornate clock on the mantelpiece had struck midnight, smiles were flowing more intimately, expressing social acceptance, if not overt encouragement. Even the anonymous faces in their gilt frames seemed to brighten up, the goggling stags' eyes to wink at me from the wall. 'Well done!' a sculpted angel with a gilt trumpet blared at me. In the distance, I heard wedding bells ringing . . .

I deliberately shifted my thoughts to my grandmother's cosy flat where no one asked questions, then to the various athletic youth championships in which I was soon to compete, and for which I would have to be in good form if only to please local news-papermen who liked to take photographs and write about me in their sports columns. Next week I would practise some flying starts on the track, and there was no reason why with some extra training I should not clear 1.50 metres in the high jump . . .

A sense of proportion and reality returned.

'Another glass of wine, Marianne?'

The young Doberman licked my hand, and took me back to the bridal show where smiles had assumed a proprietorial air.

'Come on, son,' the count told Klaus, 'ask Marianne for another dance!'

'You two make such a handsome couple!' the countess stated sweetly. Hot Benny Goodman music filled the hall. I was ready to glide, to float, to fling my arms around all and everybody. Yet I heard my voice asking permission to withdraw, professing tiredness, a headache.

I curtsied expertly to the countess and tried not to fall over my legs taking my leave of the count and his friends. Klaus saw me to my room in the west wing, but I gave him no chance to steal a kiss. Thanking him for a lovely day, and feeling very mean, I slipped into the room and locked the door behind me.

'Don't forget the shoot tomorrow morning!' Klaus cried through the door. 'I'll have someone wake you.'

I looked at my flushed face in the mirror.

'I won't,' I cried back, and opened the window wide to let in the crisp night air.

I never knew how the news had leaked out. The moment I got back to Potsdam, the baroness was waiting for me in the library. Seated on a dais, and with a look of incensed royalty, she loftily informed me that my weekend escapade had made my further presence in the house undesirable.

'I've already asked your father to seek new accommodation for you during the summer holidays. Now, go to your room!'

As I looked at the tower of anger, I suddenly saw the baroness divested of all the pretensions of her class, vulnerable as any mother who was seeing her own plans foiled.

I stayed silent, for I knew that over the weekend I had put to the test more than good table manners.

CHAPTER 8

Benvenuto in Italia!

Shortly before the summer holidays and my departure from the baron's house, I was summoned to the *Bannführerin*.[1] The wording of the official letter left no doubt that I was in for a serious reprimand rather than congratulations as the new multiple-athletic youth champion of the Land Brandenburg. I had a good idea who had informed on me, as did the class, for Gudrun, the blue-eyed *Gruppenführerin*,[2] class speaker and watchdog, had often threatened to report me to local BDM headquarters for sloppy greeting habits and for such openly defiant gestures as leaving my right arm stubbornly in my pocket or on the handlebar of my bike. Gudrun did not like me. She made no secret of it. And I suspected that if I had let her beat me on the track once or twice in the past, she might be more favourably disposed towards me.

Heftily built, with high cheekbones and a chin pointed like a goat's beard, she wore her hair neatly plaited and pinned into a bird's nest. She was slow to smile, deep-voiced and angular in her movements; there seemed indeed to be nothing gentle about her. Relying heavily on her Hitler Youth rank and political convictions, she had long been imposing her 'Big Sister' image on the class. Somehow we never questioned her leadership, for her authority plainly equalled that of the form teacher. The class secretly feared her, while teachers treated her with tact and made sure they never said anything which could be misconstrued or distorted.

Not surprisingly Gudrun lacked a sense of humour, a deficiency which matched her political make-up and was suitably reflected in the brown and mustard shades of her clothes. She pretended to

---

[1] Head of the local BDM (Bund Deutscher Mädchen [girls' section of the Hitler Youth]).
[2] BDM group leader.

have read *Mein Kampf*, and given half a chance would have cheerfully lectured us on national socialism and the role of the individual. Not content to check on the respectful observance of the '*Heil* Hitler!' in class or rebuke some wretch for poor attendance at cadre and group meetings, she examined the uniforms of her classmates like a sergeant major whenever a school display of solidarity had been ordered by Party or Hitler Youth leaders, objecting to a smudgy blouse, to an emblem sewn on too high or too low, or to shoes whose lack of shine could, in her eyes, only imply gross disrespect towards *die Fahne*.[3] There was no doubt about it: Gudrun was in control. Mutely accepted or furiously resented, she brought the kind of power into the classroom which hitherto had been the sole preserve of teachers.

At BDM headquarters – a stately villa and one-time Jewish property – a broad-chested bulldog of a woman was seated behind a massive desk with the expression of a prison wardress. Her blonde hair, pulled back tightly and knotted in the nape of her neck, added to the severity of her appearance, while a row of metal badges heaving on her starched, Persil-white blouse intimidated, rather than elicited respect.

I felt myself shrinking; my shoulders sloped forward, and I stammered my name. A voice which clearly did not expect, nor was likely to tolerate, any contradiction, censured me for not having attended meetings for weeks, and for failing to offer the official salute with due decorum.

Her question came like a pistol shot. 'What have you got to say?'

I was lost for words. How could I explain to this martial woman that the greeting was such a bore, or the infinite boredom of lectures and the constant demand to prove one's allegiance to the Führer? How could I define the process of disenchantment with the movement over the years – a process like growing from childhood into adolescence, with perspectives changing, and a more rational appraisal showing up flaws and stains in the political fabric? There was a war on, and here I was on trial for trifling with the salute, and for frequently leaving my chair at meetings empty. It didn't make sense!

Yet, undisputable power was sitting behind the desk and waiting for an answer, and I remembered the image which the

[3] The swastika flag.

Völkische Beobachter had created of me as a young, talented athlete for whom they would be looking out in the months to come. My confidence returned.

'It's my athletic training sessions,' I protested quietly. 'I have spent every free minute getting fit in the hope of qualifying for the National Youth Championships.'

Now a smile crept over the bulldog's face as if she had remembered all of a sudden that Potsdam's athletic ace was standing before her, and was calculating the prestige which my win, or at least a good placing at national level, would lend her own leadership.

'Yes, it is true, you have done very well so far,' she said at last. 'At the *Gaumeisterschaften*,[4] didn't you run the 100 metres in 12.5 seconds, one tenth of a second over the national women's record?'

'*Ja, Bannführerin!*'

'I still think the pentathlon is your strength. You seem to be an all-round athlete. I shall be watching you in Breslau. Remember, you'll be fighting for Potsdam!'

'*Jawohl, Bannführerin.* I'll do my best.'

Shifting from one foot to the other while my inquisitor perused a file, I saw myself racing my bike to the swimming pool in the hope of meeting Andreas, the most sought-after date from the *Realgymnasium*.

'Well, obviously you can't be in two places at once,' the voice continued, 'and I think we might take your recent athletic achievement as compensating for your absence at meetings. However, it has been reported that often you do not raise your arm for the salute, and in some instances have actually made a downright mockery of it. This is, of course, a serious accusation. You see, with your sporting record, Marianne, you must always try and set an example. I trust I won't have to reprimand you again. *Verstanden?*'

'*Jawohl, Bannführerin!*'

'Right, you may go now.'

With a '*Heil* Hitler!' of which the Führer himself would have been proud, authority dismissed me, and I felt like clicking my heels as I returned the greeting in snappy style.

The Munich–Rome express was steaming through Austria, carrying in two special coaches the pick of German Hitler Youth

---

[4] Regional championships.

athletes. Sitting by the window, I watched the Alpine autumn scenery unfold, and uniformed boys and girls flitting back and forth through the corridor, squeezing, jostling past the open compartment door and drowning the soporific hum of the train with their chatting and fooling about.

Although I recognised in my companions' effervescent mood and quicksilver faces my own excitement, I remained withdrawn in my corner. 'I'm proud of you,' I remembered my father saying not long ago, when I was chosen to represent Germany at the 1942 European Athletic Youth Championships in Milan, and I could not deny that I had been walking ten feet tall at the prospect of participating in an international event for the first time.

'There'll be competitors from twelve nations, all Europe will be there,' the selectors had boasted – adding, as an afterthought, 'with the exception of the countries with which we are at war.'

In its sports section, the Potsdam edition of the *Völkische Beobachter* had devoted a long article to my selection for the forthcoming games, and I knew my father would have shown the newspaper clipping to all his business friends: 'Here, read this, it's my daughter they're writing about!'

The powerful closing lines were still dancing before my eyes.

' . . . and now all boys and girls from Potsdam and the Land Brandenburg will be keeping their fingers crossed that in Italy Marianne will yet surpass her recent fine performance at the Breslau National Youth Championships for the glory and honour of Germany's youth.'

Yes, the article certainly imposed obligations, and left no room for defeat.

My thoughts strayed back to the first school games, when I had suddenly found myself out-running and out-jumping my classmates, and throwing the rounders ball out of reach of the tape measure. It had not been long before Hitler Youth leaders had discovered my prowess and calculated my potential.

I entered the world of competitive athletics at the age of fifteen. 'Marianne came, saw and conquered' was how a local sports columnist described my arrival on the scene, and I had been flattered to be noticed, if not exultant at being allowed to step out of anonymity. Now, at seventeen, I knew that my ambition to excel – perhaps a healthy and legitimate trait – had been aimed, in the first instance, at removing the institutional label of my upbringing and gaining recognition as an individual.

Right from the start I had been marshalled into the sprint distances and the pentathlon, and as my speeds, leg power and throwing range began to feature on the local sports pages, amassing points for the home team and prestige for Potsdam's leadership and the *Leistungs-sport*[5] promoters, I found myself being entered for a whole range of one-day competitions. I did not mind, for, despite my mean diet, I felt fit. In the end, a local sports reporter drew official attention to the risks involved. Following a meeting in which I had won all eight events, he expressed his concern for my health: 'Care should be taken that Marianne, with her bones and joints still at a growing stage, is not made to compete in too many disciplines!'

Over the years I had stood on the top tier of rostrums, receiving prizes, certificates, smiles and handshakes from prominent Party and Hitler Youth leaders, yet at no time had I been driven by an inner compulsion to compete in order to win. Neither had I allowed track training, or the emotive atmosphere of a stadium, wholly to take over my life. More than anything, it had been fun: the cheering of the crowd, the tension, the concentration, the fight for tenths of seconds or a decisive centimetre. The track events had perhaps been the most dramatic: shooting out of the starting hole or block, feeling every muscle in my body responding, and a voice inside me shouting, 'Run, Marianne, run like hell!' Beating down the track, not looking left nor right, and being speeded along by the crowd and often by my father's yell, 'Ma-ri-an-ne!' Then the final thrust across the finishing line. Officials with stopwatches and impersonal faces. A pat on the back or a handshake from the runner-up. A loudspeaker announcing results. Applause. Hitler Youths surging towards me, brandishing pens and autograph books. Clicking cameras, reporters and my sunniest smile – the same smile which next day would be looking at me from the sports page of the *Völkische Beobachter*.

The jumping and throwing had been good fun, too, even if each attempt to add an extra centimetre to a jump, or to part with a javelin, a shot or a discus at the right moment, angle and speed, was usually preceded by a wrenching in my guts.

I had always been a good loser. When I had not made it to the top tier, I had not sulked, turned my back on the winner or thrown my spiked shoes in a corner in a fit of self-disgust, yet I

[5] Competitive sports.

could not deny that I had enjoyed cheers and applause as much as my favourite *Schlager*,[6] and that winning, while holding all the exhilaration and loneliness of a child sitting in the crown of a plum tree, had made my world seem a better place – war, school, exams, being a boarder and all.

Outside, the mountains were edging closer . . .

'Isn't it strange to be going abroad in the middle of the war?' asked Thea, the relay reserve-runner, a girl afflicted with acne and a constant desire to compensate for her facial shortcomings.

'Yes, isn't it?' cried the other girls in my compartment, and the remarkable fact prompted a new line of thought.

It was indeed strange to be going abroad, and to be concentrating on matters of sport and national prestige, at a time when the grim reports of the firebombing of Hamburg were still playing havoc with one's imagination, most goods were strictly rationed, clothes were beginning to acquire a much-worn look and few people did not worry about next week's groceries or the prospect of another hard winter. Besides, contrary to official prognosis, wasn't there talk that the war would drag on and, in the process, intensify?

Yet, a month ago, at Breslau, the host city of the annual National Athletic Youth Championships, the *Reichsführer*[7] had said in his closing speech, 'If our enemies had seen the Games, they would realise that victory is on our side.'

What was one to believe?

'I say, Marianne, you did well at Breslau, didn't you?' The voice belonged to Lena, our hurdling weasel.

An elbow nudged me. 'Eh, wake up!'

'Yes,' I replied, not too convincingly, 'I came second in the pentathlon. If I'd thrown the javelin a few centimetres farther I would have made champion. But then I clocked in the fastest time in the 100-metre heats!'

'They picked you for the second leg of the 4 × 100-metre relay. Right?'

'They did. I'm afraid there won't be a pentathlon event in Milan.'

'Ah, but then they say the relay is the most important event;

---

[6] Hit tunes.
[7] Head of the Hitler Youth.

95

you know, *Deutschland, Deutschland über alles*, and let's show the other nations how strong we are!' The speaker was Renate, high-jump champion and daughter of a German aristocrat.

Now everyone advanced her own theory.

'I heard the Dutch girls have some real buzzers in their team!'

'The Roumanians have some good sprinters, too.'

'The Norwegians . . .'

'Don't underestimate the Italian team, they'll have massive home support!'

Renate rose. She did so as gracefully as if she were wearing an evening gown and someone had asked her for a dance. 'Excuse me, ladies, I'll go and stretch my legs a bit.'

'I say!' cried Käthe, the second long-jump candidate, who had not been able to sit still ever since we had boarded the train. 'Why don't we go and have a chat with the boys?'

There was a rush towards the door. I did not move.

'Aren't you coming, Marianne?'

'Later – I'm afraid someone might pinch my window seat,' I joked. I was glad the girls were taking their loquaciousness into the corridor. There was so much, after all, to be seen outside, now that the train was climbing higher up the mountainside past steep rock-face and precipitous terrain which, once it opened up, drew the eye to the greyness of jagged peaks, to a blue stream sneaking through a green valley, and, in the distance, to water spouting over sheer rock, exploding on impact in a cloud of spume and running downhill in silver veins.

The train, as if it were running out of steam, reduced its speed to a walking pace. I pulled down the window and greedily inhaled the clean mountain air which held the scent of pine and wild flowers, and the warmth of sun-baked rock.

My senses felt airborne.

'The mountains elevate our thoughts to their altitude,' I remembered my father saying, and I wished the train would creep along just a little longer. Instead, it picked up speed again.

'Everybody back into their compartments!' shouted the team leader, a no-frills, poster image of German womanhood. 'Fifteen minutes to the frontier. Tidy yourselves up, girls!'

At the Brenner, the German frontier station, armed police grinned and waved. There were no formalities, and the train soon started moving again to the calls of 'Good luck!' and 'Victory for Germany!' The next stop was Sterzing, the gateway to Italy. Uniformed *carabinieri* were sauntering along the platform, pointedly ignoring the sixty-odd bright faces hanging out of windows like trussed-up grapes. The team leader looked into our compartment.

'Get back into your seats, girls, and don't talk to the guards on the platform! Be on your best behaviour! Remember, you are Germany's young sporting élite ... you're representing the Reich!'

'I'm so hungry!' Gisela wailed.

Soon, boys and girls dressed in the uniform of the *Gioventù Italiana*[8] were handing small rattan baskets through the windows, and all of a sudden it grew very quiet on the train.

I did not look up and, bent over my roasted chicken half, hardly noticed that the train had started moving again. I cleaned the meat down to the bone, and polished off a stick of crusty white bread and a chunk of salami sausage before attacking grapes, large and sweet from hot summer sunshine, and a peach as huge as a man's fist. When I felt juice trickling down my fingers, I licked them with the delight of a child lapping up melting ice cream.

'My God!' I cried, leaning back and folding my hands over my stomach. 'I'd forgotten what real food tastes like!'

Gisela sighed. 'So had I!'

Nor did the other girls hold back with their comments.

'It was my first peach ever!'

'I didn't know that grapes came so large and sweet!'

'Hm, if this is Italy's welcome, I'm going to love every minute of it!'

Happy and replete I concentrated on the passing landscape south of the frontier, looking out for any features that might mark them as 'Italian' or 'foreign'. But the mountains still looked as impressive, the valleys still as green as on the Austrian side, except that sheltered, south-facing slopes were now tightly staked with vines.

This then was Italy, I thought, smiling inwardly at the romantic notions I had nursed of the country as a child. History, art and literature classes had in time painted a realistic picture, and now, for me at seventeen, Italy was more than spectacular sunsets over azure waters and the magic of Axel Munthe's Anacapri, more than dark, handsome men singing 'O Sole Mio' or serenading on the Grand Canal, more even than pasta, salami

---

[8] A fascist youth organisation.

and sun-sated fruit. It stood for sculptures and friezes, churches and palazzi, the Colosseum and the Leaning Tower. It provided the stage setting for Romeo and Juliet, and had once fed my winter-starved imagination in a cold classroom with Goethe's famous poem 'Mignon':

> *Kennst du das Land, wo die Zitronen blühn,*
> *im dunk'len Laub die Gold-rangen glühn . . .*

But Italy was also Il Duce and fascism. School and Hitler Youth lectures had extolled the virtues of modern Italy, by portraying Mussolini as a wise and powerful leader whom Hitler had invited to form an alliance against their common 'bolshevist foe'. School books, too, were stressing Il Duce's economic, social and political achievements, devoting whole pages to what their authors considered to be one of his finest feats: the draining and cultivation of the mosquito-ridden river Po basin, a topic seemingly important enough to be set for a history exam. As for his army, which we were taught represented a fine, courageous fighting force, I did not quite know what to believe, recalling a recent conversation between my father and one of his business friends.

My father was treating me at a Berlin Löwenbräu restaurant to a hearty Bavarian-style lunch for which he was happy to sacrifice a week's meat coupons. *Herr* Wagner, a high-calibre salesman and business friend of my father's joined us at table, and soon the conversation between the two men revolved around an Italian steel contract. But not for long. By the time our pork knuckles and sauerkraut arrived, they were speculating, low-voiced, about the fighting capabilities of the Italian army.

'Mind you, they perform best on a parade ground and in operetta.'

'Too much wine and long siestas, if you ask me. I'd say their temperament is just not suited to fighting a real war!'

'Hm, I like the Italians, they're good fun, but their soldiers . . .'

'Yes, not enough steel in their muscles!'

'Mussolini . . . let's face it . . . he's just another puppet of you know who!'

Bending over their plates, coiling up strands of kraut on their forks like spaghetti, they had nodded agreement with each other's cryptic remarks, leaving me to wonder about the obvious discrepancy between my own obedient notions about Italy as Germany's Axis partner and comrade-in-arms, and the undoubtedly well-informed views of two bright, sober-headed businessmen.

Their conversation had in fact added new impetus to a suspicion first planted at the baron's house, and steadily growing, that not all one heard, or read, or was being told, was entirely true, and could often be statements twisted or manufactured.

Milan. Special coaches to take the girls to one hotel, the boys to another. Bustling streets, hooting motorcars, colourful shop windows; well-dressed pedestrians sauntering along the crowded pavements, their girths suggesting that the time for notching belts tighter had not yet come.

I pressed my nose against the coach window. Apart from shop and street signs in Italian, the scene was as yet devoid of anything distinctly 'foreign' – and where was the war? A certain peacetime quality seemed to hover over the streets, reminding me of pre-Olympic Berlin, and of the first time my parents had taken me for a stroll along the Kurfürstendamm, where my amazement had known no bounds: a string of cafés, restaurants and cinemas; elegant ladies in white gloves and straw hats; fine-suited, -hatted and -gloved gentlemen buying posies of violets from fat flower vendors for their high-heeled companions. A café in which the sight of palatial decor and mountainous cream *Torten*, the sound of intimate voices and discreet cup-tinkling, had made me walk on tiptoe and speak in church whispers . . .

The hotel, a superior establishment judging by the gold-braided porter, jumped to life the moment the coach disgorged its load of hungry teenagers. Staff steered us straight into a large, empty dining room where a fleet of waiters shot into action. We had roast chicken and fruit for a mid-afternoon meal, after which the team leader read out the next day's training schedule and the week's individual starting times. No one, she said, raising her voice one decibel, was to leave the hotel.

'We don't want you to get lost in this big city. After all, none of you speaks the language and you have no lire.'

A voice. 'Why weren't we allowed to take any with us?'

The team leader weighed her words carefully.

'We thought . . . we thought it wiser to let you come without your own money . . . we don't want you to traipse around the streets and shops. Anyway, all you need will be supplied free. Any questions?'

There were none.

'You may go to your rooms now, unpack, wash, have a rest. Dinner is at seven. Afterwards we shall meet an Italian Youth delegation. So make sure, girls, you are presentable. *Heil* Hitler!'

The chorus which answered the salute sounded somewhat feeble. Perhaps this was due to Italian staff standing around, or did the greeting not find a willing echo in a foreign hotel lounge?

I shared a room with Renate, the high jumper, and it was not long before we shared a joke and found ourselves thinking along the same lines.

'I don't like the idea of remaining cooped up in here for the rest of the afternoon,' I said, 'I wish we had some lire.'

'No problem!' replied Renate. 'I can get us some.'

She looked quizzically at me. 'What do you think? Shall we slip out? We still have hours to go before dinner.'

'Yes, let's!'

We left the hotel by the backstairs like burglars, unnoticed by the team leader and a busy receptionist. The street was noisy, the air hot and sticky. Passers-by stared at us and at our uniforms, unsmiling, not offering assistance when Renate consulted a street map.

'We're going to see a friend of my father's,' she said. 'Uncle Vittorio is a banker. He always stays at our house when he has business in Frankfurt. You know, the way he talks he doesn't seem to think much of Mussolini. Back home he would have been put away long ago for his loose tongue. My father thinks he's the brother or cousin of some cabinet minister. I think he's awfully sweet, really.'

In the foyer of an imposing bank, Renate gave her name and asked to see '*il direttore, il mio zio*'. Instantly we were whisked through several doors into a soft-carpeted room which gleamed with glass, leather and polished wood. A heavy-set man in a pinstriped suit rose from behind a mammoth desk and came forward with outstretched hands.

'*Cara mia!* Welcome to Milan!' he greeted Renate. '*Come sta tuo padre, il mio amico?* Is that your friend?' He shook my hand. 'Sit down, the two of you! Would you like some *aranciata?*'

Renate explained the reason for our visit and why we were not supposed to walk around on our own.

'Sounds a bit like a lame excuse,' she said, 'after all, we're not

100

children any more. But then, father has been pretty reticent lately about the general state of affairs.'

'Ah,' said the banker, scratching his shiny skull and looking rather uneasy. Like the team leader earlier, he weighed his words as if they were rationed.

'You see, *cara mia*, one can't help noticing certain . . . antiwar sentiments. Mussolini's position . . . he hasn't made a public appearance for some time. Also, there are rumours that a big battle is about to begin in North Africa, and this at a time when we haven't come to terms yet with our own heavy losses at the Eastern front. And there is the bombing of German cities – dreadful, dreadful!'

He dabbed his forehead with a monogrammed handkerchief despite the pleasant coolness of the room.

'I'm afraid the days of the blitzkrieg are over, and the Russian army is only waiting for the next winter. No wonder many of our people are tired of war, and resentful. Perhaps this is the reason why your leader has instructions not to let you loose on the city on your own.'

An hour later, Renate and I stood in the Piazza del Duomo at the foot of Milan's magnificent cathedral. Each of us had one thousand lire in her pocket.

I was fascinated by life in the piazza and quick to note that surrounding shops were not only displaying fine-textured and colourful garments, beautiful leather goods and exquisite glassware, but that pedestrians were sporting clothes of fashionable design and free of threadbare or mended patches – a sight that had grown rare in Potsdam and Berlin.

'This must be the famous Galleria!' Renate said, and turned into a glass-roofed and marble-floored Arcade lined with smart shops and cafés. 'Come on, let's taste that famous Italian ice cream!'

We sat down at an outside table of a *gelateria*.

As we spooned up our cassata to moans of delight, I continued to watch the passers-by, taking in every detail of their dress, their volubility, the eloquence of their gesticulating hands. Here at last was something superbly 'foreign', I thought: but wasn't it strange that, while people stared most indiscreetly at us from neighbouring tables, they did not smile nor engage us in friendly conversation, the way Berliners had demonstrated their spirit and hospitality during the Olympics? In the light of what the banker had said, were our Hitler Youth uniforms perhaps making us unwelcome visitors, as the representatives of a country which had drawn Italy into a war which most Italians might frown upon?

Such questions spread a shadow over the white marble table. I looked at Renate.

'I feel eyes burning holes into my jacket.'

'So do I.'

'It's our uniforms, of course.'

'It's what Uncle Vittorio tried to tell us.'

'Let's pay and go back,' I suggested. My mood had gone flat.

The opening ceremony of the Games, with its flag raising, fanfares and massed display reminded me of the Berlin Olympics six years before. Much water had since flowed down the river Havel, as Berliners liked to allegorise the passing of time – years in which I had made it from a terrace seat down to the stadium track. Now, instead of the Führer, Count Ciano, Italy's minister for foreign affairs, took the salute in the march past of the participants and, after a rousing speech, declared the Games open.

For days we commuted by special coach between the hotel and the stadium, the ride taking us through tree-lined avenues and – according to an informed Renate – past many of Milan's historic landmarks. Nor did it bypass the industrial suburbs, where soot had blackened tenements, people's faces looked grey and smoke was dimming the sunlight.

For days we lived on sandwiches, roast chicken and veal; for days we feasted on grapes and peaches, while in the Italian sunshine my relay squad easily qualified for the finals, and the stadium brass-band was given frequent opportunities to improve its rendering of the German national anthem.

However, on the day of the sprint and relay finals a case of diarrhoea had broken out among the German delegation – something amounting to a major catastrophe in the eyes of the two distraught team leaders.

'I bet they've put something in our food, to weaken our prospects,' Elfi, the third-leg runner suggested, but nobody laughed, feeling positively under par, and the way our team leader was glowering at the hotel staff seemed to suggest that she did not altogether discount such a theory.

I alone did not suspect Italian sports fans or patriots of having sabotaged our fitness. I remembered plum-picking time at the

Home, and I knew that our own gluttony was to blame, our craving for fruit that had either long disappeared from ordinary German households or never reached the shops in Hitler's stringent prewar economy.

The stadium, over which earlier rain-showers had formed a dome of humid heat, was packed with thousands of spectators in a rally mood which reached fever pitch the moment the girls' 4 × 100 metre relay finals were announced.

I crushed another glucose tablet in my mouth, blocked any further thoughts of bed and mint tea, and took up my position. It started to rain again. I swore and continued my warming-up spiel, bobbing up and down, accelerating leg-work in a mock sprint, flexing and relaxing limbs and shoulders, before taking a final deep breath and allowing my mind to freewheel. Suddenly I felt my body rising to the occasion, and now there was nothing but the straight lying before me – a hundred metres, waiting, challenging . . .

An expectant silence settles over the terraces. The gun goes off, the first runners shoot out of their starting blocks. Brunhilde takes the bend, and I begin to calculate the moment when to start running, in order to effect a swift baton-change – not too fast, lest I overshoot the line, not too slow, lest I lose valuable tenths of seconds. The sky, however, does not give a damn about the dramatic minute ticking away on the ground and opens up a torrential downpour. Seconds later, I feel a wet baton placed in my outstretched hand, and I thrust myself against the wall of blinding, pelting rain which is washing my face, seeping into my mouth, tasting of nothing. The stadium explodes. Cheers are showering the Italian runner in the neighbouring lane, ecstasy is pulling the crowd from their seats, is threatening me. And now I am not running for myself, but for Germany, my fatherland, the country of pine forests, Silesian mountains and Rübezahl legends, of Schubert impromptus, noble Beethoven symphonies and romantic evening songs; the country of Goethe and childhood stories, of apple pancakes and *Nusstörtchen*, horse chestnuts and giant sunflowers . . .

Then it is all over. I smoothly hand over my baton to Inga and, as through a net curtain, watch her going into the bend and Maria sprinting home for victory on the final stretch. In true mocking style, this is also the moment it decides to stop raining, and it does so as abruptly as if someone has turned off a shower tap. A shout behind me: '*Wir haben gewonnen!*'[9]

The loudspeaker blares out the result in Italian and German, proclaiming 'Alemagna' to be the winner and the German team's time of 48.8 seconds to be a new European record. The announcement is greeted with measured applause from the grandstand, to be joined seconds later by a roar from the terraces, when 'Italia' is named as the runner-up.

I take off my running shoes. This is it then! We have won! We have done our bit, I have done mine. Now let's see what Italy has to offer. And, *du lieber Gott*, am I hungry!

But first our relay team has to step on to the top tier of the rostrum for the prize-giving ceremony. I stand in front and in full view of the grandstand from where Count Ciano – uniformed, bemedalled and oozing southern charm – descends to make the presentation. A moist, flabby handshake, a screen smile, a medal and a silver cup for each member of the squad. The German national anthem resounds in perfect brass harmony. The sun is breaking through the clouds, turning the cups into flashing beacons. With our heads held high, our arms outstretched, we watch the hoisting of the flag . . .

In the changing room, an exultant team leader pats backs and shakes hands. 'Well done, girls! Well done! Now, listen: on points, the German girls' team has come first in the championships, far ahead of the Italians and the Dutch. Congratulations to you all!'

' . . . and the boys?'

'Second,' the team leader replied, looking suddenly piqued, not wasting another syllable on such humiliating news, but packing into her final statement all her pride and gratification: 'At least *you*, girls, have not let the Reich down!'

At the evening's gala concert our delegation occupied the front rows at La Scala, the city's opera house. One day, I thought, I shall tell my children about its stunning gold decor, its circles of boxes swathed in red velvet, the stare of opera glasses, the ladies' elegant robes and jewellery; I shall recall a setting which choked any thought of war in the bud and made me forget about the increasingly spartan way of life back home. Happily, I surrendered myself to Puccini's languishing music.

[9] 'We've won!'

Back at the hotel that night, the team leader called for attention. 'Tomorrow, the German delegation will be taken to Lake Como. Italian youth leaders and officials from the city of Milan have prepared a surprise package for us. We'll be treated to a steamer ride, to lunch at one of the grand lakeside hotels and a visit to the famous Villa Carlotta. So let's all get a good night's sleep, and make sure, girls, you're looking spick-and-span tomorrow!'

A beautiful September morning was flooding the Piazza Cavour with light. Open towards the lake and adjoining the steamer quay, Como's large square was lined with cafés and hotels, and on sun-strewn terraces elderly men were sipping coffee and reading newspapers. Palm trees. A blaze of trailing, carpeting flowers set amid all the whiteness. The faintest of breezes wafting ashore, mingling with scents sweet and tangy, and with the smell of the jetty where wood and tar and fresh paint were baking in the sun.

Rounding up some stragglers, the boys' team leader shouted:

'Come on, you lot! The boat is waiting.'

'Don't slouch, girls!' our team leader added. 'Remember, you have won the Games!'

Leaning against the deck railings, next to Renate, I watched the steamer heading out into the shimmering waters of the lake against which the lush shoreline vegetation and the blue hues of the distant mountains were clearly delineated.

The view was breathtaking, light, water and expanse creating the kind of setting in which a poet or writer might not have to wait for his creative spark, nor a painter for the first stroke of his brush.

My enchantment found words: 'God must have been generous when he created this landscape,' I said.

Renate seemed strangely unmoved. 'I've been here before,' she said, 'with my parents, just before the war. I remember white sailing-boats and a fleet of steamers plying back and forth.'

I wished I were on a dinghy, alone with oars and the lake.

Behind me, the voluble Italian guide, who had given up translating superlatives into broken German, opened his arms and, looking out towards the lake, cried, '*Bellissimo!*'

Tremezzo. A lakeside *palazzo*-sized hotel. A fairy-tale tableau. In a sumptuous banqueting room sunlight is trapped in mirrors and chandeliers. A long table heaves under silver, candlesticks and lavish flower arrangements. Trusses of grapes and vine leaves

105

trailing from terraced stands resemble the Hanging Gardens of Babylon.

While Italian youth leaders and pot-bellied dignitaries delay the *hors d'oeuvres* with speeches about Italy, the Reich and the merits of physical training, boys and girls, desperate for the serving signal, keep a close watch on the fleet of waiters sailing into the hall with silver platters and tureens.

Later that afternoon, tiptoeing through the splendour of the Villa Carlotta, replete and happy, I listened only half-heartedly to the guide's running commentary on the history of its art treasures and when my chance came, slipped out into the sub-tropical gardens where the sleepy heat-haze had lifted and the sun was casting shadows again. I was spellbound, a child to whom access to a magic garden had been granted.

Cypress-bordered alleys, exotic flowers, lawns dotted with palm and rustling bay-trees. A scented lemon-grove. Secluded walks where light and shade were dancing on marble benches and white grottoes. An archway wreathed with roses and over time-worn steps, leading down to a formal box-edged rose-garden. Here, the magic was complete: a fountain, fragrant air filled with vapour and rainbow colours, a marble balustrade with crimson flowers cascading from ornamental stone vases, and – at the foot of it all – the lake which had turned into a sheet of silver in the afternoon sun.

I felt tempted to open my arms and cry out, '*Bellissimo!*'

The platform at Milan's glass-roofed central station was crowded. Other northbound delegations stood or sat around in orderly groups, each keeping strictly to itself and speaking its national language. Around us trains were arriving and departing, carriages being coupled or uncoupled, engines sounding their steam whistles. Yet all the familiar hubbub of a mainline station did not drown the ebullient, stentorian voices of Italian families who – sometimes three generations strong – had come to see a traveller off.

From a Berlin–Milan sleeper train, clean-shaven, smart-suited men, many German and Italian officers among them, and elegant, self-assured women stepped out on to the platform and called for porters.

On another platform, a slow train chugged in from the south, disgorging, from third-class compartments with slatted, wooden

106

benches, kit-shouldering soldiers, stocky, wild-looking men with cardboard suitcases and shapeless women weighed down by luggage and infants, or pressing bundles to their bodies like crucifixes.

Then a special train arrived, and we settled down in first-class compartments for the journey home. As we passed through the north Italian countryside, I found little to hold my interest. Not only was the corridor deserted, but the girls in my compartment looked positively morose and were fighting a yawning epidemic. It seemed reasonable to assume that no one in our coaches would burst out singing 'Deutschland, Deutschland, here we come!'

My hopes that the Games, and the girls' team victory, had made splash headlines in the national newspapers did not materialise.

My father met me at the station.

'I'm afraid they've given it only a few lines,' he said, handing me two newspaper clippings. Ignoring the throng of people on the platform, I raced through them.

One article from the *Völkische Beobachter* dealt briefly with the girls' 4 × 100 metres relay record and their proud team-victory; another, from the paper's Potsdam edition, carried a few extra lines congratulating me on my successful participation. In both, the failure of the boys' team to return with the coveted victory over Italy had been passed over in silence.

'It looks as though the boys committed an unpardonable sin not coming first!'

I looked at my father, but he did not, with a grin or a sideways glance, take the acerbity out of his remark. Steering me towards the exit, and clear of the crowds, he added, 'There's another reason for the modest coverage. Right now everybody's eyes are fixed on Stalingrad. The papers say our summer offensive there has been halted by strong enemy resistance. Also, there is no more talk about the imminent fall of the city, and it looks as if the Sixth Army will be stuck out there for months. And there is the increasing bombing terror ... Altogether, *Kind*, I'm afraid we might all be in for a hard time.'

'Gosh!' I said. 'I feel as if I have been away for weeks, in another world!'

'Oh yes, you must tell me all about it.' My father patted my hand. 'I'm very proud of you, but first I'm taking you to your new home.'

CHAPTER 9

'Hath not a Jew . . .?'

'*Herr* Benjamin is a Jew,' my father explained on the way to Potsdam. 'A year ago he was taken away, and he has not been heard of since. His wife is Aryan, which makes their three teenage children *Halbjuden*. But even *Mischlinge*[1] are having a hard time now, so I hear. Two of the Benjamin children had to leave school, the eldest is barred from university and army service, and like many others in similar positions they would find it impossible to get a paid job.'

'But won't they hate me for . . . being different?' I asked.

'I'm afraid it was the only place I could find for you . . . I mean, in a respectable household. Rooms are scarce now, and the house is not only splendidly furnished but is close to Sans Souci Park and to your school. I'm sure the family will treat you well. After all, they need the money I'll be paying them for your room and board. Heaven knows what they live on. Though *Frau* Benjamin, as an Aryan, has been allowed to keep the house for the time being, the bulk of their estate has been confiscated, which leaves them without adequate means of support. I suppose that's why they advertised for a lodger. Mind you, they must have been immensely rich. *Herr* Benjamin was a city banker, and bankers – particularly Jewish ones – always knew how to make money!'

My room at the Benjamins' villa confirmed my father's assumption about the family's former wealth. In fact, on entering my room, I felt as though I were stepping into one of Sans Souci's royal chambers, into a room which seemed to react with mild condescension to my cardboard suitcase and to the idea of

---

[1] Children with one Jewish parent.

108

having to accommodate a schoolgirl. Was it my imagination, or was the soft-shaded carpet crying out with indignation under the tread of my none-too-clean shoes? I glanced around. A long, gilt-framed mirror reflected my tanned face as well as the sparkle of a crystal chandelier whose pear-shaped cut-glass pieces tinkled in the draught like a glockenspiel. Candelabras on silk-covered walls, a marble-topped table with bow-legged chairs and a glass cabinet containing very fragile-looking porcelain, vied for dominance in the room, while a huge brass bedstead, discreetly tucked away in a corner behind a silk hanging, did not diminish its *petit salon* atmosphere.

A small grizzled woman in drab, loose-hanging cotton introduced herself as my new landlady. I looked into troubled eyes, at the grey shadow of a woman whose delicate shoulders were sagging under an invisible weight.

'I hope you will be comfortable, Marianne.'

'I'm sure I will, it's a lovely room,' I replied politely, not mentioning my dismay at finding its two front-facing windows fitted with iron bars.

'Come, let me show you the other rooms on this floor,' said *Frau* Benjamin, and the grey shadow led the way.

The ground-floor apartments, including a black-tiled bathroom with an oversized marble bath, marble floor, gilt taps and a toilet seat of polished oak, repeated the affluence of my own room. So did the lounge and the dining room where dark, wooden panelling and thick velvet curtains – drawn just enough to let in a slant of daylight – created the dignified gloom of a funeral parlour. By the time we had completed the tour the atmosphere of the rooms, in which sorrow, anxiety, resentment and hope-against-hope seemed to have settled like dust, had rubbed off on my mood. However, when my father got ready to leave, I did not communicate my uneasiness to him, nor did I ask him to find a cosier home for me. I suddenly noticed how much he had aged lately, how his own apprehensions had burrowed deep lines into his face. I stayed silent. I would cope. I would show him that I had grown up.

Back at school the following day, the headmaster paid me a special tribute during the general assembly, stressing my own part in the recent achievement of the girls' athletic team in Milan. Hundreds of eyes were upon me.

'. . . and we are proud to have in our school an athlete who has represented the Reich's colours abroad!' he ended his speech, inviting me to rise to the applause of the school. In class, *Herr* Banter, our history teacher, probing for evidence of how the Milanese had demonstrated their friendship with the Reich, asked me to give a detailed account of the championships and describe the sights I had been privileged to see, before he returned to history and, strutting about the classroom with his hands folded behind his back like a latter-day Bonaparte, lectured on the Napoleonic Wars.

Milan and Como suddenly seemed continents and light years away.

At the Benjamin house, I became aware of the plight of children from 'mixed marriages' for the first time, thus forcing me to sound out my own feelings on the subject.

Over the years I had forgotten about the disappearance of one or two familiar faces, just as my eyes had got used to anti-Jewish posters and newspaper caricatures, and my ears to *Aufklärung*[2] tirades by propagandists. Preoccupied with the demands of my own life, in which sporting success had gradually propelled me from the classroom corner into the school's limelight, I had never quite accepted, nor altogether rejected, the doctrines on 'race purification' as propounded at Hitler Youth meetings and – in the light of Mendel's laws – in biology class. Besides, years had gone by since that morning when I had witnessed uniformed hatred unleashed against the possessions of a mute minority.

Indeed, ever since the Star of David badge had disappeared from the streets of Potsdam, and the rain of several seasons had washed anti-semitic slogans from walls and hoardings, was it not as though the city's Jews had never existed? The film *Jud Süss*, on the other hand, highly recommended on thematic and dramatic grounds by schools, Party and Hitler Youth leaders, had often pulled the last nail out of people's consciences and rekindled or cemented their anti-Jewish sentiments by depicting the 'eternal Jew' as an obnoxious, scheming creature, a cancer feeding on the German economy and the very essence of Aryan life? And had the film, with its unequivocal messages, not made many a cinemagoer ask himself whether the expulsion of Jews from German society might possibly be justified?

[2] (Racial) enlightenment.

I did not have much to go on – a whisper here, a remark there. No more. For most people shunned the subject in conversation, and few dared to voice their views outside their own four walls.

'People are afraid,' I remembered my father saying, 'afraid for their own lives. There's nothing we can do, anyway. After all, the death penalty is not only for *Wehrkraftzersetzer*[3] but also for the *Feind im eigenen Land*.'[4]

Hans, Jürgen and Ruth, *Frau* Benjamin's *Mischling* children, accepted me into their family with smiles sustained by polite reserve. Having been left with a house, but otherwise with nothing but loads of free time, the boys went about selling family trinkets and growing fruit and vegetables in their back garden. Still hoping she might one day perform on an opera stage, Ruth took free singing-lessons from a singer whose own defective Aryan pedigree had banned her from public appearances.

All three listened tensely to round-the-clock news and special bulletins; they looked at old photographs, played stacks of records or invited their friends to dance to muffled boogie-woogie and jitterbug music until the early hours of the morning. And sometimes they would ask me to join them for an evening of what they called 'dancing on a volcano'. 'Life is short,' they said. They did not add that, for them, it had never been more uncertain, never more frightening.

Although my ration card boosted the family rations, food was always scarce on the dining-room table on which a fine damask cloth and heavy silver cutlery looked strangely at odds with the humble fare offered in *hors d'oeuvre* quantities on gilt-edged dinner plates. Still hungry after a meal I would steal into the garden to pick an apple or two, while looking forward to more satisfying meals during weekend visits to my father or grand-mother.

'How do you manage always to look so cheerful, Ruth?' I asked the red-haired girl with the blue eyes one day.

Ruth quietly changed a record and took a bite from a crust of bread. Her voice was firm, perhaps too firm for a fifteen-year-old.

'Tears, Marianne, are for the privacy of your bed. We might have no legal rights, and one day we might end up like my father,

---

[3] Citizen undermining fighting morale.
[4] The enemy at home.

111

but we needn't wear the Star yet. Besides, we still have our home and some freedom. Most important of all, we still have our radio. Nevertheless . . . I do envy you . . .'

Hans had quietly entered the room.

'Tell her!' he shouted. 'Tell her how much you envy her for being Aryan, for having the unadulterated blood of the master race in her veins!' He strode aimlessly through the room. 'Don't mind my sarcasm, Marianne, we know you're a nice girl, but this is the way things are, and we like to call them by their name. You see, they call us *Mischlinge*, hybrids, and they search our faces for any semitic traits. The SS, of course, would just love to pin the Star on our chests, to warn you people that we, too, are dangerous to your genes, to your children, to the economy, to Germany's culture and what else!'

He took a few steps towards me.

'You know, Marianne, they treat us as if we have no hearts and no feelings, or as if we were born as genetic freaks. Have you read Shakespeare in school?'

'Some of his plays,' I said, calculating the paces to the door.

'*Der Kaufmann von Venedig?*'[5]

'No.'

'Of course not! Wait, let me read you a short passage from it.' He took a leatherbound volume of Shakespeare from a book shelf and straddled a chair. 'Listen to this! This is what Shylock, the Jew, says: "*Hat ein Jude denn keine Augen? Hat ein Jude denn keine Hände, Organe, Sinne, Gefühle, Leidenschaften? Ist er nicht das Gleiche, wird von den gleichen Waffen verletzt, von den gleichen Krankheiten heimgesucht, von den gleichen Medikamenten geheilt wie ein Christ? Kühlt oder erwärmt ihn nicht der gleiche Winter und Sommer?*"'[6]

He snapped the book shut and came towards me again, in his eyes the rage, the torment of many days and nights. 'Do you know what they do to the Jews in concentration camps?' he shouted, the veins behind his temples swelling and turning bluish.

---

[5] *The Merchant of Venice.*
[6] 'Hath not a Jew eyes? Hath not a Jew hands, organs, dimensions, senses, affections, passions, fed with the same food, hurt with the same weapons, subject to the same diseases, healed by the same means, warmed and cooled by the same winter and summer, as a Christian?'

I backed away.

'They are treated like rats!' he went on. 'They are herded into trucks and railway waggons, in camps they are starved and tortured, and who knows how many are killed every hour in . . . in . . .' His voice broke.

'That's enough, Hans!' Ruth cried, looking hard at her brother. 'Marianne is only two years older than I am!'

'*Ja, ja, tut mir leid*,'[7] Hans said, his arms expressing the futility of his anger. 'I didn't mean to upset you. I was thinking of my father. You see, it's the Jew in me who needs to cry out at times.'

Embarrassment flooded my face. Stammering words of regret, I sneaked out of the room like a child caught in the act of stealing. I knew I would need time to sort things out. I was conscious all of a sudden of a twinge of guilt for having allowed my sunflower philosophy to ignore or doubt the truth of rumours, and the fate of Jews and half-Jews to occupy as much space in my mind in the past as news of civil war in Spain or the eruption of a South Sea volcano. It had all seemed so far removed from my own doorstep – until now. But then, I thought, how many people are ready to take rumours at their face value, particularly if they stretch the imagination to its limits?

[7] 'I'm sorry!'

CHAPTER 10

Sebastian

Two weeks after I had moved into the Benjamin household, Sebastian entered my life. The young lieutenant, who was serving in the Panzer Corps,[1] and now convalescing from a leg wound on an island in the Havel, literally appeared upon the scene as if he had been waiting for me.

I woke to a calm and sunny morning early in October, the kind which opens windows wide, sees housewives hanging up their first vats of steaming laundry before breakfast and brings a whistling postman to the door. The weatherman, forecasting meteorological superlatives for the weekend, spoke of a freak return of summer, and I knew that – in defiance of the calendar – women would hastily retrieve clothes already stored away for winter, thus adding, for a day or two, some sprightly colour to the copper shades in the streets.

I decided to wear a flower-patterned frock and to miss school.

'May I have your canoe for the day?' I asked Jürgen.

'Sure, Marianne, just make sure you don't sink it – there are enough boats going down around us right now as it is.'

The two-seater canoe was waiting for me at its river moorings. I changed into my swimsuit and was soon paddling up river towards the island of Hermannswerder where a former exclusive boarding-school, enclosed by parkland, had been converted into a military hospital. Choosing the quieter arm of the river to round the island, I passed a jetty on which a young, fair-haired man in an army shirt was staring out across the water. On catching sight of me he waved and limped closer to the edge of the planks.

[1] Armoured Regiment.

'Hello, pretty one!' he called over to me. 'What a way to spend a lovely day like this. I envy you!'

I rested my paddle, and the boat began drifting slowly downstream and into the direction of the jetty. The caller cocked his head and smiled.

'I suppose, *Fräulein*, you wouldn't consider taking me on board . . . just for a short ride? I could do the paddling for you. I still have the full use of my arms. And you would do a good turn to a semi-invalid – an infinitely bored one, I should add.'

I remained silent, not quite sure how to react to such a bold request from a stranger. Did the fact that he had been wounded in the service of his country, or the lovely river landscape, perhaps entitle him to relax the normal rules of etiquette?

'My name is Sebastian,' the young man continued, '*Oberleutnant* in a tank unit . . . in line for promotion. Got wounded out east, but the damned leg is on the mend now. I've been lucky . . . almost lost it. What's your name, *Fräulein?*'

The canoe pressed closer to the jetty.

'Marianne.'

'Marianne!' the young officer echoed, making my name sound like a term of endearment. 'You see, I've been cooped up on this island for the best part of a month now. It's nice enough once you're allowed to hobble around, but there is a limit to what you can do. I like coming down here. The rest of the world . . . the war . . . it all seems far across the water. But what about that ride? I'm afraid when it comes to the fatherland's gratitude, they give you the Iron Cross or promote you, but no one lays on a canoe ride with a pretty girl!'

He sat down stiffly on the steps of the jetty, took off his shoes and socks and dangled his feet in the water.

'The water is still quite warm for October. What I wouldn't give for a swim!'

I drifted closer, studying the tanned, open face which smiled so engagingly, and I decided that this man, who called himself Sebastian, was not only stunningly handsome, but that his unpretentious, shortcut approach – which in the streets of Potsdam I would have ignored with the modesty of my age and with what my elders called 'middle-class' respectability – held an endearing and compelling note.

My canoe touched the tip of the landing stage.

'You are pleading your case very well, *Herr Oberleutnant!*' I said, laughing. 'Oh well, I don't see how I can refuse a canoe ride to one of our convalescing heroes! But not for long, mind you! D'you think you can get in without upsetting the boat?

'I'll try. But please call me Sebastian. Eighteen months in the army, and in the war, and one forgets the sound of one's Christian name.'

Climbing somewhat awkwardly into the seat behind me, and taking over the paddle, he quickly directed the boat back upstream with forceful, rhythmical strokes . . .

There is an absence of words between us as if sudden proximity were keeping words at bay, or as if they might break the slow-flowing peace and tranquillity that is only fractionally broken by, and immediately absorbs, the sound of the paddle as it smacks the water, one, two, one, two.

An arm of the river, no wider than a channel, separates a tiny, reed-obscured island from dense riverbank vegetation. Here, the water seems to be standing still, the air to intensify the illusion of a midsummer day. Sebastian puts down the paddle, and suddenly words cascade from our lips as we talk about ourselves, about the war and about things past and present. Imperceptibly, obeying a slight underwater current, the canoe drifts closer to the island. As the minutes tick by, talk grows reluctant again, self-conscious, ceases altogether. Sebastian's hand touches my shoulder as if by accident, returns and stays on it. The silence between us begins to tremble.

'Come!' Breathing his request on my neck, he gently pulls me backwards until my head lies in his lap and his face is towering over mine. And somehow, incomprehensibly, I know things are as they should be, and I do not resist the touch of his hand on my warm skin, nor rebuff that same hand when it slips under the top of my swimsuit to cup my breast.

The sun is standing at its highest for October. A mallard, her offspring in tow, her yellow bill trained at the drifting canoe and its silent occupants, is passing by at close range. An involuntary flutter of my hand, already regretted, sends the young brood cackling into a zigzag flight. But calm soon returns to the water, and so does the floating quality of the moment. Minutes later, however, the canoe chafes against a stockade of reeds. Sebastian finds his voice first.

'Let's find an inlet and go ashore to stretch our legs, shall we? How small it is! I've never set foot before on a dwarf's island. I bet its diameter is the size of Gulliver's boot!'

116

A narrow passage through the reed bed reveals a stretch of sand and, beyond, some elevated grassland. Sebastian, his trousers rolled up to his knees, and exposing the scarred battlefield of a shin bone, pulls the canoe ashore, then holds out his hand, bows and sings to the tune of Don Giovanni's famous aria, 'Come o come, my lady, join me on my desert island'.

'I warn you, I'm familiar with Giovanni's little schemes,' I joke, welcoming the change of mood, but too embarrassed to look into the face of the man whom I have allowed to touch my breast. I unpack my food parcel.

'Would you like a lard sandwich or an apple?'

Later, lying lazily on our grass bed, we turn our faces away from the sun and towards each other, and when Sebastian kisses me, he does so as a worshipper might put his lips to the picture of a saint, or an Olympic champion to his gold medal. And when he does so again, he does so as a man, and his hand knows how to caress, and how far to travel, without shocking, or corrupting, or having the door slammed on it. And I respond with all the wonder, the urge and the restraint of one whose heart is in her first kiss.

Finally, loosening our embrace, I look at my companion of still countable hours and minutes.

'I . . . I don't understand,' I stammer, 'I hardly know you, Sebastian. Only a short while ago you were a complete stranger . . . and here I am . . .'

Sebastian looks at his watch, strokes my hair.

'We've known each other for an eternity – for exactly two hours and twenty-two minutes. You see, war somehow changes one's concept of time. If two people meet, and feel drawn to each other, and if they know the hours they may have together are numbered, normal conventions tend to fall. There's no time for waiting, no time for etiquette. The day seems to have twenty-three hours, if not less, and one grabs and tries to hold and treasure every hour that will lift one above the rest. And one also learns to let go again. The war is a hell of a teacher!'

A kiss sealed the lecture.

'I hope I didn't sound too much like a philosopher. And now, my pretty, I'm afraid we'll have to go back. Will I see you tomorrow?'

I try to smother the eagerness in my voice. 'I can pick you up again. Same spot? Same time?'

'Roll on tomorrow . . . and Monday, Tuesday, Wednesday.'

'School finishes at two.'

'Whereabouts do you live?'

'Next to Sans Souci Park, not far from Schloss Charlottenhof.'

'Well, then we can meet in the park in the afternoons. Next week they'll let me take my leg into town, and in three weeks' time I'm likely to be discharged and posted back to my unit.'

Three weeks can be a long time! Suddenly, Sunday, and the days to come are lying before me like numbered, gift-wrapped parcels.

Luckily, the weather on Sunday did us proud again. On Monday, however, autumn returned with a vengeance. Winds gathered and, sweeping across the town, broke up the mosaic of red and gold which had been dominating parks and streets. Yet, although heavy grey skies warned of rain, showers were miraculously holding back, allowing Sebastian and me to meet in the deserted park.

Golden foliage mingling with the claret shades of aged copper beeches. A sudden calm spell, a simultaneous break in the puffy clouds. A park seat instantly transformed into an oasis of sunshine amid the wilting flowerbeds. Sebastian and I racing towards it like hungry sun-seekers.

I played with the buttons of my dress. 'Will I see you again, Sebastian, some time, after the war?' I asked, instantly regretting the artlessness of my question, and biting my lips, before slipping into his arms.

'I'm afraid the future doesn't exist for me as long as the war lasts,' he replied. 'It has never looked more fragile, never more obscure for anyone. Only the present is real, the process of living from one hour to the other, from one day to the next. I feel it's the only way of thinking these days – a brutal, twenty-four-hour philosophy, you might say, yet one that helps to preserve one's sanity. Do you understand what I'm trying to say, Marianne?'

In reply, I picked up a stick and drew two lines on the ground, two paths crossing and running alongside for less than a shoe's length, before diverging, one line deflecting strongly to the east.

'That's you and me!' I said, seeking Sebastian's arms.

'I'm afraid that's us!'

There were more afternoons when, walking along the sheltered paths, hands linked, or snuggling up to each other in a recess of the Chinese tea pavilion, we did not talk much, as though words might

118

shorten the hour or detract from its quality, and whatever talk there was between us pointedly shied away from the future. Sebastian had made our position clear, and I was happy enough to keep my part of what seemed an understanding not to waste precious time on blowing soap bubbles.

As the days went by, I increasingly neglected my homework and in class was frequently reprimanded for staring out of the window. I failed my maths and physics class test, and I did not care. I was happy. Meanwhile, the expression on my face and my marked lack of attention was confounding my classmates.

'You look as if you were walking on clouds, Marianne! Who's the lucky boy? Anyone we know?'

But even though I wanted to shout it from the rooftops, I did not tell anyone about Sebastian, about my dates with an officer who had been decorated and might soon be a *Hauptmann*,[2] and whose looks would have had the class swooning, used as they were to the pink, pimply faces of the senior boys from the nearby *Realgymnasium*. Somehow, I was loath to share with anybody my first tender romance about which there had been a finality from its very beginning.

Three weeks after we had met on the Havel, Sebastian was posted back to the Eastern front where, he said, they needed every able-bodied man even if he walked with a limp.

He now wore the insignia of a *Hauptmann*.

I was standing by the open window, looking through the bars into the garden and across to the park. My thoughts were not on my English essay; with Juliet's farewell from Romeo still fresh in my mind from a recent literature class, I now knew that parting was not so much 'a sweet sorrow', but – as the French put it – '*mourir un peu*', a saying perhaps more poignantly valid in wartime.

Suddenly, the clouds, which perhaps in sympathy with my low spirits, had been hanging low for days, burst, and rain stabbed through the air, each drop a dagger driven home with pent-up fury. Within minutes, the street was transformed into a sea of murky, broiling water, the garden paths into muddy canals, and when the rain finally stopped, and only dripping leaves, a gurgling drainpipe, and the smell of drenched soil and

[2] Captain.

119

vegetation still spoke of the downpour, the air had a deliciously clean and bracing quality, the last autumn colours a freshly washed look. But the shower had done more: it had diluted my heartache and, in an odd way, straightened my perspective. And had Sebastian not promised to write? In my own letters did I not have the power – for as long as it took him to read a page or two – to drown the noise of shelling, to soften the touch of naked steel, to paint pictures more pleasing to the eye than a battlefield? In handicraft class I would knit him a scarf, and this weekend I would walk beside the river, even if it was steel-grey and flowing fast. And later, I would retrace my steps in the park to the rose pergola under which Sebastian, amid a flurry of white, wind-torn petals, had kissed me goodbye with the tenderness that had never asked for more.

I closed the window. My essay was waiting, so was some laundering and the mending of clothes which, under the textile rationing scheme, had no prospect of being replaced, not if I was saving up for that much-needed winter dress. But first I would go and listen to the afternoon news bulletin. With Sebastian somewhere out in Russia, the fighting in the Caucasus, on the river Don or in the depth of the eastern plains had suddenly assumed a new importance in my life.

For days a watery sun struggled vainly to pierce the cold mist which had risen from the river and surrounding lakes, and one morning the town lay steeped in a thick fog which seemed to creep into houses through every crevice, every loose floorboard and roof tile. When it finally lifted, the air had acquired a sharp edge, while – in true November fashion – the wind was going through the trees with a fine toothcomb.

I received my first *Feldpostbrief*[3] from Sebastian: '. . . For days the sky over this vast, flat monotony has been as muddy as the ground, and the wind is so fierce that it can keel a man over. The temperature is dropping, and if it wasn't for the dirt, sweat and engine oil around me, I could swear I can smell snow in the air. And I can't help thinking of a small sun-drenched Havel island, and of afternoons in the park with a certain schoolgirl! . . .'

In some letters lines had been blotted out by an army censor,

---

[3] Forces letter.

in others Sebastian's thoughts had unashamedly gone back in time: 'I shall never forget you, *mein liebes Mädchen*. I see your smile, your soft hair before me, and my lips remember every centimetre of your face . . .'

In one letter he spoke of the onset of winter, and in his sparse comments managed to communicate a coded apprehension of things to come: '. . . It has been snowing for days, and there is nothing around us but a whiteness in which a man is as conspicuous as a tree.'

Others brought the frozen landscape right into my room, so that I shivered in a wind which was 'spiked with ice crystals' and 'clawed at the face', or I stared, by the writer's side, into a night which was 'still and unclear and incredibly bright', yet held a strange sense of foreboding.

'It will be Christmas soon,' he wrote one day, 'a time I always associate with my childhood in Pomerania – with carols, hot punch and a crackling open-hearth fire; with the smell of pine, roast goose and spiced cookies fresh from the oven, and visits to neighbouring estates by horse-drawn sleigh . . . I might not be able to write for some time now, but I shall be thinking of you!'

And I was aching with the thousands of miles between us.

The British had recaptured Tobruk, the Allies had landed in North Africa. Air raids on German cities were causing large-scale destruction and heavy losses among the civilian population. The Russian counter-offensive had begun at Stalingrad. Actively campaigning against so-called rumours that a turning point in the war had been reached, Goebbels and Party and Hitler Youth officials denounced the negative and subversive attitude of some *Volksgenossen*[4] as treason.

At Hitler Youth meetings songs still stressed a commitment to which voices failed to lend the sparkling eagerness of earlier years.

> *Wir marschieren für Hitler*
> *durch Nacht und durch Not,*
> *für die Fahne und Freiheit,*

[4] National socialist term for a German citizen.

für Leben und Brot.
Unsere Fahne flattert uns voran . . .[5]

During the weeks of Advent, cadre meetings were suspended in favour of carol singing in Potsdam's hospitals and a variety of door-to-door collections.

In history class, Napoleon had long died on Elba, *Herr* Banter – contrary to his normal attention to historic detail – having pointedly skipped through the chapter dealing with the annihilation of the emperor's Grande Armée on the frost-scourged Russian plains and the ice floes of the Beresina. Much to his chagrin, the further study of nineteenth-century Europe was shortly replaced by a series of lectures by the headmaster on socio-political economy – periods during which I used to cover my note pad with sunflowers and smiling mannikins.

At the Benjamin house, the radio was now left on all day and would be besieged by every member of the household for the evening news. Collated, so as to play down any disquieting or demoralising element, news of British and American terror raids on German cities, and the intensifying battle at Stalingrad, were set against minor German territorial gains or retaliatory strikes – the kind of news snippets, which, delivered by the reader in a higher-keyed voice and given ample coverage, Hans called 'morale-boosters'.

However, the Benjamins had learnt to read between the lines and to interpret innuendoes, and while no gleeful comment was ever passed in my presence, the flicker of a smile on my landlady's face, a meaningful wink between the brothers, or Ruth walking more light-footedly through the room, reflected the state of the nation more accurately.

Christmas Eve 1942. The small local church is packed for the carol service, and my mother and I manage to get the last two seats in the back pew. And yet more people are thronging into

[5] We are marching for Hitler
through the night and through adversity,
for the flag and for freedom,
for life and for bread.
The flag is flying ahead of us . . .

the church until they spill from the aisle through the open door into the night where it has started snowing.

The minister tries to make his voice carry the message of the Christmas story through the church portals. The organ leads a keen congregation in 'Silent Night, Holy Night'. More carols, carols triumphant or reverent, reaching centuries back, and churning up emotions and childhood memories.

Ending the service, towering over a tableau of bowed heads, the minister remembers the dead. He prays for the men on the battlefield, for the wounded and those in captivity; he prays for those who mourn the loss of a son or a husband, for all men and women at home who are fighting the war with weapons of the heart and the spirit. Finally, his plea goes out for peace and goodwill among men – '*Friede auf Erden und den Menschen ein Wohlgefallen.*' For the first time, and with a sudden lucidity, I see something bizarre, even ambiguous, in such pleadings in times of war. Are not congregations in enemy lands addressing identical appeals to their God at this very hour, and with equal sincerity and fervour – to a God who does not, through some divine formula, as arbitrator or negotiator, bring about peace between warring nations, just as He does not award victory to the side which prays best or loudest?

My arguments, together with a Bach prelude, trail behind me out of church into a night which has turned white.

Back at my grandmother's house, a Christmas tree has been decorated with peacetime tinsel and a month's candle ration. An exchange of gifts. For me, an alarm clock, a book and, what bliss, a red handbag. White table linen, crystal and silver candlesticks salute a modest meal. On the radio, carols, Beethoven, Palestrina. In her armchair, my grandmother clutches a ten-week-old forces postcard from my uncle. My mother, smiling, eagerly welcomes the man she calls 'the major' – a lean, middle-aged aristocrat whose World War I injuries have banished him to a ministerial office chair, and who is putting his arm around my mother's shoulders as if he had a right to.

Christmas 1942, and no further word from Sebastian.

On my way to school at the beginning of February 1943 I came across some baffling sights.

Following a sudden fall of temperature, heavy overnight snow had brought out house owners and shopkeepers with snow shovels. Few of them, however, were actually engaged in clearing snow. People were standing around in groups – a practice normally discouraged by the police, who viewed with suspicion, and firmly dispersed, any gathering of citizens considered to constitute a crowd, unless they were required to line the streets for a march-past, or to demonstrate their support for a rally. Young children, delighted with the fresh fall of snow, and noisily expressing their rapture, were being hushed by their mothers and sent back indoors. More mystifying scenes: two women comforting each other in a doorway; an elderly man rushing up to another, raising his hat and going through the motions of condolence; a woman, the world's anguish on her face, storming out of a baker's shop, pursued by the slow beat of march music, shouting into the street, 'My son, my son!'

Stalingrad had fallen.

In school, there is a special assembly this morning. A symphonic funeral march forms the overture to a special radio communiqué: '*Der Kampf um Stalingrad ist zu Ende . . .!*'[6]

A voice that seems offensive in its forced detachment announces that the Sixth Army, under the exemplary leadership of *Feldmarschall* Paulus, has succumbed to superior forces and to adverse conditions.

'*Ich hatt' einen Kameraden . . .*' The national lament fills the hall. The school stands up and joins the chorus, then the headmaster takes over. His shaking voice pays respect to the emotiveness of the hour.

'Sit down, school! This is of course a disaster beyond all comprehension. The Russian winter . . . the superiority of the enemy . . . our losses.' He clears his throat, fingers his tie, reassumes *Haltung*.[7] 'And what can we do? Well, in the months to come, we must try harder than ever to prove ourselves worthy of the men who gave their lives out there, worthy too of the wounded, and of the men now entering Russian prison camps . . .'

I am no longer listening, and I feel as if the mothers, wives and

---

[6] 'The battle for Stalingrad has ended.'
[7] Formal bearing.

sweethearts of the men in Stalingrad have chosen me as the receptacle for their grief. Images come running: legions of snow-covered corpses, endless columns of exhausted, half-frozen prisoners stumbling east into a cold whiteness that has no horizon. And the wounded . . .

I feel sick, I feel like standing up and screaming, from the centre of the hall where I am sitting. 'Why? Will someone please tell me why?'

Instead I probe my pocket for a handkerchief. The girl on my right is noisily unwrapping some paper, the one on my left is playing with the buttons on her dress. The headmaster's voice rattles on: 'Three days of national mourning have been declared, during which the school will remain closed. Now, leave the hall quietly, and go home. Remember, girls, this is a very sad day, a national tragedy. School dismissed. Heil Hitler!'

'Heil Hitler!'

Back at the Benjamin house, Ruth was sliding down the banister of the sweeping staircase.

'Stalingrad has fallen, Marianne!' she cried, landing with a thud on the parquet floor, then racing back upstairs to repeat her ride.

Nobody seemed surprised, nor came to fetch me, when I did not turn up for lunch.

The nation mourned. In the streets, swastika flags flew at half-mast; classical music bridged the intervals between frequent news bulletins. Sitting around the radio more tensely than ever, Hans, Jürgen and Ruth made no effort to conceal their optimistic mood, and during mealtimes even *Frau* Benjamin was less reticent.

At a mass rally, broadcast to the nation, Goebbels declared 'total war', and the lusty yells of thousands seemed to support his demand that every man and woman should be involved in the war effort.

Over the coming weeks, the street scene changed visibly. Bars, dance halls, many shops and restaurants closed; older men were called up, women without young children and within a certain age group were drafted into factories, sent to farms or trained in defence units. Except for the presence of old people and children, and of soldiers walking on crutches or with limp sleeves pinned to their uniform jackets, Potsdam's streets now looked deserted during the day. Rations were cut once again, the collection of money and expendable clothes stepped up.

At school, the headmaster, who taught maths to the *Oberprima*,[8] wrote an extract from Goebbels' latest speech on the blackboard: '*Durchhalten ist alles!*',[9] Frederick the Great's motto which, in true Prussian spirit, he explained, combined the elements of fortitude, suffering, endurance and tenacity of purpose.

By the time the daffodils and tulips had burst into bloom, newspapers were still swollen with obituaries. In German literature, the class studied Goethe's *Faust*, devoting several periods to the seasonally appropriate 'Osterspaziergang':

> *Vom Eise befreit sind Ströme und Bäche*
> *Durch des Frühlings holden, belebenden Blick,*
> *Im Tale grünet Hoffnungsglück* . . .[10]

A peacetime mood of spring and joy pervaded the classroom for an hour – chaffinches danced on the windowsill, desks were bathed in sunshine, and even *Herr* Baumann's bass voice assumed a higher pitch. Then the bell rang and reality returned.

Out of school reality stayed close at hand too. Hans and Jürgen were picked up one day and sent to a labour camp. Party officials inspected the villa and declared their intention of using it for offices. Ruth and *Frau* Benjamin got ready to move in with friends. I packed my suitcase.

I never heard from Sebastian again.

[8] Top form (upper sixth).
[9] 'Endurance is everything!'
[10] Freed from the ice the brooklet flows,
Touched by the spring's life-giving glances,
Hopeful the valley's green advances . . .

CHAPTER 11

'And all about was mine, I said . . .'

A quiet residential street lined with cherry trees in their May
bloom, a handsome white villa built in the austere style of the
Thirties on the banks of the Heiligensee. *Herr* Mangert had
chosen the site for his residence well, and, as a distinguished
architect he could afford to. Besides, the area was highly
favoured by Potsdam's professional élite. Here, name plates
were ostentatious and of polished brass, heavy iron gates carried
'Beware of the dog' signs, and prewar notices discouraged
beggars and travelling salesmen, and directed legitimate tradesmen to discreet side-entrances. Thick privet hedges screening off
properties from the road and from each other ensured maximum
privacy. And who would not be intrigued by living a stone's
throw from a lake noted for its beauty and for the serenity that
comes from restricted public access, and which was bordered by
parkland on one side, villas and gardens on the other?

Now that refugees from the eastern provinces were pouring
into Berlin, and Potsdam was trying to absorb its quota of
homeless people, *Herr* Mangert – like other householders with
more than a specified number of rooms per head – was required
under a local government directive to take in a lodger, or to have
one or more refugees compulsorily billeted by the town council.

Needless to say, this was an unpopular measure and, not
surprisingly, the Mangerts – a childless couple – preferred the
first option which seemed less arbitrary and would leave them
with control over who was to live under their roof. They had
advertised for a lodger. My father and I went for an interview.
Herr Mangert, a balding, thin-lipped man in his early fifties,
took us on a tour of the house, through rooms beautifully
furnished and carpeted, filled with antiques and paintings, and
complemented by a tasteful and expensive-looking decor.

127

'Of course, I'm sorry for them,' he said, explaining to my father his unwillingness to accommodate refugees. 'I don't want to sound like a snob, but I hear most of them are really no more than peasants, people not used to our style of living. And, if you take in one, you're likely to end up with the whole family. They'll clutter up the house with pramloads of personal belongings, from pots and pans to rusty bicycles; they'll want to spend hours in the kitchen and hang up their washing on the lawn. And imagine children swarming all over the place! Crying babies, nappies, bottles!' *Herr* Mangert held up his hand in terror. 'I'm afraid my wife is very delicate. Not that we have no hearts — we've just donated money and a trunk full of old clothes! *Man ist ja kein Unmensch!*[1] As I was saying, I feel sorry for the poor souls. What a barbaric war!'

'Yes, I understand,' remarked my father politely, though he looked as if he didn't. 'I'm sure my daughter would be no trouble. After all, she's no stranger to your kind of milieu.'

He introduced himself as the sales director of a famous steel company and pulled out an impressive visiting card. His immaculate shirt, sedate silk tie and boardroom suit did the rest, and in no time I was declared bona fide as a lodger.

'You can have the use of the garden and the rowing boat, Marianne,' he said, as we stepped out on the white, stone-flagged terrace which overlooked the lake, while *Frau* Mangert, a woman of pale and diaphanous beauty, added all too hastily, 'But the kitchen for only a short time. Erna, our housekeeper, is very sensitive about her kitchen! You wouldn't want to do much cooking anyway, would you?'

'No, not really,' I replied, seeing the range of self-cooked meals drastically reduced.

Herr Mangert patted my shoulder. 'I'm afraid I also have to insist that you keep to your own room and make yourself as unobtrusive as possible . . . a matter of privacy, you understand.' He gave my father a man-to-man look while his wife offered me a saccharine smile as a palliative.

I was angling for a vaguely polite reply, seeing before me an exquisite home in an enviable setting, and staring in disbelief at skin-deep smiles and at two people in whose self-centred universe charity seemed to be nothing but a Christian catch-phrase.

[1] 'After all, one is no monster!'

A week later, just before my eighteenth birthday, I moved into the converted attic room where a large oriel window, besides framing a generous view of spring-clipped lawns, meticulous borders and blossoming lilac-trees, offered a wide-lens picture of the sleepy, shimmering lake and the park opposite.

This is not a dream, I kept reminding myself. I was free now, released at last from a regimented mock home-life. No more barred windows for me! No more rooms which chilled with their waxed, scrubbed brightness, with a spirit-clipping gloom or with the opulence of crystal and marble. No more curtseying where deference was not due. No more awkward moments, riding out humiliation as a 'commoner' or as the object of envy or resentment for being Aryan and 'different'!

Before I unpacked, I ran into the garden and cut an armful of lilac for my room.

I was no less intoxicated with the new mental and physical space around me and – once the school bell rang – with being mistress of my own time. I spent afternoons in seeking the spell, if not the total dominance, of the lake and I idled away evenings in the cinema, trembling with the heroine of love stories or escaping into the glittering confectionery world of German film musicals. Sometimes Benji, the boy next door, who was waiting for his call up, asked me over for a party, and we would dance behind closed windows to swing music and American hits of the Thirties – music pronounced 'decadent' and forbidden by the Party.

Suddenly bored with competitive sports, I no longer attended athletic training sessions and often invented excuses for my absence from the various summer events. Physically, I felt I had no more to give, constantly hungry and often tired as I was. A diet of thin restaurant soups, cabbage or fried potatoes for lunch, skimmed milk puddings or mean sandwiches for *Abendbrot* did little to promote physical fitness or a desire to spend my existing resources on the sports field.

Mentally, too, I had changed. Years of competitive athletics had taught me more than self-discipline and self-respect. I no longer kept my eyes fixed on the ground, on my plate or on an institutional dress, but knew how to take my own bearings. My ego no longer clamoured for the cheering of the crowd as a panacea for loneliness, nor for the awed whispers of local competitors in the changing room – 'That's her . . . over there . . . we won't have much of a chance!'

129

Yes, I was a big girl now! Not only did I wear a bra and size six shoes, but teachers used the third person singular when addressing me – the outward acknowledgement of adulthood. And what better proof had I of having outgrown adolescence than being content with small doses of happiness, because to ask for more at a time like this was surely greedy and foolish. Had I not learned how to let Sebastian go without tears, and without the promise of a *Wiedersehn*?

Summer was exploding around me and the lake was waiting outside my window. All of a sudden life seemed infinitely exciting, even against the background of the war and the boredom of school and Hitler Youth commitments.

I gave no thought to the future, for all the elements propitious to sound planning and personal ambition were missing. With two months to go before my *Abitur*[2] I was resigned to the fact that my life, like those of my classmates, would be manipulated for the duration of the war. On leaving school we would be drafted into the labour service or into one of the women's auxiliary services, while university entrance was restricted. Indeed, now that the war had entered a new and terrifying phase, there seemed to be no point in counting one's steps even to the next corner.

Commuting between school and the lake every day, I soon resented the need for organised, single-minded study and, not unexpectedly, found my marks, which had been steadily declining over the years, dropping to an all-time low within weeks.

'Pull yourself together, Marianne!' said *Studienrat*[3] Wolter, self-consciously fingering his new Party badge. 'I realise you have to cope on your own, but I can no longer ignore your appalling work in maths. What have you got to say?'

I stared silently at the floor. How could I explain the enchantment which had entered my life, the need to return day after day to a lake, to a corner of a paradise discovered, and not yet lost, while the fine midsummer weather lasted and the war was still keeping its distance?

[2] Matriculation.
[3] Senior teacher in secondary school and civil servant.

Summer reigned supreme that year. Back from school in my hot attic room, I went straight to the window. Below, tantalisingly close, were the lake and the dinghy tied to its mooring. I knew the seat would be hot from the sun, the oars longing to move smoothly across the sheet of reflected light, parting it with less sound than it takes to turn the page of a book. 'It has a soul,' the child in me would claim, and the young adult agree. Now nothing could hold me back. Forgotten was *Herr* Wolter's warning, forgotten my resolution to tackle the seemingly insurmountable problems of higher maths. I dumped my books, changed into a swimsuit and raced downstairs.

The lake is mine this summer. No other boats intrude upon its idyll, no human voices pierce its calm, while the lazy passage of the dinghy, and the swans and ducklings which never venture far from the bulrushes that provide shelter from the glaring sun, cause no more than the slightest agitation of the water.

Rowing and drifting through the heat haze, watching, marvelling. Fish jumping for midges, minnows weaving about in emerald water, gauze-winged dragonflies hovering and darting over its surface in pursuit of insect prey. Watching and marvelling, before manoeuvring the boat through a cascade of weeping willows into a tiny bay where the water laps placidly against its bows.

Here then, the afternoon is complete: on the bank, forget-me-nots, marigolds and wild irises; on the water, the lush green plates of floating duckweed; above me, sunshine streaking through the skirt of plying branches, creating a crocheted pattern of light. A scent of jasmine, a water-mole diving into the water, a startled warbler escaping to a higher branch . . . Time, too languid to move, low-keyed afternoon sounds attuned to sun-drenched tranquillity. I am seized by a sense of wonder and elation which is longing for expression, and now words are coming, tentatively at first, then flowing freely, tumbling on to paper, taking shape and falling into rhyme – my first shaky lines of poetry.

Later, when the sun is about to set behind the century-old trees in the park, it is time to row over to the small island at the far end of the lake, to take off my swimsuit and glide into the water from a hidden inlet.

The warm velvety water caresses my naked body, makes my breasts swell, and in the ecstasy of swimming in turn above

131

water through the last burnishing shafts of light, and submerged, with eyes trying to penetrate the aquarium world of fish and quivering, writhing pond-weed, I wish I could store time in a glass jar like seashells or marbles.

For years, *Studienrat* Wolter, my tormentor in maths, had managed to keep his name off the Party's membership roll. No one knew how he had got away with it for so long. A reputedly gifted pedagogue, and applying the standards of the old school, he thought mathematics indispensable to a girl's good all-round education, if only to enable her to move within an abstract sphere of thought and so sharpen her analytical and critical faculties. At the risk of dismissal he constantly refused to have any of his classes replaced by physical-training periods.

'He's nuts!' some said. 'Hasn't he heard of "*Körperliche Ertüchtigung*"?'[4]

Modelled on the Führer's much-quoted demand for a German youth which was not only slim and strong, but 'swift as greyhounds, tough as leather and hard as Krupp steel', the Reich's fitness-orientated policies had been rigidly enforced in schools for years, inevitably at the expense of academic subjects, and it was no secret that good performances in the gym, in the rowing team or on the sports field were credited against poor marks even in major subjects. I for one had done well under this system of compensation. As a result, by the time I reached the *Oberprima*, formulae, equations and physical laws had become a brick wall against which I banged my head in vain. *Studienrat* Wolter, of course, would have loved nothing better than to see me repeat the year, if only for failing to grasp the intricacies of the subject he taught with such excellence. But at the end of the school year, faced with my recent accomplishments on the track or the parallel bars, the powers that reigned in the staff room would promote me to the next form.

For his private vendetta, however, *Herr* Wolter was not bound by Party or government directives, and whenever I handed in blank sheets at a class test, he would crumple them to the size of marbles in front of the class, and hurl them into the wastepaper basket. Yet despite such theatrical gestures I could not help liking him, and I felt sorry for letting down such a dedicated

[4] Attainment of physical fitness.

teacher who, I was sure, would never forget me for embodying the Reich's *Körperliche Ertüchtigung* scheme.

For years, Party and Hitler Youth propaganda had been levelled against Jews, Bolshevists, German communists and the country's western enemies. Now, with the war in its fourth year, it seemed that the time had come for schools to play a more effective role in the campaign against the enemy without and within, for the tenor of the messages suddenly drummed into the classroom made it quite clear that someone high up, if not Goebbels himself, had poked his finger into the curriculum of the *Oberprima* and had found it lacking in *Feindpropaganda*.[5]

Subjects were chosen to provoke the mind, to breed contempt or mockery: the Boer War. The *Engländer* as the originators of concentration camps. The ruthless master role played by British colonial traders and administrators. Henry VIII, the syphilitic Bluebeard. Victorian child labour. Drudgery in mills and mines. Life in the slums of foggy London. The exploitation of the English working class by bowler-hatted, fox-hunting men. American slave-trading and slave-keeping practices. US capitalism. The list was long – and we pricked up our ears, stifled yawns or shuddered with appropriate horror.

A special period dealt with the role the Jews had played in the German economy, and the threat they represented to the master race. To back up the lecture, a film was shown which portrayed the archetypal Jew as a suave, potbellied and shifty-eyed city type posing beside gargantuan moneybags. Alternatively, he was depicted as a long-bearded, sunken-eyed scarecrow of a man who inspired fear and revulsion. The soundtrack spat the film-makers' contempt into the classroom: 'The Jews are eye-sores on the German landscape, boils on the back of the German people, a subhuman species comparable only to rats!' A voice seething with chilling hatred: 'They must be eradicated!'

Next class, German lyrics. Hölderlin and Mörike. Stanzas echoing with spring, music and eternally valid thought, poetry painted with the lightest of brushes, requiring the class's empathy and transposing our minds into a romantic world which, for an hour, wiped out the spartan, slogan-filled present.

One day a documentary designed to ridicule our English enemy evoked unwanted reactions. To the superimposed sound

[5] Propaganda against the enemy.

of hearty English voices singing 'We're going to hang up our washing on the Siegfried line', English prisoners-of-war were seen hanging up their shirts and socks on a string fixed to the barbed wire of a German POW camp, and not – as the commentator stated sarcastically – on the Siegfried line.

It was the first time I had seen English soldiers, and my immediate reaction was that they did not look very different from our own, except leaner and more hollow in the cheeks. And it flashed through my mind that each of them would be loved by someone somewhere in England, by someone waiting and praying for their safe return. Suddenly, things no longer made any sense.

In biology, *Fräulein* Klaasen, explaining the behaviour of male sperms in mammals, made a fleeting reference to fertilisation and the growth of the human embryo.

'This is what happens when two people get married . . .'

The class strained eyes and ears.

'What happened to the stork?' someone whispered.

Fräulein Klaasen kept her eyes on the blackboard on which she hastily sketched the biological consequences of intercourse between a man and a woman, and while she carefully avoided the term 'sex', and cleverly talked her way around the technicalities of the act, she did not fail to point out the social stigma attached to practising such intercourse, or to conceiving, out of wedlock.

'A decent girl doesn't do it before she is married.'

Giggles. Paper missiles darted across the rows of desks, and a flushed *Fräulein* Klaasen quickly switched to the Reich's racial doctrines and their genetic objectives – a subject on which she appeared to be on firmer ground.

Music classes were held in the assembly hall. This term, the *Oberprima* practised the chorus 'Ave Verum', listened to gramophone records of Mozart's 'Kleine Nachtmusik' and rehearsed a buoyant song possibly chosen by *Frau* Peitsch – music teacher and fanatical Party member – for its patriotic theme:

> *Heilig Vaterland, wenn in Gefahren,*
> *Deine Söhne sich um dich scharen . . .*[6]

[6] Holy Fatherland, when in danger, your sons are rallying around you . . .

Similarly, in the course of a single morning, we might have to shift from a study of Dürer's 'Praying Hands' or Michelangelo's 'Pietà' to lectures in Bolshevism and national socialism; from Kant, Nietzsche or Homer to the blood and soil philosophy of the Third Reich; from Goethe, Hölderlin or Verlaine to writings recommended by Party educationalists; from English and French prose, or the Prussian wars, to an examination of Germany's claim to more *Lebensraum*.

Out of school, newspapers, radio and newsreel coverage took over where books and lectures left off: the V2 bombings on London, and Anglo-American air raids on German cities; scenes from the Russian front, with German soldiers smoking and smiling at the camera during a break in the fighting; the Führer visiting his troops – 'We shall wring the final victory from the enemies!'; close-ups of disarmed prisoners, of enemy tanks burning, planes crashing and ships sinking. Music to forget the war: '*Wenn in Capri die rote Sonne untergeht*',[7] '*Kann denn Liebe Sünde sein*'.[8] Songs sweet and sentimental, often with erotic innuendoes but always without any element of tristesse. '*Achtung, Achtung!*' A special news bulletin. A German flying ace killed in action. The lament. Beethoven, Schumann, Wagner. The news. Meditations on a philosophical theme. '*Achtung, Achtung!* Enemy bombers approaching from ...' A rousing speech by Goebbels. '*Sieg Heil, Sieg Heil!*' A fairy tale for children. Outside in the street, a marching column. '*Nun lasst die Fahnen fliegen!*'[9] Left, right, left right! *Zack, zack!* A constant stream of messages bombarding the mind.

To me, these had never been more conflicting, more bewildering.

The fine weather continued, but the nights soon formed a stark contrast to my carefree afternoons.

At the beginning of the war, shortly after the first sirens had been tested during an air-raid drill, *Herr* Mangert – a man of obvious resources and forethought – had an underground shelter built at the bottom of the garden, which was not only wired and comfortably furnished but contained gas masks, a steel safe, a

[7] 'When the red sun is setting on Capri'.
[8] 'Can love be a sin?'
[9] 'Now let the banners fly!'

schnaps cabinet and, on its wall, a valuable painting of a sinuous nude. I suspected I had been given access to *Herr* Mangert's private bunker not so much out of magnanimity, but because he was afraid of what the air-raid warden might say. However, never feeling quite comfortable about being shacked up with the Mangerts for an hour or two at night, and realising how much they valued their privacy, I often slipped out into the garden to watch enemy bombers on their way to Berlin passing over Potsdam through a criss-cross pattern of search beams and flak fire. Unperturbed and in perfect formation, they resembled a flight of chimerical and seemingly inviolable silver birds.

Later, when the all clear had sounded and the sky had again grown calm, the fierce glow on the horizon which marked the extent of the raging firestorm in the nearby capital, pursued me to bed and into a leaden sleep. By the next morning, a north-easterly wind might have turned the air acrid and left particles of ash on windowsills, on freshly-laundered sheets and tender rose-petals – telltale signs which, like the nightly droning chorus, reminded Potsdamers that their city was vulnerable too. Its time might come tomorrow, some said; after all, was Potsdam not regarded as the birthplace of Prussian military spirit and glory, and had it not retained its reputation for over two hundred years? Besides, every child knew that from the air the city was not only mottled with lakes, peaceful parks and palaces but with huge barrack complexes and military depots.

'It would make a perfect target for enemy bombers,' *Herr* Mangert stated one night in the shelter. 'If the *Amis*[10] or *Engländer* seek us out one day, it won't be Sans Souci they're after but our Prussian heritage. Militarily, the place is like a bloody beehive, and there are too many potential targets for comfort, I'd say!'

'Oh, stop it, darling!' *Frau* Mangert cried with mock indignation. 'Don't paint the devil on the wall!'

'I'm afraid I might be right, Louise.' *Herr* Mangert poured himself a schnaps and lifted his glass. '*Prost! Lasst uns geniessen den Krieg, denn der Frieden wird fürchterlich!*'[11]

This popular, if pugnacious joke, which combined ambiguity with cynicism, had been circulating through households for

[10] Slang for Americans.
[11] 'Let us enjoy the war, for the peace will be terrible!'

weeks, for German humour, having turned black and gone underground, often reflected the state of the nation. Perhaps the defeat at Stalingrad had set people speculating about the possibility of defeat. With daily reports of heavy air-raids on German cities, the recent retreat of the German *Afrikakorps* and the Allied landing in Sicily, the formerly outrageous idea of the country losing the war had suddenly, frighteningly, become feasible.

'It's not much of a joke,' *Frau* Mangert said, 'more of a defeatist statement. It demoralises one.' She shivered, and in the dim light of the metal-cage bulb, her face had the look of faded voile curtains.

'I'm not sure, Louise,' her husband continued ponderously. 'I think the prospect of losing the war, and of living under enemy occupation, if not enemy terror, might build up moral resistance in some people. Ha! It might even be some devilishly clever slogan planned by "the little man"[12] and his propaganda big wigs . . . if you know what I mean!'

He looked sternly at me. 'Not a word to anyone outside, d'you hear?'

I nodded. I was listening to the pounding of anti-aircraft guns.

In outward appearance Potsdam seemed untouchable in the shimmering July heat, just as if its peace was impregnable, its beauty indestructible and its lease on time would never expire. Its splendid baroque and rococo palaces, churches and town houses still bore witness to an era in which *Hohenzollern* kings had not only fought wars but lived graciously, cultivating architecture, literature and the fine arts.

The garden at Sans Souci, said to have been modelled on Versailles and to be one of the finest examples of Italian landscaping, still revealed Frederick the Great's penchant for French and Italian culture – a fact which, with possible reverence for his statesmanship and for Prussian military history, had not been suppressed in school books after 1933.

But history was not only present in Potsdam's striking sights: it lived on in its quiet alleys, in the quaint, cobbled streets of the old town and their low-storied, half-timbered houses, and it lurked around iron street pumps with decorative handles and in

[12] Goebbels.

the shade of ancient mulberry trees. Nor was it only artists who flocked to such places with their easels. Many a fine summer morning, equipped with folding chairs and drawing pads, and chaperoned by *Frau* Klingelmann, our arts teacher, my class and I went sketching in one of the narrow streets which still seemed to echo with the clatter of hooves and the voices of the King's fusiliers. Or we had tried to catch the spirit of old Potsdam in the regal aspect of the Stadtschloss, its lyricism in one of the ornamental iron parapet bridges which spanned the city's sleepy, tree-lined canal.

Now, slowly but irretrievably, Potsdam's time was running out as the war intensified on all fronts.

The night seemed to store the heat of the day in which temperatures had soared to a midsummer high. Despite a ventilator shaft, the air in the garden bunker was stifling. *Herr* Mangert constantly wiped his forehead and replenished his glass, while his wife, draped on a divan in her negligee, cooled her face with a Chinese fan.

I slipped out into the moonless night and crouched at the edge of the pitch-black lake which, in its nocturnal silence, seemed to exude a strange hostility. Only minutes later real hostility filled the air. This time I did not see gleaming birds moving majestically through a mosaic of light, but hundreds of heavy bombers which had taken over the sky and, flying at a lower altitude and in what looked like closer formations, droned in a more sinister way then ever, uncaring, unmolested by the white puffs of smoke exploding around them, and bent only on their mission of terror. They came in waves, and the sky was alive with them. For an hour? For two? What was time in the face of such magnitude?

Later, much later, when the horizon reddened, when the great fire, kilometres away, lifted the darkness off the lake and breathed its faint reflection over it, I thought of my father who lived in the heart of the city, and an overpowering desire for sleep reminded me of the oral *Abitur* exams I would have to sit in a few hours.

I wake to excited voices on the landing – strange sounds indeed in a house which never comes to life before I go to school. Steps labour up the staircase. A knock. My father is standing in the door.

Normally he fills a doorframe with his imposing build, but today he seems shrunken, his skin parched. The large, protuberant eyes which dominate his face, are those of an old, tired man, yet I can read in them the bewilderment of a child whose favourite toy has broken. One glass of his rimless spectacles is cracked, his jacket sleeve is singed. Clutching his briefcase in one hand and a portable typewriter in the other, he takes a few steps forward, drops into the nearest chair, and exclaims:

'Oh, *Kind*, I've lost everything!' And my father, a man of Silesian stoicism, pulls me towards him, buries his face into the pit of my stomach and weeps.

An incendiary smell fills the room.

Having shared my breakfast of mint-tea, rusks and jam, my father relates his lucky escape from his burning house through a street on fire, and his narrative, delivered in a faltering voice, evokes the images of a horror film: incendiaries setting rows of houses alight, follow-up bombs explode, spreading the blaze, turning whole streets into furnaces. Survivors axe their way through the lightly-cemented emergency cellar exits, each time finding the staircase of the neighbouring house blocked by fire, smoke or rubble. At last, an unobstructed stairway leading into the street. A ferocious firestorm drives people towards an opening in the inferno, their flight often thwarted by collapsing structures or slowed by whirling ash and giant sparks. Eventually, a street that has been spared, an open space through which to file, where breath comes easier and clothes don't catch fire. Terrified, screaming people, running, lurching, stumbling away from the conflagration, or slumping down on the pavement – a suitcase or a briefcase in their hands, a child in their arms or, more often, empty-handed . . .

'My flat . . . the whole block . . . all gone!' my father cries, restoring his grip on briefcase and typewriter.

'You're alive, *Vati*,' I say firmly, 'that's all that counts!' I tentatively touch the singed jacket-sleeve, the scorched strand of hair, the withered cheeks. Suddenly I feel the stronger one, the comforter. Events have reversed our roles.

They have also brought the war into my room.

My turn came last. In the holy of holies, which had held every student in awe for years, the fully assembled teaching staff was seated behind a gleaming table as for a tribunal. The headmaster was in the chair. Ten minutes of oral grilling were set aside for each subject which, in the written exams, a candidate had failed, or passed with poor marks. It was up to me to make good, to convince, to bluff my way through sixty minutes.

I tried to wrench from my sluggish mind all I knew about eighteenth-century France and her cultural and political impact on Europe; I fumbled for verbs and adjectives in an effort to translate a passage of French; I described what I feebly remembered about geological fault formations and the climatic influence of the South American rain forest on global weather; I got lost in the maze of chemical compounds, and desperately searched my memory for the equations that applied to gravitational law and the speed of light. Finally, asked by *Studienrat* Wolter to solve a number of mathematical problems, I saw myself marooned in the desert, my inquisitor, and the hushed silence behind him, turning into waiting vultures. Then it was all over, and I rejoined my fellow candidates in the sun-drenched classroom where everybody talked and nobody listened.

I stared out of the window. The nail-biting time had begun. The hour of judgement arrived at noon with the tinkle of the school bell. The first candidate was called into the staff room and returned with a beaming smile. So did the second, the third, one after another.

'Hurrah!' they cried, jumping over chairs or flinging themselves across desks in one last display of schoolgirlish boisterousness, in a mood too self-indulgent to take heed of me, the last one to be summoned.

As I crept towards the judges of my academic inadequacy I noticed with a strange detachment that a shaft of sunshine had turned the headmaster's bald head into a shiny dome and the Party badge on his lapel into a flashlight.

'I'm sorry,' he said, rubbing his closely shaved chin, 'you have not passed, Marianne. We have carefully considered your excellent sporting record as well as your fair marks in music and art, but we feel that these do not compensate for your wholly unacceptable, your abysmal standard in the science subjects. However, you will be pleased to learn that you will be allowed to repeat the year. Well then, we'll see you in September. Better luck next time! Heil Hitler!'

I acknowledged the salute with a raised arm, not quite sure whether I ought to express gratitude for being given another

140

chance, or to show remorse by bursting into tears. *Studienrat* Wolter, pointedly staring at something of immense interest on the ceiling, and smiling as if he were rubbing his hands under the table, decided the issue. I stormed out of the room, obsessed with getting away as quickly and as far as possible from the site of my failure.

Cutting corners, mounting the pavement, my bike races through the almost empty streets as if speed could shake off my sense of shame. I know my father is waiting to hear the good news which would temporarily divorce his thoughts from the events of the night before. Suddenly a pit opens up and sucks me in; and now all urgency has gone. I leave my bike inside the gate of the Neue Garten, and my legs steer me through a deserted landscape of lawned, sun-grilled space, past patrician oaks and copper beeches towards the white marble steps of the Marmorpalais,[13] which sweep right into the water of the Heiligensee – my lake of many weeks, my friend, poet and magician.

Taking off my shoes and socks, I walk down to the last submerged step which, though still visible in its cool whiteness, falls off sharply into an opaque abyss. The warm water reaches my knees, mirrors my face. My foot strikes out, cracking the image and tossing angry ripples over the greenish blackness. Arguments. Will the water take me? Will it drag down the body it caresses in the afternoons? The voice of common sense: 'Get your perspective right, girl, and stop dramatising! Anyone who has learnt to fight for points, tenths of seconds and centimetres should be capable of tackling a minor personal defeat!' The language is plain and sobering, tidying up an emotional shambles. As I glare back over the years, I see myself merely eddying along in school, not to speak of this summer of indulgence, of homework hours spent in sweet, irresponsible idleness and romantic daydreams.

I blow my nose. The pit is ejecting me, and closing up. The grand catharsis is over. Late afternoon sunshine strokes my head and shoulders, shadows are lengthening, the marble under my thighs begins to cool.

A park warden appears on the top of the steps.

'Eh, *Fräulein*, time to go home. Park'll be closing soon.'

I feel ravenously hungry.

[13] Friedrich Wilhelm II's former summer palace.

The Mangerts greeted me with raised eyebrows; my father sighed with relief and took me into his arms.

'Thank God you're back, child!' he said. 'I was so worried. Where have you been all this time?'

He held me at arms' length. 'I know you didn't pass. I called the school.'

I started sobbing.

When he spoke again, his voice took on a prophetic lift. 'Never mind, *Kind*, you never know what it might be good for. Providence has many faces, and it often blesses us in the strangest of disguises. Actually, odd as it might sound, I rather welcome the idea of your repeating the year. The way things are going you'll be safer here, at school.'

The hand which had spanked me when I had jumped onto a moving milk cart, which had pointed out tigers and lions in the zoo, or repaired broken toys, now touched my hair. And all I could think was how amazing, how utterly unpredictable life could be. Once again, within hours, our father-daughter roles had been reversed. Having climbed out of his own despondency, my father was now the comforter, even though the smell of his jacket still held ugly reminders of last night's holocaust.

Next morning my father returned to Berlin, to seek new accommodation and to pretend – in line with Party and national defence propaganda – that from urban ruins and ashes Germany would rise again and win the war. I resigned myself to the thought of spending another year at school and to afternoons being tutored in maths and physics. First, however, my summer holiday was being mapped out in Hitler Youth and Party quarters.

I received an official letter from the *Kreisleitung*.[14] It stressed the great war effort and the individual's part in the country's total commitment, and it contained instructions on where and when I was to report for a six-week service stint on a farm where, together with another *Primanerin*, I was to look after small children, make myself generally useful in the house and help bring in the harvest.

The letter left no room for arguments or evasive action. One did what one was told and, at best, shrugged one's shoulders or cursed at being deprived of the freedom of choice. But then,

[14] Regional party HQ.

wasn't it only fair to expect a *Primanerin* – particularly one in my position – to give up her summer holidays at a time when food and labour were getting shorter every day? Besides, there were several pleasing aspects to the scheme: being city-born and bred, I might discover new horizons in the country where the nights were quiet and without fear, where there would be horses and the smell of clover, hedges that came alive with crickets at sunset, and where, at the first light of dawn, a rooster would wake the sleeper. And there would be meat and *wurst* and creamy milk and butter and real eggs and – I could almost smell it – freshly baked, crusty farm loaves the size of cartwheels.

I spent the last day before my departure on the lake, but the prospect of finding it drastically changed on my return cast a strange gloom over my mood. Somehow, as with the passing of childhood innocence, I knew that I would never quite recapture the lake's magic in its present intensity. One morning the lake would wake up to the first autumn mist, and it would then not be long before buffeting winds bared the trees and whipped up the slate-grey water, and winter froze my lake into silence.

CHAPTER 12

Pitchfork Manoeuvres

Nobody could fail to take notice of Ingrid, and nobody could fail to like her. Easy-going, and forever obliging with an impish smile, she enjoyed great popularity in the classroom and the schoolyard for her masterly imitations of teachers, and for her whistling skill which was compared by avid cinemagoers in the upper forms to that of Ilse Werner, the whistling heroine of many film musicals.

Judging by her side-splitting performance in earlier school plays, she had a flair for acting, notably for Chaplinesque comedy. But far from aiming at a stage career after the war, her ambition was to study tropical medicine and to work in one of the former African colonies. Rumour had it that she had a boyfriend who was a Luftwaffe cadet, which – true or not – added a certain spice to her fair Gretchen looks.

Ingrid, I learned, was to be my companion for the next six weeks, and I congratulated myself on my good luck, for with her easy-going ways, and her sharp sense of humour, she promised to be a lot of good fun during our enforced working holiday.

Ten minutes before the train was due to leave, Ingrid arrived at our meeting point outside Görlitzer Bahnhof panting hard and her hair flying.

'Marianne,' she cried, nudging me in the ribs. 'Fancy being paired up with you. I suppose I could have done worse. Well, are we all ready for some refined country air?'

'. . . and for pitchfork manoeuvres!'

'. . . and for outside loos!'

'. . . and for those dear cows!' I made milking motions, singing, '*Zipp, zapp, strull, ist der Eimer noch nicht voll!*'[1]

---

[1] 'Zipp . . . is the bucket not yet full?'

Ingrid laughed. 'Ever mucked out a byre before?'

'No. Have you?'

'No. Oh well, here we come!'

Our flippant mood died the moment we entered the station, where a naked steel frame was all that was left of its former glass dome. Thousands of refugees were crowding the concourse. As we pushed our way towards the platform, I brushed shoulders with human misery for the first time – with women and old men who looked bewildered, frightened or apathetic and spoke with a strange accent, a grey mass of people clutching children, belongings and sleeves, while being registered, labelled, grouped, fed, watered and routed on before the next air raid was due.

Ingrid and I managed to squeeze into a carriage, reached the corridor and turned our suitcases into seats.

'Did you see the ruins on your way up?' I asked, when the train started moving.

'I did. I had no idea. It's really nightmarish. And many blocks were still smouldering. You know, my father says people often suffocate in a firestorm, sometimes they get stuck in the melting asphalt! It's too awful to think about. All that rubble, the burnt-out buildings, the smoke which is hanging over the streets . . . it makes Potsdam look like a peaceful resort, doesn't it?'

The train crept out of Berlin, sometimes inching its way over recently damaged and hastily repaired tracks. It passed huge craters, grotesquely bent steel, crippled sidings and rolling stock. When two hours and two changes later we finally arrived at the tiny rural station in the middle of nowhere, my eyes rested gratefully on a landscape which, sane, peaceful and as yet untouched by the turmoil of the war, instantly blotted out thoughts of ruins, fire and refugees.

Trees lined the country road. A few scattered farms poked through the flatness of the land as if through paper. Long strips of beet and potato crops adjoined miles of corn that stood golden and high and heavy. Yet there was no monotony. Hedges looked as if they had been embroidered with crimson, dark pinks or ripe yellows; rooks were sweeping low over the fields; swallows seemed to fall from, and immediately surge back into, a sky in which the sun had reached its zenith.

'Isn't it gorgeous!' I exclaimed when the train had puffed away and we found ourselves alone on a narrow slab of a platform covered with grasses and dandelions.

'It's all right, I suppose,' Ingrid said. 'A bit too quiet for my liking. You can practically hear yourself thinking.'

An elderly farmer was waiting behind the station shed beside a horse and cart. His working clothes, and his boots covered with dried dung, extended a bouquet of farmyard smells.

Smiling broadly, he lifted his cap and held out a huge, calloused hand. 'Welcome, *Fräuleins*, I am *Herr* Hansen.'

Ingrid and I introduced ourselves.

The farmer ponderously stroked his chin and cocked his head as if he were seeing two pretty city-girls for the first time and, perhaps, assessing their working potential.

'*Na, dann klettert mal rauf!*'[2] he said at last, pointing to a seat in the back of the cart, and stacking our heavy suitcases like bales of hay.

'*Hü!*' he called out, and the horse moved away with a start.

I nudged Ingrid's ribs and whispered, 'I bet he's wondering whether we're strong enough to lift a pail.'

Ingrid giggled. 'I think he looks damn pleased with himself, as though he'd bought two heifers at a bargain!'

After a short trot down the country road, the cart turned off into a lane, and presently we stopped at a sizeable whitewashed farmhouse flanked by two giant chestnut trees, and connected to outhouses in horseshoe fashion.

A dark-clad woman in her forties, wearing a scarf tied behind her head and an apron around hips which had clearly never worried about conventional dress sizes, detached herself from the welcoming committee which had assembled at the front door.

'There they are, the *Stadtfräuleins*,' she cried, and came forward with outstretched hands, followed closely by two apple-cheeked, thumb-sucking youngsters and three slightly older children with equally glowing and well-fed looks.

Frau Hansen squeezed my hand like a wet sponge, then summoned the eldest boy.

'Bernd, give the *Fräuleins* a hand with their luggage. And now, the rest of you, come and say "*Guten Tag!*"'

Her authoritative voice left no doubt that the farmer's wife would be taking things from here.

---

[2] 'Well, up you go then.'

Two rickety iron bedsteads took up almost the entire space in our attic room. Sagging mattresses, resting on worn-out springs, formed hammocklike depressions, while a feather bed – the heavily inflated version of a duvet – covered the foot of each bed.

Two plain chairs, a washstand with ceramic jug and bowl, an enamel bucket, a cracked mirror throwing back distorted images, and a washing line strung up between walls and sporting four grotesque hangers, completed the frugal furnishing. At the sight of an outsized chamber pot at the foot of each bed, and clearly visible from the door, I had no heart to ask for the whereabouts of a bathroom.

'*Das Klo ist auf dem Hof*,'[3] said *Frau* Hansen, as if she had read my thoughts, 'and there is a tub in the wash house.'

'Well, it isn't exactly the Excelsior,' Ingrid said as she started unpacking.

Despite the sparse light which the dense foliage of one of the chestnut trees allowed into the room, a framed proverb, cross-stitched in large Gothic letters, showed up clearly on the wall: '*Morgenstunde hat Gold im Munde.*'[4] I winced.

A croaking voice from downstairs, belonging to grandmother Hansen, called: 'Come down, *Fräuleins*, you must be hungry!'

That evening we met the entire household at the long, scrubbed kitchen table for *Abendbrot*. Grace. A steaming meat stew. Thick slices of crusty bread. Dripping thick with onions and apples.

'That's Janislav down there, he's Polish,' *Frau* Hansen said, pointing to a shy-looking, dark-haired man at the bottom of the table. 'Some call him *Fremdarbeiter*,[5] others *zwangsverpflichtet*.[6] He says he was picked up by SS-men in his native village and carted off to Germany to work. Isn't that so, Jan?'

The Pole nodded. *Herr* Hansen put down his spoon, wiped his mouth with the back of his hand and addressed himself to Ingrid and me.

'You might as well know the rest, girls. When they brought him here, they left instructions on how he was to be treated. Jan is not allowed to go to the next village, not even to church. He is

---

[3] 'The loo is in the yard.'
[4] 'Morning hour has gold in its mouth.'
[5] Foreign labour.
[6] Forced labour.

not supposed to listen to the radio or read a newspaper. He must not sleep under the same roof with us and should take his meals in the shed where he lives. They told us not to get chummy with him . . . there are hefty penalties for that sort of thing. But I say "bull-shit" . . . sorry, *Fräuleins*. We all think Jan is a damn decent chap and a good worker. He's more like a member of the family. Eh, Jan?'

Keeping his eyes on his plate, the Pole nodded and smiled.

'Out here,' *Herr* Hansen continued between spoonfuls, 'a man is as good as his work, and as trusted as he proves himself. I will not have a man treated like an animal on my property! That's my motto, and to hell with those who tell me otherwise. Mind you, when *Herr* Stiller is here – he's the rural inspector, *Parteigenosse*, a real fanatic, they say . . . you know, "Heil Hitler!" here, "Heil Hitler!" there – I shout a bit at Jan, to make Stiller think I'm keeping Jan on a tight rein.'

Now the Pole looked up. 'You all good people, *panie*. I . . . I grateful.'

'Do you have family?' I asked.

'*Ja*, wife and two children. Long time not seen . . . not since I come here.'

'When was that?'

'Three years ago . . . long time!'

I stayed silent. I felt ashamed of being German, ashamed of those who categorised people and treated some like inferior beings. I remembered a history lesson in school, *Herr* Banter speaking with indignation of the abduction of African Negroes and their being shipped to America as slaves – a sentiment which had clashed only too sharply with the doctrines propounded by Goebbels, *Reichführer* Himmler and Hitler Youth leaders on the racial inferiority of Jews, Poles, Slavs and Gypsies, of people labelled '*Untermenschen*'.

'And this is Kurt.' *Herr* Hansen pointed his spoon at an elderly man with swift blue eyes and a skin like parchment. 'He's been with us since as long as I can remember eh? World War I veteran he is. Getting a bit stiff in the joints these days, aren't we, Kurt?'

The farmhand grinned and bared stumps of teeth. Now *Herr* Hansen pointed to the woman next to me, about whom everything seemed to be pink and round.

'That's Trudi, our dairymaid. She lives two kilometres down the road in the village. She'll show the two of you how to milk a cow.'

148

Trudi giggled and held her plate out for a second helping.

Having introduced the rest of the household, *Herr* Hansen proceeded to dig heartily into his stew.

It was *Frau* Hansen who with a single statement broke the jocular mood at the table: 'Our eldest son was killed at Stalingrad.'

In the weeks to come, Ingrid and I tumbled into bed at night too tired to notice the shortcomings of the room. We soon fitted into our new routine, even though rising at the crack of dawn held no particular attraction. We looked after the toddlers, peeled potatoes, hung up washing; we stacked hay, fed poultry and pigs, and helped clean out the cow shed; we were shown how to milk a cow, how to make butter and how to pluck a chicken. Yet despite the long hours of hard, unaccustomed work we found ourselves in a constantly jocular mood which was only waiting for a chance to explode in riotous laughter. And there was always time to mount a horse for a gentle trot, to fool around in the hayloft or chase the Christmas goose around the yard.

Sometimes, at the end of a day, when the yard had gone quiet and Ingrid was celebrating her nightly hairbrushing ritual – fifty strokes no less – I felt the need to step outside the strictly daily pattern, by wandering down to the small stream in the meadow where the noise of frogs and crickets competed for dominance, and the air was sweet with foxgloves. Here, at sunset, under a sky streaked or flushed pink, it was easy to empty the mind of all things mundane, and no one could see me if I opened my arms towards that last solemn glow of light.

The lack of modern conveniences provided Ingrid and me with a never-ending source of amusement. As on most farms a communal earth closet at the back of the yard – vulgarly termed '*Plumsklosett*' – served everybody's needs, and Ingrid and I would remark on such medieval backyard facilities through the heart-shaped hole in its door until laughter threatened to choke us or a male voice announced its owner's urgent call.

One day, not long after we had arrived on the farm, the old proverb which claims that the last laugh is always on the loser was confirmed for me, and for days Trudi's detailed account of my first milking effort provided a topic at the *Abendbrot* table where, after a day's work, minds were all too ready for a spot of jesting and leg-pulling.

'How did Elsa behave today, Marianne?' someone would ask, alluding to the morning when I had first confronted Elsa.

Squatting on a low stool, my head resting comfortably against the animal's warm flank, I had tried to make the warm, distended udder release its milk, hissing '*zipp, zapp, strull* . . .' Yet to no avail. 'There's no milk coming!' I called over to Trudi.

'Then just stop tickling the good girl,' she replied from her corner from where I could hear the unmistakable sound of milk swishing into a pail. 'Try harder, Marianne! Elsa likes it. Just give her teats a good pull, the way I showed you.'

So I did. In response, in what appeared to be a movement intended to remove some troublesome flies, the cow's tail flew round and into my face, as did the first spurt of milk. With a shriek I toppled backwards towards the hindleg of the neighbouring cow who was not amused and, possibly to demonstrate her consternation, began to relieve herself with gusto not far from my head.

The weeks passed quickly. Hungrier than ever from manual labour and fresh air, I gorged myself on thick meat stews, potato pancakes and soups enriched with hefty chunks of smoked pork. The *Wurst* was home-made, the bacon farm-smoked; milk came in jugs straight from the cows, butter from the churn. At weekends, there was *Topfenkuchen*, a cake rich in butter and eggs, while in baskets all over the house the season's first fruit was waiting for the bite of teeth.

Not surprisingly, the conversation at mealtimes centred mainly on farming matters and the events of the day. The war, it seemed, was too indigestible a subject, one still too far removed, geographically, from the Hansens' own doorstep, still too evocative of the loss of a son, to be discussed at table.

In the evenings, *Herr* Hansen liked to listen to the radio's daily farming programme and weather forecast, before briefly tuning in to the news. The local paper was always slow in arriving on the kitchen table, and when it did the news had always been overtaken. But nobody, except Jan, the Pole, took much notice of the outside world which, to the Hansens, as part of a self-reliant and self-contained community, stood for loathsome government regulations, a clichéd Party jargon, production quotas and supervision by men like *Herr* Stiller, whose powers over farming and slaughtering matters, while fiercely resented, *Herr* Hansen had learned to turn to his own advantage.

Herr Stiller, a pompous, rotund Party official and regional agricultural inspector appointed to spot check on home slaughter and to ensure the timely delivery of fixed quotas, called at the Hansens on the flimsiest of pretexts at least twice a week, although in his official capacity he was required to make his rounds less frequently.

Never a man to mince his words, *Herr* Hansen called him '*Schmeissfliege*' – for, buzzing around like a tiresome blow-fly, *Herr* Stiller liked to boost his own rations and would conveniently relax the rules he was supposed to enforce for the good of the people. He was in the market for favours and counter-favours, and it was understood that he would pay in his own currency for the well-wrapped parcel he so eagerly accepted at the end of each visit, by his absence on home-slaughtering days, and no questions asked.

One day, slapping the dough she was kneading as if it were *Herr* Stiller's pot-belly, *Frau* Hansen summed up her contempt for this reputed model of political perfection: 'That man would sell his daughter for a pound of butter and a dozen eggs!'

The Hansens did not pretend to be other than plain farming folk, and although their smiles came as easily as their talk about farming matters, there always remained a certain awkwardness in their conversation with us, the two *Stadtfräuleins* who were learning English and French, and who had no need for pen and paper to divide, subtract, add or multiply simple figures, and who must therefore be very clever. But although their own schooling might have been limited to the rudiments of reading, writing and arithmetic, the Hansens were no fools.

With petrol and textiles severely rationed, and no more colourful market days to lure the Hansens into the district town, it was now up to *Herr* Stiller, to Willy the milk collector and Heinrich the postman, to bring local gossip, rumours and legitimate information to the farm – not counting the weighty men who came in lorries or in shiny black Opels to collect produce, or pin Party and police notices on the stable door. However, not given to fear, anger or morbid speculations about the state of the country, and blatantly not caring whether Adolf Hitler was in power, or men in dark suits and top hats ruled a Republic, or a Hohenzollern headed a monarchy, the Hansens did not mind living on the fringes of local and national affairs.

And somehow, this lack of concern seemed to suit their notions of self-sufficiency.

One evening, when the first puffs on his pipe had cleared his perspective, *Herr* Hansen summed up their 'rural island' philosophy in two sentences: 'Out here, we have our own government, we've had it for generations. Our soil, our livestock need us and we need them, no matter what bloke or political party runs the country.'

It was easy to see that such interdependence and loyalty was not only breeding values unlikely to be found in city life, but that despite back-bending labour throughout the daylight hours of the seasons, the Hansens' rewards were not measurable in Reichsmark. Instead of paying heed to Party slogans, and raising their arms in the '*Heil* Hitler!' salute, they folded their hands for grace at table and for harvest thanksgiving, and served their own God behind the plough, in byre, pigsty, stable and kitchen.

CHAPTER 13

Beetroots, a Bechstein Grand and Party Matters

After a memorable summer, autumn was sweeping over Potsdam, and soon weather more appropriate to November settled upon the town. The lake thus no longer tempted me, and I set about repeating my final year, determined to engage in a period of serious study. Indeed, for a while it seemed as if my course, instead of meandering, was leading straight ahead. My motto was simple: no romantic daydreaming, no misuse of after-school freedom.

But the odds were against me.

After school one day, *Frau* Mangert called me into her bedroom, and I tiptoed into this most sacrosanct of places with a fair degree of curiosity. I was not disappointed. A full-length wall-to-wall mirror gave an impression of space, reflecting a regal bed and varnished period furniture. Printed curtains and uphol-stery matched the cream, gold and pink decorative theme to perfection. On the dressing table, a silver vanity set, china figurines, carelessly discarded jewellery, and flacons and jars formed an untidy collection of objects softened by a bouquet of pink roses in a china vase.

Wearing an exquisitely embroidered, very flimsy piece of silk, *Frau* Mangert was sitting up in bed. A featherweight quilt revealed the slim outline of her body; sleek, silver-blonde hair and a lace-edged pillow of the daintiest pink framed her alabaster face, while her eyes reminded me of spring skies. Surely, I thought, in her sea of pastel hues, lace frills and perfumed privacy, my landlady looked as fragile and as beautiful as her Dresden figurines.

Frau Mangert did not bother to offer me a chair for her short address. 'I'm afraid, Marianne, I shall have to ask your father to find new accommodation for you. I'll need your room at the end of the month, to put up a niece of mine who is coming to live with us. I am sorry!'

A delicate hand fluttered towards me as she added, in the voice of exhausted royalty, 'Off you go then.'

By the time I had closed the door I had accepted the news with equanimity, realising once again that good things do not last or are, at best, variable.

Cold November mist was steeping the streets when I moved a hundred metres down the road into a private boarding house for girls, run by an elderly widow who was rumoured to have French blood in her veins and was locally known as 'Madame'.

The pompous villa — a mock-baronial structure combining several architectural styles and boasting battlements, turrets and gargoyles — stood like a fortified castle in grounds where weeds had long taken over. A heavy, iron-clad front door associated itself with a former drawbridge and, instinctively, my eyes searched around for the remains of a moat.

As I walked up the gravel path to my new abode, its aggressive and hostile character reduced even a tall elm to size. Gothic stories came to my mind, and I found a strange reassurance in the sight of blackbirds fearlessly picking their way over a carpet of wet leaves.

The house was as gloomy inside as out. Even in daytime, heavy curtains kept the public rooms in a cheerless twilight, while the dark, solid furniture, unsmiling portraits and a collection of marble objects emanated an aloofness that matched Madame's chilling regimen and was not relieved by the presence of five bright-eyed and lively schoolgirl boarders.

From the moment Madame opened the front door and forced her thin bloodless lips into a welcoming smile, I knew this was a place where I would not be growing roots, and I was confirmed in my presentiments when Madame showed me into my room, which reeked of mould and cats' urine, and where my attempt to chase three cats off the bed failed miserably. Reluctantly uncoiling and arching their backs, they hissed at me with a ferocity in character with the house, and without conceding a centimetre of bed space. I rushed to open the window.

'Keep it shut!' Madame commanded. 'We mustn't waste warm air.'

'But the room is not heated, and . . .' I argued.

'Never mind. There's a war on! We can only afford a fire in

154

the lounge.' She stroked the cats. 'Come on, my sweeties, mummy is going to light her stove.'

The cats jumped off the bed, rubbed their bodies against Madame's rough-stockinged legs, and stalked regally out of the room.

That night I went to bed with half my suitcase still not unpacked.

As the widow of a wealthy German industrialist who in the Party's heyday had actively and financially supported the movement, and had acquired the property not long before his untimely death, Madame was unlikely to have any monetary worries. But there were a lot of empty rooms in the house, and under the emergency housing regulations the building would have been ideal for refugees and bombed-out families. A handyman, repairing a fused plug in my room, made no bones about Madame's decision to take in young boarders, intimating that it had not been prompted by loneliness, unfulfilled motherly instincts or financial considerations, but by a desire to avert the 'calamity' of *Zwangsbelegung*.[1]

'She's a clever one,' he said, 'adores cats . . . well, you can smell them all over the house, can't you? A cats' home, that's what she's running! Mind you, I just come in for the odd repair job . . . need the extra money. Name is Kunz . . . Franz they call me. But what's a girl like you doing in a place like this? I wouldn't want to live here, not with her and all those cats around. She gives me the creeps. Keeps her own quarters firmly under lock and key . . . only the cats are allowed in. If you ask me . . .'

Madame stood in the door. Her voice cleaved into *Herr* Kunz's back.

'Haven't you finished, man? Get on with it! Don't you know there's a war on? And you, Marianne, tidy up your room!'

She shuffled away, keys rattling, a chatelaine who, haunting her own corridors, seemed to leave sudden draughts and sepulchral shadows behind.

Except for an elderly, half-deaf charwoman, Madame had no staff to help her run her boarding house, and the question arose why local authorities had given their approval to such a venture – assuming that Madame had sought it in the first place. As it was, her empty rooms were now occupied by young lodgers and housing regulations had been satisfied. However, while providing far from ideal home-surroundings for adolescent girls, it

[1] Compulsory billeting.

seemed to have escaped official notice that Madame was no wizard in the kitchen. Her cuisine made a mockery of her alleged French background, and her menus consisted of a range of beetroot dishes for which one would have looked in vain in traditional cookery books. The hot dish of the day was always predictable, and my co-boarders and I used to make bets on whether the vegetable would appear on the table stewed, fricasseed, breadcrumbed and fried, pickled or mashed up with potatoes. Indeed, there seemed to be no end to the disguises in which Madame's meat substitute could be served for human consumption, while the range of her deserts remained deplorably limited to sour garden apples dished up stewed, puréed or hidden in farinaceous jackets. In the meantime, Madame's ten plump, contented cats provided the answer to the diet's shortcomings.

Five weeks later, I had lost the weight I had gained on the farm and my suitcase was still not fully unpacked. One day I rang my father and told him I would not stay a day longer in a place where cats prospered on my rations and where a ghoulish house-mother ruled with beetroots, sour apples and a chain of rattling keys. With the Christmas holidays about to start, I packed my belongings and took a hurried leave, half running, half slipping down the staircase, and slamming the door like a released prisoner.

By chance an elderly couple down the road were advertising for a lodger. Accompanied by my father, and determined only to settle for a place which held connotations of home, I went to meet my prospective landlords.

In the empty street, a soft carpet of snow muffled our footsteps, and as we approached the villa I could hear someone inside playing Beethoven with a professional touch. A house where music reigns would surely provide happy lodgings, I thought, and made myself as agreeable as possible to *Herr* Bartsch, a former concert pianist, and his wife. The couple admitted that since they had never had time to have children of their own, they were quite excited at taking in a schoolgirl.

A decorated Christmas tree added a homely touch, and the room to be let, though small, was comfortably furnished and had no window bars. I was allowed to admire the gleaming Bechstein grand in the music room, and, yes I could have the use of the kitchen! *Herr* Bartsch's eyes rested paternally on me, his wife was generous with smiles and ginger biscuits, and a young boxer rubbed its nose against my knee. I decided this was a good place to pitch my tent.

But once again, my hopes of turning a furnished room into a home, and landlords into a family substitute, failed.

Soon after I had moved in, *Herr* Bartsch urged me to resume my piano practice and offered me free lessons. I was thrilled to have a chance to play on a Bechstein and to have a teacher of concert-hall standard. However, it was not long before his proximity on the piano stool turned into embarrassment. For whenever he invited me to watch him tackling a difficult passage, he inched closer to me on the stool until his thigh touched mine and his breath was pumping like a pair of bellows. Or, demonstrating the correct technique of a finger exercise, and sweeping with his left hand up and down the keyboard, his right arm might casually glide around my shoulders, and his face – as by accident – brush my cheek.

One afternoon, *Frau* Bartsch caught her husband *in flagrante*, with his arm around my shoulders, and with no room to wedge a sheet of paper between his housecoat and my flannel dress. I was not surprised when she told me – once she had restored her composure – that her husband needed more rest at his age and would, regrettably, no longer be able to teach me.

From now on, *Frau* Bartsch watched like a Cerberus over her husband's good behaviour and always seemed to be in two places at a time. The door to the Bechstein sanctum and to the living room remained closed, and my landlady's conversation restricted to the weather, the use of the kitchen stove or the payment of the rent.

'What would you like to do after school . . . I mean once you've finished your war service?' my father asked me one day. 'I remember when you were twelve you wanted to become a female detective, at thirteen a tap dancer, at fourteen another Mata Hari.'

I laughed. In the past I had always modelled my ideas on the heroines of the films I had seen. Now, with only eight months to go before my repeat *Abitur*, I reckoned I might make a good journalist and told my father so.

'There's a college of journalism in Berlin,' he said, 'but in order to get in you'd have to know the history of the Reich by heart and be thoroughly familiar with all aspects of national socialism. Besides, you'd have to join the Party, and I'm not sure this is a good idea, not the way things are going. In fact, I'd rather you didn't.'

We had not talked about it any more. However, one day, in an impulsive mood, which overrode any compunctions and any thoughts about its possible future implications, I completed a membership application form. After all, it was little more than a piece of paper, I thought, a small price to pay for the fulfilment of one's ambition. And had not my father reasoned along the same lines in 1936?

To speed things up, I decided to hand in the form personally at the local Party headquarters. Yet not until I had climbed the three-metre board for my second somersault did I remember the crucial papers in my pannier bag. Cursing my forgetfulness, I resolved to pass the offices on my way back, and got ready for a neat dive.

An hour later, I stared at the mess in my hand. Close contact with my damp swimsuit had made the ink run across the pages. But tomorrow was another day. I would pick up a new application form. It was getting late and I was hungry. Perhaps Walter would ask me over to a secret dance party . . .

However, week after week went by without my carrying out my intentions. One morning I realised that my journalistic dreams had gone the way of my other plans for a career. I did not know then how providential the careless packing of my swimsuit and my subsequent forgetfulness would one day prove.

Although Christmas had proclaimed once again the hopeful message of 'peace on earth', spring 1944 saw what would later be termed 'the final reversal of the country's fortune of war'. Air raids on German cities continued to destroy, disrupt, paralyse and demoralise. Survivors supplied gruesome details of people blown-up, buried under rubble, suffocated, incinerated, widowed or orphaned. Rations were cut further, Führer headquarters admitted significant withdrawals on the Eastern front and heavy losses on both sides. In their broadcasts to the nation, Hitler and Goebbels promised final victory, alluding to the devastating power of a secret weapon which would soon be ready for use. Rumours flourished, morale-boosters flooded hoardings, walls, the cinema screen, radio programmes and newspapers. School started earlier in the morning, to make up for lost time spent in shelters during daytime alerts. And as more clouds of ash and gloom drifted over from neighbouring Berlin, so Potsdam's face seemed to grow ashen and gloomy, and to fail, like myself, to respond with earlier vigour to the stirrings of spring.

In school my continuing high marks in English and French revealed a flair for modern languages and encouraged me to think of studying them at university level once the state allowed me to determine my own future.

One day my father visited me after school. I was pained to see him looking grey, troubled and tired.

'Have you applied for Party membership yet?' he asked.

'No, I forgot,' I said. 'Anyway, I've changed my mind. I should like to study English and French.'

'Splendid! I am relieved!'

'Why?'

'Oh, I've heard things.' He went to the door, looked out and shut it firmly before easing himself back into his chair. 'I suppose I shouldn't tell you, it's too horrendous, too risky if passed on carelessly. But then, you're old enough. Promise me you won't talk to anyone about it?'

I did.

'It's the Jews,' my father began, 'I have it from a reliable source that they are carted off to special camps to be killed by gas, whole waggon-loads of men, women and children.' He folded his hands. 'As God is my witness, when I joined the Party in 1936, never in my wildest dreams did I think that it would come to this! There's more – and if it weren't so serious I might be inclined to see the whole thing as a huge joke.'

My face was a question mark.

'I got into disgrace with the Party,' my father said, and recounted how, summoned before a special tribunal, he had been charged with conduct unbecoming to a member of the Party, such as failing to greet other *Parteigenossen* in the street with a raised arm or to wear his badge in public, not to mention his absenteeism from Party meetings over the years.

'In my defence,' my father said, 'I pointed out that I was working late every night on steel contracts – they were free to check up on this. I stressed how difficult it is nowadays to get enough steel, and that we needed steel to win the war, an argument they accepted. However, on other points I was found "guilty", one being the "impertinence" of my having referred to the block warden as a pompous ass, another telling jokes about *Goldfasane*[2] – jokes, they said, which were clearly directed

[2] Nazi 'big shots'.

against Party authority and bordered on the subversive. I couldn't very well deny the latter charges – obviously someone had denounced me. The trouble is there are now as many *Goldfasane* and pompous asses around as informers.'

I laughed, but my father's face remained grave.

'It didn't take them long to consider their verdict. "You've let the Party down," they said, and expelled me. And now I am being posted to a place near Warsaw to run a steel mill. It's manned entirely by Polish and Russian forced labour, supervised by German foremen and guarded by the SS. I'm afraid it smacks of a suicide mission, for the Polish underground is getting stronger with every kilometre the Russians are gaining. That's why I wanted to see you, *mein Kind*, one never knows . . . things have never been more uncertain.'

As he took his leave, I hugged my father as if I were seeing him for the last time. I knew he was right. Nothing was certain anymore, nothing beyond being alive at this particular moment.

In a letter to parents the headmaster explained that, under new regulations issued by the ministry of education, students in secondary schools over the age of seventeen who had completed at least five months in the top class were deemed to have reached maturity and would be awarded the *Abitur* certificate and pre-semester university entrance. The object of such educational curtailment, he stressed, was to set young people free for war service.

None of my classmates protested. On the contrary, some were only too happy to squeeze through on poor assessment marks, while others, who had long been pining to leave school behind, looked forward to entering an adult world no matter how many risks were attached.

Our last morning at school. A brief ceremony, smiles galore, handshakes from teachers. The open classroom door pointing to the big, ugly, beautiful, exciting world outside, a world from which we knew there was no return to scratched desks and ink wells. None of us wanted to be the first to cross that awesome threshold. The school bell shrilled for the end of the morning break, but not for us. We had already been summoned elsewhere.

'And where are you off to, Marianne?' asked Roswhita, the daughter of a high-ranking Treasury official.

I fingered the letter in my pocket. 'I got my travel orders this morning,' I said. 'Gustl and I are to run a kindergarten in the

Berlin 1936. The author at her school desk.

Top 2 The author at the age of five. 3 On the steps of the primary school. *Bottom* 4 The study in the author's grandparents' house: the author's mother is behind the desk. 5 The salon in the same house.

Top 6 1936: The Berlin Olympics. Gala show of the opening ceremony in which the author participated. *Bottom* 7 The flagged Unter den Linden.

Top 8 Potsdam as it was before the Allied air raid. *Bottom* 9 Potsdam as it was before the air raid, with the dome of the Nikolaikirche in the background.

op 10 The Home. 11 The author at the age of ten. *Bottom* 12 The author's secondary
*hool in Potsdam, which she attended 1936–44. Note the bricked-up window of the
asement, which served as an air-raid shelter. 13 The author at the age of fourteen in the
iesengebirge.

Top 14 The baron's villa in Potsdam. *Centre* 15 The lake and the Marmorpalais in Potsdam. *Bottom* 16 The author in Potsdam stadium, 1942. 17 Potsdam, 1942. The author being interviewed by a sports reporter of the *Völkische Beobachter*.

op 18 Running a rural Kindergarten. *Centre* 19 Cocoa time.
ottom 20 Playing games (*'Ziehet durch...die gold'ne Brücke'*).

Top 21 Tangermünde, the council chamber, used at the end of the war by respective US and British town commandants.
22 Tangermünde, 1945. *Tante* Bertha's house.

Centre 23 Gandersheim, 1948. The author shortly before going to England. 24 The author's mother in 1950. *Bottom* 25 The author's father.

Oder-Neisse region,[3] some village way out, it's so small that it is not even on the map.'

'Lucky you! I've got to do my stint in the *Arbeitsdienst*[4] somewhere in Pomerania,' Roswhita replied, and told me how one year in the service had made her sister's cheeks chubby and her hips as broad as the flanks of a cow. 'Camp life absolutely fagged her spirits. And the drill! I know it's going to be an absolute bore. Rising at 5.30 a.m, PT, a cold wash, bedmaking, flag-hoisting and some "tra-la-la", a bread-and-jam breakfast followed by a day on a farm. In the evening, a stodgy *Abendbrot*, camp chores, political lectures, more singsongs . . .'

'Poor you!' Erika chipped in, a girl whose face belied food rationing and made me think of prewar Nivea advertisements. 'I'll be trained as a *Flakhelferin*.[5] And I shall be wearing a uniform!' She looked chuffed, but I wondered whether it had occurred to her that flak barriers were favourite targets for low-flying enemy aircraft.

Renée, born with all the advantages of a famous family name, bemoaned the fate which was sending her to a Berlin ammunition factory, to work – her granny would turn over in her grave – with steel, grease and gunpowder; while Liselotte was being allowed to go on straight to university because of some liver or heart or other condition.

'Doctor's certificate,' explained Anneliese, nicknamed 'the professor', not only because she was top of the class but because she knew the answer to everything. 'You've got to have been ill recently, or be on a diet, to be exempt from war and labour service. Mind you, even a grumbling appendix would get you out of it temporarily, or boils or scabies or a touch of TB . . .'

Outside the school gate we waved each other goodbye. For the last time I looked at the grey building with its walled yard, at the classroom window through which, year after year, my attention had strayed.

As the cloistered school days retreated into the past, and an inhospitable March wind tousled my hair, I felt suddenly very unprotected.

[3] Region between rivers Neisse and Oder (now Poland).
[4] Reich Labour Service.
[5] Women's auxiliary service in anti-aircraft units.

CHAPTER 14

'... *durch die gold'ne Brücke*'

The moment I entered the village nursery I knew that in Gustl I could not have chosen a better working companion.

Blue-eyed, soft-spoken, and with blonde, wavy hair which still seemed to mourn the recent loss of its long tresses, her fine-boned, pretty appearance contrasted with her practical no-nonsense ways, such as were more likely to be found in a midwife or a mother who had been decorated with the Führer's golden *Mutterkreuz*.[1] She now strode confidently into the converted village hall, whereas I hung back, overcome by the abrupt change of environment and reversal of roles.

Two days ago, I had still been sitting at my school desk, controlled by my teachers and by Gudrun, the *Gruppen-führerin*. Now, in the harsh light of the morning, a mass of children, from tiny tots to those of primary school age, were waiting to be taken care of, to be formed up in lines for the toilet, comforted, played with, exercised or generally kept amused until their parents picked them up on their way home from the fields or the nearby brickworks. With no time to draw breath, I had exchanged a classroom for a kindergarten, schoolmates for young charges, a pupil's role for those of nurse, playmate and teacher.

'My God!' I cried, seeing myself at the mercy of twenty youngsters, and experiencing a strong sense of inadequacy and helplessness. 'How can we ever get them under control?'

'Oh, come on!' Gustl replied, moving with ease and authority through pandemonium. 'They won't bite you! Haven't you got any brothers and sisters?'

'No, I'm afraid not.'

[1] Highest decoration for mothers with eight or more children.

'Poor you!' She proceeded to roll up her sleeves and tie an apron around her waist.

'Have you?' I enquired.

'Oh, yes! I'm the eldest of six brothers and sisters. And now, let's get on with it, shall we?' She planted her hands on her hips, grew a few centimetres and called out:

'All quiet now! Quiet, I said. That's it. Good morning, children.'

'Good morning, auntie.'

'Now listen: this is Marianne, and I am Gustl. We are going to look after you for a while. And I can tell you right now, we're going to have a lot of fun together. This is what we do. First we wash our hands and have a cup of cocoa, then we'll go and find out whether the scarecrows in the fields are really frightening away all those hungry blackbirds. And perhaps we'll come across some rabbits and the first spring flowers . . .'

The children began to crowd around her.

'. . . and after lunch, when you've had a rest, we'll play "*Ziehe durch, ziehe durch, durch die gold'ne Brücke*" and other games. And we'll work with bricks and plasticine. And I know so many lovely stories and songs . . .'

Gustl, the inconspicuous girl, who had never been very articulate or outgoing in class, and had seemed content to remain on the fringes of classroom popularity and activities, the same Gustl was now superbly in control.

I rolled up my sleeves and donned an apron. 'All right, let's start!'

The weeks passed as if on stockinged feet. We had no radio, seldom got hold of a newspaper and received no mail. Come Sunday, we knew another week had passed. Yet even if we had had a calendar, I doubt we would have bothered tearing off the pages every day. A strange timelessness prevailed. Food, though plain, was plentiful, the nights were long and sleep sound. As if we had been divorced from history in a sea of awakening fields, no harassing tales, no intimidating sounds, no sights of urban hell plagued our minds. And if to begin with I had resented impatient fingers, pasted with semolina pudding or plasticine, tugging at my skirt, or turned up my nose at sour dribblings or dirty pants, I now dealt with such matters as if I had grown up with a platoon of younger brothers and sisters. In fact, each new

163

day surprised me with flashes of self-discovery which, brought about by a trusting smile or tiny arms reaching out for my neck, or by drying tears that seemed to stem from all the misery of this world, made something vibrate inside me where nothing had ever been sensitive or receptive before.

Halfway through April the countryside was still devoid of lusty spring colours, and the acres of stacked tiles and loam blocks which marked the site of the nearby brickworks still spread bleakness for miles around. For this was brickmaking country where in the drizzle even the lime-green shoots took on the colour of clay soil, and low-hanging skies created a mood of desolation. As many men from the village were working in the clay pits and at the kilns as in the fields, but none of them looked any younger than fifty except Oskar, the village idiot, who – so everyone agreed – owed his life to an administrative oversight by SS and Party authorities.

During the week, the villagers were people of few words and temperate voices. On Saturdays, however, and although the taproom served nothing more stimulating than sour, lemonade-coloured beer, the men would make the *Gasthaus* come alive with arguing, laughing and the sound of cards being slammed on tables. On Sundays, after service, the women would linger outside the small brick church, trying to cram a week's chit-chat into the time it took the men to smoke a pipe. As the weeks went by, their passive and submissive attitude towards the war and their own future was replaced by a mood of concern. Would the time come when they would have to choose between leaving their village and staying on, between the existence of uprooted, homeless refugees and what the newspapers called 'the bloody terror of the Bolshevist beasts' in the villages they had overrun? Perhaps by the grace of God, they said, they would know what to do when the time came.

Sunday afternoon would have been dreary for Gustl and me had it not been for *Herr* Wernicke, farmer, elected *Bürgermeister*[2] and unenthusiastic *Parteigenosse*.

'Had no choice!' he explained one day. 'Anyway, one PG in the village keeps the pack away.' He added that he had long lost his

---

[2] Mayor.

badge and outgrown his uniform, and his right arm was far too painful with arthritis to raise it in a '*Heil* Hitler!' salute, even if he were to meet the *Herr* Gauleiter[3] himself! At least one snickering old man in the village recalled how before 1933 their beloved *Bürgermeister* used to hum the 'Internationale' and at least once, during general elections, had hung out a red flag from his window!

Herr Wernicke taught Gustl and me skat,[4] but once we had mastered the rules of the game, far from showing the two novices any mercy, he treated us like two old card wizards. The regular Sunday afternoon game seemed indeed to form his own high spot of the week, judging by the way he rubbed his hands before a new game and by the roguish smile which split his face each time he called '*re*' or '*contra*'. And it was clear that it was only for our sake that he tolerated the untimely disruption of the game by his wife who, halfway through the battle of cards, served coffee and home-baked *Rosinenkuchen*. If, at the end of such a welcome break, the children insisted on showing us the latest addition to the henhouse or the rabbit pen, he would mock resentment, crying, 'Just when I know I have a good hand coming! Don't be long! I'm shuffling the cards in the meantime.'

Later, over *Abendbrot*, freshly-baked bread and home-cured ham were served amid a plethora of questions to which we knew no answers.

Rooks started building nests, farmer Reichert's apple tree burst into clouds of pink blossoms, May sunshine took the sting out of the day's chores. Gustl and I got hold of two rusty bicycles which, despite their antiquity, managed to take us in our spare time over bumpy tracks through meadows teeming with cowslips and buttercups and pastures speckled white and black with grazing cattle. As we pedalled along and soaked up the tranquillity of the land, it seemed inconceivable that one day tanks might roll, shells blast and an army of heavy-booted men trample across such a scene of rural peace.

Allied forces had landed in Normandy. In the village, two families were mourning for sons who would not return. An

[3] Head of NS administrative district.
[4] A three-handed card game.

165

elderly farmer died in bed, a baby was born, *Herr* Wernicke cut his thumb on a scythe, which, sadly, prevented him from holding a hand of cards. To top the bad news, Gustl and I received new posting orders.

A few villagers came to see us off.

'Where are you going next, *Fräulein*?' a woman asked me.

'Home first,' I said, 'then I'll have to report for another spell of service. It'll be organised by the Hitler Youth and the *Reichsarbeitsführer*.'[5]

'Oh, yes,' the woman said slowly, 'they know how to organise!'

A farmer came forward. 'Well, as long as they don't send you too close to the Russian lines, girls.'

Other voices:

'Thank you, *Fräuleins*, for all you've done. The children are going to miss you!'

'So shall we all!'

'Here, take this, you won't get it on your ration cards!'

For the last time I pulled up little Rudi's socks and tied Gerti's shoelaces. I blew kisses to some of the children whose eyes were wondering how some people could be here today and gone tomorrow. A hand tugged at my dress, tiny fingers held out a bunch of daises.

'Here, auntie, for you.'

As Gustl and I waved our goodbyes from *Herr* Wernicke's gig, I furtively wiped away a tear and decided that I would have at least three children – once I was married, of course.

[5] Head of the Reich labour service.

CHAPTER 15

By Order of the Reichsarbeitsführer

A week later, I was packed off east again, this time in a special train loaded with other boys and girls in Hitler Youth uniform. According to rumours circulating through the compartments, we were heading towards the Wartheland[1] to a destination known only by the engine driver and the two leaders in charge – an *Obergefolgschaftsführer*, a sinewy and very Aryan-looking man who seemed to be in overall command, and a *Ringführerin* whose scrubbed face and no-nonsense air perfectly matched her thick hose and man-sized walking shoes, and whose innocent remark at the onset of the journey that the boys were outnumbering the girls by five to one – a mere slip of the tongue – had instantly given rise to wild speculations and adolescent jokes.

As we left the city I tried to shut out the sight of devastation on both sides of the track. And I remembered the journey to Italy not long ago, when the high spirits of my companions had spilled into the corridor, and the mountain scenery held me glued to my seat. In contrast, the mood on this train seemed strangely subdued, and the countryside – for the best part of fifty kilometres – held little visual appeal for the traveller. However, once we had crossed the grey, fast-flowing river Oder, a rich pastoral view opened up: a patchwork of fields, copses and pastures crisscrossed by telegraph poles and tree-lined country roads; scattered farmsteads, hay wagons, the first wheat-stacks, and all around, harvesters at work, sticking out of the sea of proud corn, out of the flatness of the land and the delicious monotony of yellows and greens like pinheads.

---

[1] Warta area (Poland), east of river Oder.

The train slows down, comes to a halt on open track and stands waiting. Windows are pulled down. The compartment fills with the scent of June meadows and with a stillness which, as if by magic, silences all conversation. But now a rumbling is heard in the distance, growing in volume, a roar, a gust of wind. A Red Cross train steams past in the opposite direction at a speed which still allows one to register bunk beds, white bandages, limbs in traction, grey faces, the limp wave of a hand, a brave smile – flitting images backed up by the rattling of the coaches. For seconds, reality brutally intrudes; the horror of the war reels past on the opposite track, a train from hell, from a battlefield inferno, from a manmade realm of shadows. It thrusts upon us visions of blood and amputations, the moans and screams of strong men, and we instantly drop our smiles as if ashamed of confronting human wretchedness with youthful glee.

Then the nightmare passes, leaving nothing but peaceful rural views and a noiselessness which grows more intense with every second. When, finally, the train jerks back into motion, conversation picks up again, but remains glum and low-key for the rest of the journey.

Towards midday, the train stopped at a weed-infested, crumbling platform. Grasses sprouted in a former waiting-room. A derelict building disgorged, through its open roof, a swarm of excited, screeching birds. A rusty water-pump, weather-defaced signs, an arrow pointing to something at the end of the platform which was no longer there; birches, stunted conifers and miles of sunny fields, and, waiting on a dusty road, four army trucks.

As the train emptied, comments emerged loud and clear from the mass of scrambling boys and girls.

'I'm sure you wouldn't find this place on any school map.'

'I say, this is the end of the world!'

Firm voices told us to get a move on and board the trucks.

'We'll be in camp in twenty minutes.'

There was no doubt that the two leaders knew the exact location which the *Reichsarbeitsführer*, together with the army, Hitler Youth, and other organisations had fixed for some secret 'war service operations'.

Sleep was slow to come that night. I tossed and turned on my straw mattress in the top bunk of a farmhouse attic whose rafters had stored, and were now releasing, the heat of the day.

168

Straw rustled around me, strange creaking and scratching sounds combined with the restlessness of the sleepers. By midnight, moonlight was flooding the attic and all the cats of the district had formed a chorus. I wished we had been allowed to camp in tents, like the boys, or to make our beds out in the open, just as many years ago, one sultry summer night, my sleeping companions and I had exchanged a sticky dormitory for a mattress on the terrace, a bland ceiling for a moonlit sky.

An early rise, PT, a quick wash under the yard pump and bedmaking are followed by a breakfast of rye bread, *Muckefuck*[2] and ersatz jam. We know the drill even before we're through it. After years of training, the flag-raising ceremony, too, is simply routine.

'*Alles antreten!*'[3]

We assemble in the yard around a makeshift flagpole hastily erected by an obliging farmer. The *Ringführerin* looks raring to start the day. I yawn, others follow suit. The girl next to me picks straw out of my hair. A command. We straighten up and raise our right arms in honour of the flag. And now a dashing song fills the yard, scattering hens and throwing a dog of doubtful pedigree into an angry fit of barking. Someone in the house pointedly shuts a window. The *Ringführerin* reads out a poem which extols the virtues of work and comradeship. Judging from the sound of steely voices from the nearby campsite, the boys are starting their day in similar fashion.

'And now,' the *Ringführerin* says, pausing, waiting for the dog to stop barking before parting with privileged information, 'let me tell you why you're here. In a nutshell: to enable the boys to dig trenches and erect defence structures for our infantry. While they'll be out working, you'll help run the camp. I needn't tell you that a successful defence of our front and, ultimately, the repulsion of the Bolshevist hordes, may one day depend on the good job done by the boys, and it will be you who have made this possible. So whatever chores await you in the coming weeks, you will, in a roundabout way, be helping the nation to secure the final victory and – to use the Führer's own words – the survival of the western world. *Heil* Hitler!'

[2] (Slang) ersatz coffee.
[3] 'Fall in!'

'*Heil* Hitler!'

I wonder whether anyone has given a thought to why trenches have to be dug, and tank barriers erected, so close to the homeland when the front line is still supposed to be hundreds of kilometres away.

I quickly adapted to camp life – to soft soap, field-kitchen hotpots and the smell of cabbage, sweat and latrines, to duty rosters, organised leisure, singsongs and politically-orientated lectures. In the process I fell meekly into step and trod softly where objectors and grumblers, dreamers or loners were not, and could not, be tolerated. I peeled potatoes and chopped cabbage; I washed shirts, ladled soup, sliced mountains of *Kommissbrot*,[4] distributed bars of chocolate; I was taught how to read a map, how to operate a field telephone and how to sneak up on an enemy by making the best of natural cover. And then it was time again to sit in a circle, back to vats and pails, to peeling and chopping, singing and squashing mosquitoes.

In the evenings, we joined the boys around the camp fire while the camp leader told stories about Hitler Youth heroes and *die Kampfzeit*.[5] And then it was time for songs in which banners were 'flying towards a new dawn' and 'courageously leading the way to victory', or in which the new era was 'marching ahead' – songs which did not make much sense and which, in celebrating the great cause, seemed somehow no longer to form the same bond of comradeship and unity as in earlier years. But invariably, as the evening wore on, we struck up *Heimatlieder* – simple folk songs passed on from generation to generation, which created a more traditional sense of belonging, and made even the boys' voices sound more mellow.

20 July 1944 started off like any other day at camp, except that the laundry seemed to be dirtier and sweatier, the mountains of potatoes and cabbage larger than ever. Mosquitoes were stinging voraciously and Lore nearly cut off her finger chopping a head of cabbage. There was still no mail from home and, in the growing heat of the day, a mounting lack of enthusiasm showed itself in yawns, dawdling and limp horseplay. The hours stretched out

[4] Very dark, rough, army-style bread.
[5] Early years of national socialism.

170

like worn-out elastic, making even the most energetic of girls sigh for the seaside, cool mountain air or a state of sweet idleness.

The field kitchen served potato soup with smoked sausage for *Abendbrot*, which prompted a cheeky voice to ask if we were celebrating something. Soon jokes were darting around, and free hands or soup spoons waved erratically through the air in an attempt to ward off bloodthirsty midges.

We were halfway through our meal when Willy, the senior Hitler Youth manning the camp telephone and Morse-set, stormed out of his army-style tent and conveyed whispered information to the two leaders. Wasting no time, they put down their mess tins, summoned their deputies and rushed into the tent. There was a tinkle as the telephone handle was turned, the sound of muffled voices, then silence – a graveyard silence, broken only by metal spoons scraping the bottom of mess tins. But not for long. Incredulous, emotional voices erupted from the tent, which emptied quickly. The camp leader chose a tree stump for his podium.

'Attention!' he cried. 'As soon as you have finished, I want you to line up in the usual formation for an important announcement!'

For a few minutes, during which their impatience rose visibly, and a woodpecker noisily hacked away in a nearby tree, the leaders stood around, watching spoons hurriedly scooping up the last of the soup, teeth tearing off chunks of bread, and faces screwing up with suspense and speculation. By the time we had formed a tidy semicircle, some jaws were still moving, some tongues still poking around in mouths. The camp leader's dais had turned into a pulpit.

'This is a moment none of us will ever forget,' he began, 'for the day will go down in history as one on which the infamy of a few made a whole nation hold its breath!' He paused, looked around and steadied his voice. 'There has been an attempt to assassinate the Führer' – his hand went up as if to check any possible outcry – 'but we are happy to tell you that this attempt has failed and the Führer has sustained no injuries.' He held up a scribbled note. 'Here are a few lines from his broadcast which has just gone out to the nation: "An attempt to kill me has failed. I am speaking to you so that you should hear my voice and know that I am unhurt. The conspirators have been rounded up and will be severely punished. Long live our great German Reich!"'

171

The camp leader rattled on about providence, and how grateful we ought to be that the Führer had escaped the 'murderous plot designed by enemies of the Reich'.

Why should anyone want to kill Hitler, I wondered. To end the war? To remove him as head of the nation? To tumble the Party or the SS? Did some people really hate him that much . . .?

'Let us sing!' the camp leader continued, sounding not unlike a preacher who, having ended his sermon, urges his congregation to join him in prayer and thanksgiving.

'*Deutschland, Deutschland über alles . . . Die Fahne hoch . . .*'

There was no telling how high emotions were running behind the masks of singing faces, but one thing seemed clear: what had happened was something immense and, in its implications, as yet beyond comprehension.

An hour later, with free time before the lowering of the flag, I joined a group of girls playing a scouting game in the dusk, one highly favoured by Hitler Youth leaders as a pseudo field-exercise for the skill it required in stealing up to or tracking down an enemy without being detected. For me, it was no more than playing 'hide and seek' or 'cops and robbers', a childish game which, out here, with the smell of hay and soil and pine and woodfire in one's nostrils, held all the thrills of outdoor adventure.

A pale moon stood low in the red-tinged twilight, the first sounds of the night awoke, and the evening star seemed to be gaining in brilliance minute by minute. I stretched out on a pile of hay and stared into the sky. How good it was to be alive! I had forgotten about the game, forgotten about the Führer and the 'heinous' crime of the day.

'Tomorrow, a *Kreisleiter*[6] and an OT[7] inspector will be visiting us. I want the camp spruced up as if we were expecting the Führer himself. Off you go! On the double!'

The camp leader's announcement allowed no room for questions or arguments, and soon a hundred freshly-laundered shirts

[6] Regional party leader.
[7] (Abbr.) Organisation Todt = building and construction organisation, auxiliary to Wehrmacht.

172

were drying on washing lines, bunks, tents, flags and latrines were scrutinised, and a special song practice was scheduled for the evening. Although meat had so far been a rare sight in mess tins, the camp leader organised a special delivery of pork to enrich the vegetable stew of which the visitors were to partake. Throughout the day's activities, I alone seemed to be running under half-steam. A headache, a strange lassitude – symptoms for which I blamed the unrelenting heat.

After a night of shallow, restless bouts of sleep, I wake to a dawn which filters through the skylight as through a piece of gauze. I feel feverish, and my aching limbs are sluggish. An angry sea is breaking in my ears, distorting the early morning sounds in the yard – the squeal of the pump handle, the rattle of milk pails, the jolts of a cart limping across the cobblestones. In the bunks around me straw mattresses grate with every movement of the sleepers as if they are filled with metal coils.

And now I see it through my honeycomb vision, feel it climbing on to my chest, a weight of marble – no, of steel. It is pinning me down, compressing my rib cage, forcing me to take short, rapid breaths. Tentacles, shooting from its body, wriggle towards me, teasing and tormenting, without actually touching my hot skin. I hear myself whimpering like a child, but no one hears me. Gradually the torture ceases, the rider climbs off my chest, the sea grows calmer. And now there are arms, soft, rosy, loving arms, taking hold and lifting me up higher and higher. When they let go, I know exactly what to do. Using my arms like wings, I sweep through the sky like a lark, dive as daringly as a seagull, glide as effortlessly as an albatross. The sky is mine, and with it a freedom against which all the earthbound delights I have known seem to pale. Then I hear a voice.

'Marianne,' it cries, 'come back!' – the same voice which used to call me in from play just as I was enjoying myself most, or which, at a Baltic summer resort one summer, had urged me out of the sea the moment I had left all the other swimmers behind and my white cap had shrunk to a mere dot on the water – my mother's voice, the loving voice of childhood. And I know I must fly back to earth.

Taking my own time, I smoothly glide towards the voice, landing on the ground like a feather. 'Here I am!' I say.

'She's come round!' a voice calls out, and this time it does not belong to my mother.

I open my eyes. A woman's face. A white cap. A white apron.

'Hello, Marianne, glad to have you with us again. How are you feeling?'

'Where am I?'

'In hospital. You've been quite ill. The fever, you know. But now you're over the worst, and we'll soon get you back on your feet again.'

I smile. I suck some fluid through a straw while the nurse holds up my head. A cool flannel washes my face, removes a film of sweat from my body. A fresh nightgown. A change of bed linen. A comb going through my hair . . .

'I feel wonderful!' I say to the face above me. 'You know, I've been dreaming . . .'

As I turn over on my side I know that there is not going to be another flight into uncharted altitudes.

'Marianne, you have a visitor. The *Kreisleiter* has come to see you,' an overawed nurse announced.

I stared at the uniform of a high-ranking Party official, at a dark, handsome man with a generous smile.

He pulled up a chair and sat close to my bed.

'How are you, *Mädchen*?'

'Thank you, much better, *Kreisleiter*.'

A smooth hand, which smelled of peacetime Palmolive soap, touched my cheek.

'I've brought you something,' the *Kreisleiter* said, and unwrapped a few bars of chocolate. 'Now, just make sure that you get quite well again. As soon as they discharge you, you will go on sick leave, and once you've got your strength back we'll see where we're sending you next. Anyway, you won't be going back to camp. Can you draw, *Kindchen*?'

'I always had good marks at school,' I replied.

The *Kreisleiter* smiled, stroked my hair and took his leave among the bowing and scraping of ward staff.

Two weeks later, pale, thin and still groggy on my feet, I arrived in Berlin to spend my convalescence at my grandmother's house. My room in Potsdam had been relet, my old classmates had dispersed, my old links been cut. My mother, now remarried, had long since moved to Upper Silesia with her husband, a balding, bespectacled man whose imposing personality and

174

shrewd business manners disguised not only a razor-sharp sense of humour but a kind and gentle disposition.

'Uncle' Max was not a member of the Party, yet for reasons unknown he still fervently believed in the 'final victory', and considered it the duty of each and every man to serve his country to the best of his ability at its hour of destiny, irrespective of age and such minor afflictions as short-sightedness, baldness, constipation, poor hearing or flat feet. So it did not surprise my mother when after 165 days of middle-aged married bliss he was called up and, joining the ranks of other grey-haired World War I veterans, went to war with the faith of a schoolboy volunteer.

I had not heard from my mother for some time, and there was no word from my father in occupied Poland either. But there was still my grandmother, that grand old lady and accomplished cook: soft-spoken and still retaining some of the frills of graceful living, she looked like a duchess in her worn, lace-collared dress, and she sat down to her potato-and-turnip lunch as if she were dining at the Hotel Esplanade.

Once again I became a willing apprentice in the kitchen and soon learned how to cook a range of palatable dishes even if these had nothing to do with high cuisine, nor with peacetime notions of '*gut bürgerliche Küche*',[8] while in the afternoons, walks, blessed by late autumn sunshine, took us along the banks of the Schlachtensee – an unspoilt, conifer-edged lake of sombre beauty, which showed no evidence of war.

But it was not long before the first October gale stirred up the black water and ducks were riding on the foam-crested turmoil like paper boats – a bleak and blustering scene which conveyed a sense of unrest and impending change.

A week later I received my new service posting to an *Organisation Todt*[9] unit in a small town west of Posen[10].

[8] Good, plain fare.
[9] OT, a state construction organisation, since 1939 mainly engaged in military tasks.
[10] Poznan, now in Poland.

CHAPTER 16

Verlaine and the Kreisleiter

Our steps echoed through ghostly corridors from which the carpets had been removed.

'It's not what it used to be,' said *Herr* Krause, the septuagenarian caretaker and only resident of the small, closed-down hotel, 'and we haven't got much in the way of heating either. There's a stove in the lounge, and I can make you a hot-water bottle for your bed at night, and a cup of *Muckefuck* in the morning. Fancy their putting you up here! There are plenty of rooms to let in town . . . many husbands are away, and quite a few widows wouldn't mind making a few extra marks. But then, perhaps they thought you'd make good company for an old man, eh? And what job might you be doing here, *Fräulein?*'

'I've been assigned to the drawing-office of the unit . . . kind of confidential work.'

'Oh, yes, it's all pretty hush-hush in the compound, guards, gates and all. But take care, *Fräulein*, people say some of them get rather wild at the weekends!'

A ten-hour working day was waiting for me – ten hours of tracing maps and marking trenches and defence positions far to the rear of the existing front line. I took my main meal in the staff canteen, and in the evening huddled by the stove in the lounge where the cosy light of a single lamp, which did not reach into the dustsheet-covered space beyond, lent itself to *Herr* Krause's nostalgic tales about the good old days, to reminiscences which, reaching back to the turn of the century, gained in colour and detail with every pull at his pipe.

While the unit's technical and administrative staff lived in Nissen huts within the compound, my only female colleagues – two peroxide blonde secretaries – each had a room in town.

176

However, rumour had it that they had not slept in their own beds since their arrival a few weeks before, and it did not take me long to see that the duo was appreciated not so much for their two-finger typing as for being the life and soul of weekend drinking and fondling parties, if not for adding spice to working hours with their provocative glances and wriggling of hips down corridors and in and out of offices. At the sight of their shapely, high-heeled and silk-stockinged feet, many a male head would turn, many a chair creak or swivel restlessly, many a ruler be dropped with a sigh in their perfumed wake.

Not long after my arrival I was invited to one of the notorious Saturday night parties. With *Herr* Krause's warning still fresh in my ears, I adopted a guarded position, not unlike a rolled-up hedgehog. I sipped at the strong, sweet wine, always pretending my glass had just been refilled. Never having smoked before, I took no more than one hesitant puff at each cigarette offered, desperately trying not to cough, nor did I cross my legs provocatively, nor recline invitingly on the settee, offering generous views of pink thighs and black straps, like my two more uninhibited colleagues. Smiling, dancing, yet remaining tense, and always leading suggestive remarks back to mundane conversation, I finally fled from arms, mouths and loosened trouser belts, and from the scene of inebriated midnight abandonment, to keep forthwith to myself and to the harmless company of *Herr* Krause.

Although it boasted a railway station and a life-size bronze statue of a horseman galloping defiantly eastwards, and although it was the birthplace of one moderately well-known poet and, before the war, had been the home of a brass band, not to mention seven local *Vereine*,[1] in the late autumn of 1944 the former market town offered neither attractions nor distractions to the visitor.

Grey brick houses, their prim façades unrelieved by flower-boxes, gay-coloured curtains or housewives chatting through open windows, matched the appearance of their occupants as well as the low spirits of the town. Shop windows were filled with cardboard displays, the only cinema had recently closed,

[1] Clubs.

having nothing to offer but an unheated house and a sentimental film everybody had seen at least twice. A solitary café served unpalatable ersatz beverages in drab, low-watt surroundings; in the only inn still open, not more than two or three tables were occupied in the evenings by card players, none of whom was under sixty.

The weather seemed to intensify the town's mood of dark foreboding. Following weeks of melancholic skies and drizzle, winds – sharpened by sweeping across a thousand kilometres of eastern plains – were now howling over roofs and slashing heavy rain against windows. The streets were deserted long before nightfall, being braved only by the doctor and the midwife – two dark, scurrying figures in gumboots and waterproofs, each gripping a black bag in one hand and trying to steady an umbrella with the other.

Unable to go for walks without getting drenched or buffeted, my off-duty isolation would have been complete had it not been for *Herr* Krause's company. Life was also made more tolerable by a weekly staff bonus which included chocolate biscuits and a bottle of red vermouth per head. Yet while the heavily-coated biscuits were a most welcome treat, I decided that my first encounter with vermouth should be the last.

Herr Krause had been out on the night I brought my first allocation back to the hotel. A note explained that he was visiting an ailing sister and would not be back for a day or two. With no one around to share a glass of what I assumed to be a rather weak wine, I took the bottle up to my room and locked the door behind me. I had one sip and, liking its syrupy quality, steadily refilled my glass until, warm and happy, and spinning lightweight dreams, I fell asleep on my bed, fully clothed and with the best part of the bottle gone. Next morning I woke to my first violent hangover and decided forthwith to exchange my weekly vermouth ration for a carton of chocolate biscuits.

I was bending over a map one morning when the *Kreisleiter* entered the drawing office.

'*Heil* Hitler!' he said, and shook hands with the senior draughtsman before moving over to me. I stood up.

'*Na, wie geht's?*'[2] he inquired. There was a roguish expression

---

[2] 'Well, how are you?'

on his face as he savoured my surprise. 'Nice to see you all well and pretty again. I bet you didn't think you'd meet me here, eh? Isn't this better than peeling potatoes and chopping cabbage all day?'

'Yes, *Kreisleiter*!' I smiled and studied his golden Party badge from close quarters.

He looked around as if resenting the presence of other staff, then lowered his voice:

'I often call in here on my regular inspection rounds. Perhaps I can see you sometime after work?'

My tongue was in a knot. I wished someone had told me how to say 'no' to a *Kreisleiter*. But did I want to say 'no'? In desperation I sharpened my pencil, rearranged my drawing materials – anything to avoid his eyes. The room was dead quiet. The *Kreisleiter* waited. Everybody waited.

'I'll see you soon then,' he said, touching my shoulder as if sealing a secret pact. As he strode out of the room, the men stood to attention and crisply returned the salute.

The door had hardly clicked shut when warnings sounded from every drawing board.

'Watch out, Marianne, he's known as "the wolf". You're the third girl he's tried to lay in two months.'

'He's married and has ten children . . . yes, you've heard right, ten!'

'Some girls, they say, get pregnant just by looking at his trousers.'

The senior draughtsman had the last word. 'Don't mind my colleagues, *Mädchen*, they like a good laugh, as long as it's not on them. Just don't get involved. You're a nice girl, and nice girls often get eaten by wolves.'

The weeks passed like a chain of rosary beads gliding through praying hands: six days of working, eating, sleeping followed by a bleak and wet Sunday spent indoors, in bed, at the stove or over a book, days that were indistinguishable from each other.

One night, the chain broke.

The *Kreisleiter* was waiting for me in jackboots and leather coat outside the compound gate. He opened a giant umbrella.

'I thought I'd see you to the hotel,' he greeted me. 'Dreadful weather this! I've only just arrived from Berlin, and my driver has gone for his meal. I wouldn't mind stretching my legs a bit.'

Not waiting for an answer, he took my arm and steered me away from the brightly-lit compound gate into the wet street, where an early night had fallen. I was barely able to make out his features, but I smelt leather and Palmolive soap, and I heard his boots smack the pavement. And the way my body reacted to the pressure of his arm, to the dark timbre of his voice, reminded me of how, two summers ago, the waters of the lake had caressed my nakedness at sundown. I wanted to say something, but once again words failed me in the proximity of a man who was forcing his way into my life, a man – so I reminded myself – who was a member of a political élite feared, ridiculed and despised by many, and whom I ought to scorn, rather than feel attracted to.

'Don't you feel lonely in the evenings all by yourself?' he asked.

At last I found my voice. 'No, not really, *Kreisleiter*. *Herr* Krause, the caretaker, is keeping me company.'

'But what do you do with yourself on Saturday nights and Sundays? You're young, and the town is pretty dead.'

'I read a lot.'

'What kind of books?'

'Oh, all sorts, Ernst Wiechert, Charles Morgan, Binding, Rilke.'

'I used to be a bookworm,' the *Kreisleiter* said, 'but I'm afraid I haven't got much time for books nowadays. Sometimes I open the classics again, or Kant's *Kritik der reinen Vernunft*[3] – a splendid work, but heavy going. And I like to dip into Goethe's *Faust*.'

'I thought you people only read *Mein Kampf*!' The words had slipped out, unchecked and too late to retract. I stammered a vague apology, but the *Kreisleiter* shook with laughter, which made his umbrella dance fitfully over my head and water trickle inside my coat collar.

'Oh, *Mädchen*, you're funny,' he cried. 'You won't believe it but I also like poetry, and I even read Verlaine in French.'

'We did Verlaine in school,' I said, and began to quote,

> *La lune blanche*
> *luit dans les bois*
> *de chaque branche*
> *part une voix . . .*

[3] *The Critique of Pure Reason.*

'*O bien aimée,*' the *Kreisleiter* continued.

> ... *L'étang reflête*
> *profond miroir*
> *la silhouette*
> *de saule noir*
> *où le vent pleure.*
> *Rêvons, c'est l'heure* ...

Perturbed by the sudden intimacy which had sprung up between us, I tried to break the spell with a touch of flippancy.

'So you really know Verlaine! I'm impressed!'

'Look,' the *Kreisleiter* said, as if explaining a natural phenomenon to a child, 'it may surprise you but some of us can think and read and have preserved our critical faculties ... and our consciences. Not all of us show off their feathers like peacocks. Yes, yes, I know what people say, and between you and me I agree that some of their contempt is justified. But, as I said, some of us ... you're too young to understand what happened in 1933, and how, years later, a road suddenly turned out to be a cul-de-sac.'

'I think I understand,' I said. 'My father ...' I swung round. 'Here we are!'

We had reached the hotel. It had stopped raining. The *Kreisleiter* folded his umbrella and took my arm again. 'Come, let's walk a little more. Do you know when I first saw you?'

'In hospital?'

'Oh no, two years ago at the *Bannmeisterschaften*[4] in Potsdam when you walked away with all the prizes. I often saw your picture in the paper and read all those nice things they said about you. And I was there when they carried you out of camp on a stretcher. I had just arrived. I recognised you immediately.'

'All I remember is flying high in the sky like a bird, and that it was absolute bliss.'

'I think you were fighting your way back with the determination of an athlete.'

I looked across the street, through brick walls and people's living rooms and the space of years.

'Perhaps I learnt to fight when I was ten,' I said, 'and it had

[4] Local Athletic Youth Championships.

181

nothing to do with athletics. My parents got divorced and I was put into a children's home. I felt dumped. I was lonely. And I had to prove things, to assert myself, in order to survive.'

'You certainly succeeded. But why were you put into a home?'

'I wish I knew. I suppose my parents were busy sorting out their own lives, too busy to have me around. And my mother had to earn her living.'

Suddenly, as though for the first time, I understood how much courage and determination this would have required of someone like my mother who knew what glass went with which wine, what cutlery with which dish, what type of dress with which occasion; who knew how to arrange a dinner party for twelve, speak French, make polite conversation, identify pieces of music after the first few bars, play the piano with reasonable proficiency and dance the tango as skilfully as the foxtrot, but who would not have known how to deal with an ill-tempered boss, an awkward typewriter ribbon or an intricate filing system in a busy, competitive office.

'Were you very unhappy?' the *Kreisleiter* asked, and I recounted the numbness and pain which had made me refuse my food, until they made me eat, because they meant to be kind.

'But then things happened,' I said.

'What things?'

'I'd rather not say. You might laugh.'

'I won't, I promise.' An arm went round my shoulders.

And now, as I spoke, it all came back to me: September, a garden swing, leaves floating or reeling to the ground, a sunbeam turning a bed of chrysanthemums into blazing torches. A plum tree. A world conquered on my bike. Things coming alive, taking meaning, speaking to me.

'So there you are,' I said, 'and now you may call me an incurable romantic.' I skipped over a puddle.

The *Kreisleiter*'s voice had the mellowness of ripe peaches.

'I've never met a girl like you. How old are you?'

'Nineteen.'

'Nineteen,' he echoed. 'Quite extraordinary! Such a sense of perception in one so young and pretty! What you've got, *Mädchen*, is a crutch for the soul, an aid for living. It takes some of us half a lifetime to construct some sort of survival kit, and I'll bet lots of people wouldn't even understand what you're talking about. By the way, you have no idea how I, a middle-aged man, am enjoying this conversation with a nineteen-year-old girl! I sometimes wish I had my life still before me. Ah. Not to know how agonisingly short it is, not to know that it only holds – as our Verlaine puts it – "*un peu de rêves/un peu d'amour/un peu bon jour*".[5] He stopped and faced me. 'Tell me, do you perhaps believe in . . . God?' But instantly, as if regretting his question, or not wanting to hear my answer, he studied the luminous dials of his watch. 'I'm sorry, we'll have to continue our conversation some other time. My driver will be waiting. But I'll be back just before Christmas, and if you like I could give you a lift back to Berlin, to spend Christmas with your family.'

In its vehemence, my acceptance of the *Kreisleiter*'s offer resembled that of a child which has received a coveted invitation to a birthday party.

'*Gute Nacht!*'

Lips brushed my cheek. As the *Kreisleiter* turned to go, I could have sworn he was smiling, and my right arm, forever alert to shoot up, went limp again.

Three days before Christmas I was sitting next to the *Kreisleiter* in the back of his chauffeur-driven Horch. A warm blanket covered my knees, the boot of the car held a Christmas tree and a carton filled with Vermouth, chocolate biscuits, Palmolive soap, half a pound of butter and a small leatherbound volume of Verlaine's poetry.

Winter had set in. There was snow on the ground, and in the fading light of the afternoon a sharp easterly wind was whipping the bare roadside trees. Yet, in some inexplicable way I was happy, sitting beside this enigmatic, powerful man who held his arm around me. I closed my eyes and crept deeper into the nest of his shoulder, seeking father, mother, Sebastian, friend, home, peace – all in one. Forgotten was his golden Party badge, his rank and large family, forgotten the jokes circulating about people like him. I fell asleep, and when I woke at the outskirts of Berlin, I was not sure whether I had been dreaming or whether his lips had touched mine during the journey.

My grandmother's flat was unheated except for the high-ceilinged living room in which a small cylindrical stove barely

---

[5] 'A few dreams, a little love, a little happiness.'

warmed its immediate surroundings. Some of the windows were boarded up. Electricity and gas came on for a few hours, unless a nearby mains had been hit overnight. But necessity was the mother of invention, and a candle could be made to outlast the life of its wick. Food rations now stood at a bare survival level, yet the Christmas bonus of flour, fat and sugar – measured in measly grammes – went ungrudgingly into spiced cookies.

My mother arrived a day before Christmas, looking a shadow of her former self. A long tortuous train journey from Upper Silesia. Personal belongings contained in one suitcase. Lurid tales picked up from fellow refugees. And she talked, still stunned, still bemoaning her husband's sudden call-up, shivering not so much from the cold which seeped through the windows, but with the last forty-eight hours still vivid in her mind – two days of tightly packed compartments and solidly blocked corridors, of bladders and bowels opening in despair, of a stench spreading like a poison gas, of people fainting without anywhere to fall. And some, she said, had started off riding on buffers, steps and the roofs of carriages, but, losing their hold in the arctic cold, had disappeared from view or hurtled past the windows as dark, frozen shapes, until there were no more.

'I wonder if Hitler knows about the conditions on these trains?' my mother asked, not expecting an answer, and my grandmother poured us another cup of deliciously hot mint tea.

As the temperature dropped still further, we kept our coats on indoors and wore gloves to handle cutlery. In the mornings I had to make a supreme effort to leave my bed, but even more so during night alerts when the prospect of sitting in the communal cellar, in which the pipes had frozen, was even more chilling than the thought of annihilation by bombs. I often felt tempted to sleep in my clothes, and to give up washing altogether. When had I last had a bath, the luxury of steeping my body in warm water and lathering it with real soap?

The telephone – the only service which was still fully functional – rang for me on New Year's day. My father was back in Berlin and within an hour I had joined him in his flat. He pointed to a pot of coffee on the table.

'We're celebrating! I got some real coffee in exchange for cigarettes which I got for a pound of flour which I got for . . .'

I interrupted my father's black-market odyssey.

'Tell me how you got back from Warsaw.'

'It's a long story,' my father began, 'an incredible one. I'm very lucky to be alive.' And he told me how deplorable working conditions had been for the men at the Polish steel mill. A ten- to twelve-hour shift, pitiful rations. 'Pigs would have refused that muck!' Every day someone reported sick or collapsed, and when production fell, the guards did not think twice before flogging a man back to his casting pit.

'I was supposed to run the place,' my father said, 'but the SS made it quite clear that as a civilian I had no power to intervene. "You worry about your paperwork, *Herr* Gärtner, leave the men to us!" It was a command. But then they couldn't prevent me from organising extra food for the men. I used all my contacts, tapped every available source, even managed to syphon off supplies from our own army depot, in order to improve the standard and the quantity of canteen portions, and to boost each man's ration with an extra loaf at the weekends. My argument – that we desperately needed steel to win the war – worked like magic. As a result, production picked up again, fewer men went off sick and the general mood on the shop floor improved. Some of the chaps even smiled at me! Then, one morning, I was writing my report when I heard firing in the yard – the clatter of automatic rifles, screams. Before I had time to get over to the window, my door was kicked open and some rough-looking types – armed to the hilt they were – pointed their rifles at me. "Director?" they asked, and I knew then they had just shot my foremen and the guards, and that now it was my turn. But then there came loud shouts from downstairs, and a group of workers stormed into the room and argued at the top of their voices with the partisans – that's what they were, members of the Polish underground. Finally, the firing squad left and my rescuers told me to get my things and be quick about it. "Your people are finished out here, *panie*," they said. "The Russian army is on the move and nothing will stop them now. One of us will lead you back to German territory under cover of darkness." My relief must have been obvious, for they added, "You're a good man, *panie*! You're our enemy, but we're grateful for what you've done for us!" This is how I got back. But who will ever believe that Polish labourers saved my life and that, when he left me, my escort actually shook my hand?'

We sat talking until an early winter's evening banished the

light from the room. I drew the curtains and switched on the table lamp.

'And what will you be doing next?' I asked.

'I'm having my company desk back, unless I'm called up first. Come, let's drink to the new year, and that we may see the end of the war.'

The coffee pot yielded two mouthfuls of cold coffee, and we raised our cups as if they contained champagne.

A few days later I was travelling back east in an official car.

'Sheer madness!' my father had called my decision to resume my work at the drawing board. 'By the time you get there, everybody will have packed up!'

'I have to go!' I said. I knew my leave was up. But was it really a sense of duty which was driving me back against all better judgement? Did I perhaps hope to see the *Kreisleiter* again? And if I did, was I then not acting like a foolish teenager? For however brave he might be, would he not be sorting out his own priorities at a time like this and perhaps decide to stay clear of an area likely to fall into enemy hands before long?

I noticed that life in the compound had changed while I had been away. Not only was the place swarming with army officers, OT officials and dispatch riders, but canteen portions had been increased, and vermouth and chocolate-biscuit rations doubled. Every day, my male colleagues received demands for updated maps, every night there were parties – debauched affairs, according to Theo, a Spanish Civil War veteran, who admitted to being a keen reveller. For, surely, the end of the world was imminent.

'I've got nothing to lose,' he argued one morning, after being reprimanded by the senior draughtsman for falling asleep at his board. 'Certainly not my virginity, and who would shed a tear over losing this job? Look, you can't blame us for wanting to snatch a last drink or a last fuck before the ceiling caves in. Why not come and join us tonight? A last journey into euphoria, eh?'

CHAPTER 17

The Flight to Berlin

Something else had changed.

In the distance, there was now a deep rumbling sound which, never pausing and travelling unimpeded on the biting easterly wind, seemed to grow louder and more ominous every day. And with it came the Russian winter. It stopped snowing and the temperature dropped to fifteen degrees below zero.

The atmosphere in town was very tense. Some people locked up their houses and tried to get onto one of the last westbound trains. Often these did not even stop at the station, and I would watch them chugging past my office window, their engines labouring, pulling a long line of coaches covered with antlike figures, riding on buffers, running boards and roofs, and clinging to steel as if to life itself.

One day, there were no more trains. Russian units were reported to have taken Warsaw and to be advancing fast towards Posen, while German lines – so informed talk went – had been withdrawn to less than thirty kilometres east of the town.

I woke to the sound of heavy artillery, to a barrage still distant enough not to rattle my window, yet close enough to feel uncomfortable. The war, I realised with a shock, was rolling towards the town with the speed of hot lava.

There was a knock, and a breathless *Herr* Krause popped his head round the door. 'Haven't you left yet, *Fräulein*? You'd better hurry! The rest of the town is on the move. They say the Russkies are closing in . . . Posen is about to fall . . . our whole front has collapsed. Your people will be taking care of you, won't they? Well, I'm off now. Would you leave through the kitchen and lock the door? The key goes under the mat. All the best!'

I felt like laughing. Surely *Herr* Krause did not ever expect to come back, and what was a locked door to Russian boots, a lock to a machine pistol?

187

I dressed quickly. My hands trembled as I buttoned up my dress and I searched frantically for my left stocking. Outside, a red sun was rising, and when I stepped out into the back garden, the frozen snow cracked under my feet like glass . . .

There is pandemonium in the main street. I needle my way past muffled-up figures pulling rickety handcarts, past carts drawn by horses which look as though they will never reach new stables. Vehicles are piled high with pots and pans, mattresses, bedding, suitcases and sacks filled to bursting point, and at least one grandfather clock is sticking out from among someone's goods and chattels. Thumb-sucking children and old, black-swathed women are stacked on top of treasured loads, prams are heaving under the weight of toddlers and suitcases, while terrified mongrel dogs cling to the heels of their owners.

Suddenly a relentless hooting tears through the street. A German army convoy on its way to the front drives a wedge into the fleeing mass. In the resulting scramble horses neigh and trip nervously, rocking or upsetting carts. Possessions get dislodged, topple into the street, are retrieved by their frenzied owners. For a few minutes the exodus comes to a halt, and as the convoy passes through, I look into the terrifyingly determined faces of midget soldiers, into smooth pink faces whose screwed-up eyes and pinched lips seem to mimic the expressions of experienced soldiers; into faces small with fear or so innocent that they might still blush at the touch of a girl. I see boys in uniforms two sizes too large, boys who might die, calling out for their mothers or with the name of Führer and fatherland on their lips. And I have no time to feel sad.

As the trek reorganises itself, fear returns and whips people on their way – the fear of things to come if one remains, of the town being shelled, of savagery and rape, the kind of panic for which rumours have prepared the way for weeks.

In the compound, gates and doors are standing wide open. Staff and technical equipment have gone. Out of a large OT motor pool only one partly-loaded truck is left. A group of men and women are crowding around it, waiting for the driver to give the boarding signal.

'Where is everybody?' I ask a chubby man who seems to be having trouble starting the engine.

'What the devil are you doing here, *Mädchen*?' he roars. 'You should have gone in one of the Opels, like the rest of the staff. Did nobody wake you?'

I shook my head.

'Ha, typical! What about all that garbage about "*Einer für alle, Alle für Einen*"?[1] Too busy saving their own skins they were, the bastards! Where are your things?'

'At the hotel. I had no idea . . .'

The engine comes to life.

'Go and get them quickly! I'll give you five minutes, no longer. I want to get the hell out of here! Now, run!'

I reached the hotel in a mad zigzag race and, back in my room, put on as many clothes as I could fit into, before flinging the rest of my belongings into a suitcase and a rucksack. I looked in vain in my drawers for any biscuit leftovers, while a lightning raid of the hotel larder on my way out yielded only the stale end of a rye loaf. Locking the back door, and leaving the key under the mat as instructed, I plunged back into the chaos of the streets.

With only twenty yards to go, I saw the lorry moving off. It was packed to capacity.

'Wait for me!' I cried, only too conscious of the weight of my suitcase, of the freezing cold hitting my inflamed sinuses and of the sprint ahead – the race that of all races I had to win. And I wrenched every metre from the space that separated me from the vehicle and, once I had reached the cab, punched the door like a one-armed prize fighter.

A face appeared at the window. Brakes squealed. The door opened.

'Jump in, girl! Glad you made it!'

Compared with the outside temperature, the cab was warm and cosy; the noise of the engine promised speed and safety, as well as an escape from what people called a fate worse than death.

'I'm sorry I couldn't wait for you,' the driver said. 'When you weren't back after five minutes I had to push off. All hell was let loose as they scrambled into the back, all panic and elbows. It's nice up here in front, though, isn't it? You're lucky that Max, my co-driver, didn't come up with me from Berlin last night. They said he had colic. Ha! Colic indeed! *Dass ich nicht lache!*[2] Scared he was, the *Scheisskerl*! He's a hefty chap, there are at least two hundred pounds of him . . . that normally leaves no room for anyone else in front.'

[1] 'One for all, all for one!'
[2] 'It's enough to make you laugh!'

'I'm glad I made it!' I said, still panting – and I thought of the many hours spent on the track, trying to improve my sprint style and slice a few tenths of a second off my sprint or hurdle time. I could hardly have guessed then that I was preparing myself for a morning such as this, when whatever speed and fitness I still had left in the fifth year of the war would be put to the test.

'You can clean the window and help me watch the road,' the driver continued once we had left the town behind and found ourselves on an east–west arterial road jammed with refugees. 'What a trek! You can tell which of these wretches have been on the road for a day and which for a week.'

The lorry was crawling along.

'At this speed it'll take us days to get to Berlin. Low gear all the time . . . engine will overheat . . . petrol won't last. *Was zum Teufel*[3] did I let myself in for? I had a good mind not to go back yesterday, but the Party bosses don't think twice nowadays. Desertion, they call it, treason, evasion of one's patriotic duty. Ha! A loop, a gurgle and you sway in the wind. By the way, I'm Albert. What do they call you?'

'Marianne.'

'Nice name. I've seen you around in the compound. Can you drive?'

'No, I'm afraid not, I've never sat in a lorry before. But I travelled in a big car the other day, and when I was small, my father often gave me a lift in his company car – mind you, it came complete with chauffeur.'

'Hm, so you're one of those!'

'One of what?'

'Oh, nice family, nice flat with bathroom and hot water at the turn of the tap, white table-cloths, silver napkin-rings . . . and no communal lavatory on the landing, no backyard smell of cabbage and drains.'

I burst out laughing, but before I had time to reply, the lorry started skidding on a patch of ice. Albert cursed, regained control over the vehicle and gave an outsized yawn. 'I'm dead tired, girl. Haven't slept for forty-eight hours. What if I drop off? Bloody war, this! Here, I'd better show you how to drive. Come closer, I won't bite. I'm too tired for any funny business. Now, look here, these are the gears . . .'

[3] 'What the devil . . .'

190

After ten minutes of basic driving instruction Albert told me to take the wheel for twenty seconds to get the feel of it, then stated confidently, 'Now you know the drill!'

On we drove, past the endless column of men, women and children wrapped up to the eyes against the bitter cold, whose gait and the speed with which they moved, or the amount of luggage they still carried, pushed in prams or pulled in hand-carts, indicated the distance they had covered on foot. And – a sight which grew more oppressive with every kilometre – there were those who had not been able to make it any further, and who, not far from jettisoned suitcases and bicycles and mat-tresses and dolls and broken cart-wheels, had frozen into bizarre positions or were shrouded with snow.

The sun, which had reached its highest point for early February, stood pale and frosty in a white sky when, after what seemed hours of trying to steer clear of human obstacles and treacherous patches on the road, Albert's head suddenly dropped on his chest and his hands relaxed on the wheel. The heavy vehicle swerved, a ditch and the trunk of a tree came close. With no time to think I pounced on the wheel, wrenched it round and gained control. By now, Albert was snoring, but although his arms were hanging limp by his side, his foot remained stubbornly on the pedal. I veered towards the middle of the road and, terrified of Albert's foot increasing the pressure on the accelerator, and of the lorry crashing into lurching figures or into the ditch, I made liberal use of the horn. I survived the first bend, missed the hindleg of a dead horse by a hair's breadth, then found myself on a straight stretch of the road where the trek was broken for a kilometre. Now I had a moment to relax and to marvel at how the sleeper's glottal sounds managed to drown the noise of the engine.

The respite was brief. Fists hammering against the back of the cab startled Albert awake. Involuntarily, his foot pressed the accelerator and the lorry shot forward. But within seconds he was back in control and, seeing that the road ahead was clear, went into top gear.

'Must have dropped off for a moment,' he said. The hammer-ing continued. 'What the hell is going on?' he said angrily. He applied the brakes and jumped out.

Suddenly it was very quiet in the back. Then I saw the woman. Holding a tiny, lifeless bundle in her arms, she walked over to the edge of a field, awkwardly, her legs slightly apart, and very slowly as if time were waiting as her executioner. Her frail body was shaken by sobs which seemed to freeze as they reached her lips. Placing the bundle at the foot of a hedge, she hacked with her heel at the ground until it had yielded enough frosted snow to cover the body. As she stooped over it as long as it takes to say a short prayer and make the sign of the cross, standing out sharply against the grim whiteness of the fields, she struck me in the silent torment of her mourning as one of the loneliest figures I had ever seen.

A long walk back to the lorry, a last glance back to the hedge, helping hands. Then it was all over. Albert returned and restarted the engine.

'It was a boy,' he said. 'Poor woman! Didn't have a chance . . . not on an open truck . . . not in this arctic cold! There, that's the bloody war for you. I'm lucky myself . . . got four little blighters . . . lovely kids! Here, girl, take the wheel for a minute! I need a puff and a stomach warmer.'

I concentrated on the road, trying not to listen to the voice of my conscience. Oughtn't I have offered to swop places with the distressed and bleeding woman? Wouldn't it have been a nice human gesture? But – or so I pleaded with the voice within – surely it was easy to act like a good Samaritan if one's sinuses didn't throb with infection and the low temperature didn't freeze unselfish thoughts in the bud . . .?

Albert saved the situation.

'You're doing a great job, *Mädchen*! We mightn't have come this far without you!' He took a giant swig from a bottle which did not look as though it contained water.

Albert had not quite finished his cigarette when, at the sight of another struggling column, he took the wheel again. 'Right,' he said, 'let's get past this lot!'

But now the engine started spluttering and minutes later died to the accompaniment of Albert's expletives.

'That's it!' he said, following an angry monologue with the engine compartment and the fuel gauge. 'I thought the old girl would take us a little further. There are no garages or depots in these parts. I'm afraid this is as far as we go. It's all legwork from here on, everybody's on their own. I'll go and tell the others. Good luck, *Mädchen*, it was nice knowing you!'

That was the last I saw of Albert.

My sinuses cried out as the icy air struck painful membranes, and I wrapped my scarf around my head like the other refugees, leaving only a slit free for mouth and eyes. After the first kilometre my suitcase seemed to contain stones, after the second my fingers started growing numb, after the third, because I needed a rest more frequently, I began to fall back. But not for long; once I had divided the approximate mileage ahead by my present speed, common sense prevailed. I opened my suitcase and stuffed into my pockets as much as they would hold. A pair of woollen socks doubled up as mittens and, rather than part with it, I wrapped my Sunday dress around my middle.

And now I had become one of them – a member of a desperate fraternity, of an endless chain, one of tens of thousands who, having discarded their last cumbersome possessions, were lumbering on in a bid to reach the already doubtful safety of the capital, being driven only by the will to survive.

For hours we walked in a herd, measuring time in degrees of hunger, frostbite and exhaustion, and by the gradual dissolution of daylight. Colonies of crows mottled the wintry fields, in which wretches scraped the ground in the hope of finding an unharvested potato, a beet, anything edible. A buzzard kept circling over some dark object, its ghoulish cries sounding like a prophecy of doom. It was difficult to know what was more unnerving – the deep rumbling front approaching from the east and, in the tired mind, gaining in wrath minute by minute, or the shuffling and dragging of hundreds of feet over the snow-crusted surface of the road.

Night came early – a white and beautiful night, infinitely cold and cruel, in which a full moon dwelled lovingly on the chilling poetry of the naked fields and, struggling through the crowns of roadside trees, created filigree patterns on the ground, silhouettes which might look exquisite one moment, spookish another.

And now more people dropped out, collapsing quietly by the road or choosing the deceptive shelter of ditches or hedges for a place to rest, perhaps not realising, perhaps not caring, that they might drift into a sleep from which there was no waking.

I was limping in my ill-fitting, wooden-soled shoes, and my stomach was shouting insults at me for not having seen any food for thirty-six hours. But then I remembered the stale piece of bread in my pocket and I sank my teeth into it, chewing each bite ten times over. I watched with disgust, yet with full understanding, people stripping the dead of boots and overcoats sometimes long before they had frozen into rigor mortis. As time wore on, I walked like an automaton, putting one foot in front of the other, and no longer taking in details but trying not to fall behind or to succumb to the overpowering but fatal desire to sit or lie down.

At last the stars began to fade, the moon grew pallid and the sun rose once again like a blood orange on the horizon. The trek had visibly thinned out. There were fewer children now, and those who still clung to their mothers' coats whimpered or refused to move on. The air cracked with frost, turning breath into white trails of smoke.

We passed through a village which looked deserted, though smoke curling from chimneys indicated otherwise. Our knocks, however, did not open doors or windows, and barns and sheds remained barricaded.

'We have no food to spare!' people shouted from inside, and their voices sounded frightened. 'The barn is already crammed with refugees, and we're getting ready to leave ourselves!'

So we staggered on. Towards evening an armed, eastbound convoy of soldiers in ill-assorted uniforms passed us – grey-haired, unsmiling men, some with gold-rimmed spectacles, who looked as if they had been dragged from behind desks, out of classrooms or lecture halls.

'If they're our last hope, the end won't be long now,' a woman remarked wryly. 'They look as though they don't know one end of a rifle from the other.'

At last, a suburb of Berlin. Suddenly there were pretty houses with snowmen in front gardens and snow-cleared pavements – but not far behind them loomed the first bleak tenements, the first factory sites, the first grim evidence of bomb damage.

The all clear sounded. I reached a station.

'The line's been hit,' the S-Bahn guard said. 'There won't be any trains for some time.'

Aching for food and a bed for the night, I dragged myself on, and gradually the face of the city revealed some of its scars: the skeletons or the ravaged façades of tenements; streets in which, as a result of the latest assault from the air, buildings were still collapsing, and the dust and smoke made me cough. And yet, turning a corner, I might find myself in some quiet street which seemed to belong to another place and time, where faint light or radio music trickled through curtained windows, and where I could hear my own footsteps on the deserted pavement.

Underground trains were still running. As I slumped into a seat I felt people's eyes on me, but only cursorily, as one might take note of a new passenger. My wild, exhausted appearance did not startle them, neither arousing curiosity nor prompting compassionate questions. But, I told myself, Berliners had got used to the sight of refugees who had made it on foot, in farm carts or packed trains, and in their own fight for survival, how could their knowledge that every day there were fewer resources to tap and less food to go round, fewer homes affording shelter and fewer trains leaving the city, possibly generate unselfish sentiments towards those whose needs were bound to make matters even worse? Berlin, they might say, could ultimately offer refugees nothing but a dubious sanctuary and the high morale of its inhabitants.

I was wholly unprepared for the sight that awaited me, just as I was for that sense of loss which, it was said, could reduce a battle-hardened soldier to a sobbing child, and shock people into a grief which could eclipse the rest of their lives.

Black space gaped behind charred walls and window caverns where my grandmother's house had stood – a space which had belonged to rooms in which, after each weekend visit, I had left a part of myself behind. I thought of my mother and my grandmother, and the pain seemed unbearable, pleading to be released in a howling scream, yet merely seeping through my lips.

In my mind's eye I saw the Flemish chest which had contained a host of treasures; my grandfather's study where, as a small child, I had listened to strange and wondrous tales from the Far East; the salon, unforgettable for its gleaming grand piano and billowing lace curtains, for the elegance of crystal, mahogany, satin and tea roses, and – most beloved of all its pictures – Gainsborough's gilt-framed 'Blue Boy'. And my memory continued to fill the space: the heavy oak sideboard in the dining room, and the huge tureen filled around Christmastime with butter pretzels and vanilla stars; the corner in the living room where the Christmas tree had stood every year; the stately grandfather clock whose case I had searched for chocolate eggs and bunnies on Easter Sundays; the sewing table with its magical boxes of coloured and oddly-shaped dress buttons; the drawers of my grandmother's dressing table with their fascinating contents.

I groaned. My knees buckled under me, my train of thoughts

came to a halt, and I felt as if I was back on the edge of a white bed, naked, numb and shivering, as one fine September morning long ago. . . .

Shuffling footsteps. A waft of home-grown tobacco. An old man's voice.

'Been looking for family? Yes, it's been a bad week, what with one air raid after another. *Amis* dropped a lot of firebombs around here, many a fine villa has gone.' He pointed to the gutted ruin. 'This one went three nights ago . . . but they all got out in time, I heard. Let's see! Survivors usually leave a note for their relatives on the nearest tree. There are some over here. What's your name?'

'Marianne.' I heaved myself back on to my feet and in the fast-falling darkness scanned the scribbled notices. I saw initials, a message, a new address, the sweet music of my mother's handwriting.

I put my arms around the tree and sobbed, suddenly conscious again of my empty stomach, of the sharp edge of exhaustion and the lack of sensation in my fingers. The old man patted me on the back, and I thanked him for his help. A sniffing sound, the friendly rub of something soft against my leg told me that he had been taking his dog for a walk. Spurred on by the thought of a bed, of food and warmth, and of being reunited with the two people I loved, I made my way to the nearest *S-Bahn* station.

I had been on the train for less than five minutes when the sirens started wailing again. Carriages emptied quickly at the next station and with the rest of the late commuters I was sluiced into an underground shelter where, minute by minute, the air grew more foul, reeking of fear and neglected bodies, of dirty nappies and old men's leaking urine – a stench which mingled unashamedly with that untimely reminder of Germany's occupation of France, the scent of perfume.

Soon I fell asleep between the elbows and thighs of strangers, deaf to the fretful cries of children and the gruff voice of the warden, deaf even to the dull thuds overhead and the agony of the buildings about us.

When the all clear went I woke in the resulting scramble for the exit. I found the *S-Bahn* no longer running and continued my way on foot, often taking risky short cuts in my eagerness to come to the end of my trek, and forgetting the old adage that hell has many entrances.

A row of houses cut in two with the precision of a ruler. I want to retreat, but it is too late. I am trapped between mounds of rubble, smoke and clouds of pulverised masonry. I trip over a body, I flee in horror from a pair of gaping, empty eyes which are fixed on the dusty moon as in a somnabulist's trance. A few staggering steps ahead, close to a bomb crater, where the street has belched up pipes and cables, and the broken mosaic of small paving-stones forms mole hills, a woman lies twisted around a lamp post which is bent like a stick of plasticine, and not until I am clear of the body do I realise that there are no legs sticking out from under her coat. And as I climb over, or try to bypass obstacles, yet more horrors begin to crowd my yellow-dusted vision: another body; a lump of raw flesh where a face has been; the savage obscene sight of a laced-up boot sitting on top of a chunk of mortar, still enclosing the bloody stump of a foot. . . .

It is as much as I can take. I double up, my stomach turns and expels its acid content.

But now there are commands and shouts and sober voices, men carrying stretchers, searchlights and digging equipment. At last, stumbling, falling, picking myself up again, I manage to find a passage out of a street over which perhaps only one or two enemy bombers have released their lethal load.

The church clock was striking one when I finally reached the new address – a block of modern flats in a quiet, tree-lined street which, apart from blown-out and boarded-up windows, seemed so far to have escaped major damage.

I rang the bell to the apartment, but no one stirred, which did not surprise me, for surely sleep in air-raided cities – erratic and exhausted as it was, attuned to the fearsome wails of the sirens and to the explosions of bombs – was no longer disturbed by the demure ring of a front-door bell in between raids. I knocked, but still to no avail. The door mat seemed as tempting a resting place as a bed, but in a last effort I drove my fists into the door like a sledgehammer.

My mother opened the door, frowning, sleep still clinging heavily to her face; behind her, a blanket thrown over her kimono dressing-gown, my grandmother peeped anxiously at the nocturnal caller.

'Yes?' my mother inquired, slowly taking in the muffled figure in the dim landing-light, before exploding into an incredulous smile.

197

'Marianne?'

I stood and smiled back.

And now there were outstretched arms, and warm cheeks and sighs of relief, hands which helped me to undress and wash, revived toes and fingers, gave me food and made up a bed on the living-room sofa.

'We were so worried!' my grandmother said. 'Posen was taken two days ago – it was in the news – and there are terrible stories from refugees!'

'My poor child, I didn't recognise you at first . . . I, your own mother!'

'I went to Zehlendorf first,' I said, 'I thought. . . .'

'That's why I left a note. It was a terrible night, and there was nothing we could do. A canister smashed right through the roof and phosphorus spilled through the floorboards and set the rooms on fire.'

My grandmother moaned. 'My lovely house . . . !'

'Look,' my mother said, speaking to her as to a child whose favourite toy had got broken, 'we've saved the silver, clothes, pictures, most of what we'd stored in the cellar. The neighbours were marvellous. We've been lucky, mother, just think if it had been a *Luftmine*!'

Her lips brushed my cheek.

My mother's hair still smelled of smoke; her night-creamed face reminded me of the times when I had woken from a nightmare, crying, and she had slipped into my room, to smooth and stroke away the imprint of my dreams.

'How did you get this flat?' I asked, when I had been put to bed.

'When Uncle Max and I got married and moved to Silesia,' my mother began, 'he allowed his nephew to live here. Karl was an engineer with Siemens. Then he was called up . . .'

There was the softness of linen and eiderdown, of sleep waiting like a friend, and I heard my mother's voice receding, leaving scraps of information behind: ' . . . killed in the Ardennes . . . no news from Max . . . must get you a ration card . . . coke allowance . . . another blanket . . . there won't be another raid tonight. Sleep, child, sleep . . .'

A few waking moments remained – time to see the picture of the 'Blue Boy' hanging over my bed, time also to say 'thank you!' to the One in whose grace I still believed.

CHAPTER 18

A Silken Thread

I quickly adapted to life in a block of flats, and in a city in which a chameleon-like ability to adjust to changing circumstances was an indispensable aid for survival. I also modified my ideas of life and death. I no longer saw in death the final serenity of old age which knows its time had come, nor the nobility and decorum of *Vaterlandstod,*[1] as it had been glorified in school and Hitler Youth books, with no mention of its hideousness, its futility, or its anguish.

Life, on the other hand, once filled with all the coloured dreams of adolescence, now amounted to no more than a day-to-day existence which marked with gratitude every new sunrise, with humility the realisation of how little one really needed to be content, and how much, ultimately, one had always taken for granted.

My own conclusions were neatly summed up in a down-to-earth way by another tenant.

'You are alive, aren't you?' the lady countered my grandmother on the landing one day, when the latter – still a novice in the art of losing one's possessions – was bitterly bewailing the loss of her shell-inlaid coffee-table and other treasured items in the recent blaze.

Frau Karsch had just moved in after being bombed out for the third time within six months. Staircase gossip put her yellowish-brown complexion down to a serious liver disease, for how else could she have acquired a tan in February, when most windows were boarded up and no sun shone into cellars and shelters. Yet, despite her mystery illness and her light luggage, her constant optimism and sprightliness commanded every tenant's respect.

'You are alive, *liebe Frau Nachbarin,*' she repeated, 'and that

---

[1] Death for the fatherland.

is all that matters! Yes, I know it's hardest the first time. Later
... well, it gets easier, for the less one is weighed down by
personal possessions, the less one is afraid of losing them. And
you have your daughter with you, and I see your granddaughter
has safely made it back from the East. You have so much to be
grateful for.'

Rather different sentiments prevailed in the cellar one night.
Waiting for the all clear to send us back to bed, a skeleton of a
man, reputed to be an anthropologist with a doctorate,
explained why he saw in the present lifestyle of Berliners certain
parallels with prehistoric times.

'Like early Homo sapiens,' he said, 'we're engaged in basic survival. We chase around for food and for something to keep us warm.
For many hours a day and night we huddle together in cellars like
tribal communities in cave dwellings. Our clothes are shabby, and
without furs and hides we make coats from old blankets, dresses
from curtains, shoes from wood. We gather herbs, berries, nettles
– anything to supplement our diet. We hide from the enemy above
as early man from predators. In the process we've learned to
adapt. We invent, improvise, perform miracles in the cooking pot
and adjust our biological clock to sporadic sleeping hours. And
yet, in some ways, we've remained encouragingly civilised.'

'My mother still uses her silver teapot for her herbal infusions.'

The anthropologist turned to the voice as if he were
addressing a first-year student.

'I mean the way we still appreciate music and the fine arts. The
Philharmonic concert yesterday was sold out again, I hear, and
my own lecture on . . .'

It was a strange city in which I had come to live – dangerous,
dying, yet so brave.

Soviet forces were advancing fast towards the river Oder, poised
to enter the final phase of the war and the battle for Berlin.

The city's coke reserves were rumoured to be down to two
weeks' supply, and rations – averaging 1600 calories a day –
could no longer be guaranteed. The prospects looked grim.

After a heavy air-strike whole streets would be without gas,
water and electricity, and yet more people would become
homeless or return to semi-ruins and an urban Crusoe existence.
But despite the ravages of the city and the gaunt look of its
inhabitants, morale was still high. The capital's spirit seemed to

remain true to the defiant, century-old motto of the *Ur- Berliners*[2] – '*Ich lass mir nicht unterkriegen*!'[3] – an attitude which not only made men and women pick up the shreds of their lives day after day, but roll up their sleeves and clean up the mess around them as best they could. The writing might be on the wall for all to see, yet no one dared to proclaim what by now seemed to be a reality: that the war had already been lost, and that only the magnitude and the depth of the suffering still to come remained unknown.

All the same, according to informed cellar-talk, some incurable ideologists continued to cling stubbornly to their faith in the Führer and the promised final victory, while others, at the opposite end of the political spectrum, were only waiting to hang out the red flag and shout 'Welcome, comrade!'

In the daily struggle for survival, the celluloid world of the cinema provided a welcome distraction, diverting thoughts for an hour or two from the worsening military situation and from a future which defied contemplation. The few remaining city and suburban film-theatres were showing *Heimatfilme*[4] – German musicals and romantic comedies which, invariably leading to a happy ending, and being mildly erotic, brought all the glitter of show business to the screen, or transported the viewer to peaceful Alpine meadows and stag-and-Edelweiss mountains. Ilse Werner whistled through her films, Marikka Röck danced, Johannes Heesters smoothed the brows of female cinema-goers with his songs. Buxom girls with blonde plaits, bejewelled, permed ladies in silk, or demure maidens in white-collared dresses or dirndls were courted by lean, heroic men with the social polish of officers and gentlemen, or by handsome Nordic types with poetry on their lips or marriage proposals in their briefcases. In some films, darkly irresistible Casanovas made women's hearts throb with the ardour of their passion and their dishonourable intentions; in others hefty, broad-shouldered rustics in *lederhosen*, experts in lifting a stein and in handling the axe and scythe, went about conquering their womenfolk with Bavarian bravura.

'Morale wouldn't be so high if it weren't for the cinema,' so the intellectuals in the communal cellar concurred one night.

[2] Natives.
[3] 'Nothing can get me down!'
[4] Sentimental films with local colour.

'Two hours of escaping into a *heilere Welt*!'[5]
'. . . or splitting your sides laughing.'
'. . . and forgetting your empty stomach.'
'*Ja, Ja*, if they can't have bread, give them films!'
At that moment I had fallen asleep on the bench.

For many Berliners music sweetened the bitter daily pill. Special concerts were performed in churches, makeshift auditoria and even on shop floors. Orchestras, now mainly consisting of grey-haired, hunched or hollow-chested musicians, played popular tunes or performed symphonies; Tiana Lemnitz sang *Lieder* and operatic arias, Elli Ney played Beethoven, Wilhelm Kempff, Schumann. Berliners flocked to their concerts, and they did not mind sitting on hard chairs or in gloves and overcoats. Sometimes air raids provided unprogrammed intervals, and the audience scrambled into the nearest public shelter, only to return to their seats afterwards – provided the hall was still in situ.

I accompanied my grandmother to a performance of Beethoven's Fourth Symphony which, at that time, could have hardly provided a more striking contrast to the world outside. A willing passenger, I found myself taken on a great orchestral journey, and during the adagio sat with my eyes closed, suffused with magic, with music which reflected all the beauty and happiness that – it was so easy to forget – surely existed somewhere.

The radio played along in the same spirit, transmitting in between news, special bulletins and advance air-raid information popular and classical music to soothe and boost morale – music for the assembly line, for cold rooms and hungry stomachs, to help sweep up mortar and glass splinters and make the watery soup more palatable.

In a special broadcast, the Führer told Berliners that the city now resembled a huge porcupine and would be defended to its last breath, while the new secret weapon would soon bring a turn of the tide and drive the enemies from the homeland.

'*Wir werden die Wende erzwingen*!'[6] We are going to show our enemies that our courage and our spirit are made of Krupp steel. Keep up your morale, Berliners! I am with you!'

Turning the volume up, I noted with surprise that although all my

[5] A world with fewer problems and uncertainties.
[6] 'We are going to force a turn of the tide!'

senses were clamouring for peace – at whatever price – the Führer's solemn, magical voice somehow still carried a degree of conviction and managed to send inexplicable little shivers down my spine.

Yet while Berliners and the rest of the nation were waiting for the promised turn of the tide, British and American bombers were dropping their deadly loads over the city day and night. *Luftminen*, a single one of which could virtually wipe out a tenement in an instant, had recently brought a new dimension of terror and destruction to the capital. The heavy bombs whistled as they dived through the air, causing havoc within a five-hundred-metre radius, shaking the walls and cellars of neighbouring buildings and blasting loose more of the fine white and yellowish dust which hung over streets for hours afterwards.

Days and nights of anxious listening had taught Berliners that if the whistling of a mine broke off early, or if there was too long a silence after an impact nearby, their own house or block might be the next target. They also realised that they would not hear the actual explosion, but might live just long enough to feel walls and joists collapse upon them like a house of cards.

Like the rest of them, I had learned to listen and wait.

Only two hours had passed since the last all clear had released us from the communal cellar shelter when the sirens started howling again. Slowly I emerged from the kind of exhausted sleep which is deaf to the ring of an alarm clock, and to all but the loudest danger signals. I was reluctant to open my eyes, still more so to leave my bed and spend another hour in the cellar. Nor was the frost, the invisible enemy, making things any easier, seeping unimpeded through the cracks in the window boards which a single plank, nailed across the frame, was holding in position.

I was hungry, but I knew the bread bin was empty. In the morning I would queue for the weekly loaf, which bakers were not allowed to sell before it was two or three days old, so that it might yield thinner slices and, it was hoped, last longer.

I turned over and pulled the featherbed over my head.

'Marianne, get up!' my mother called from the bedroom.

I did not stir. Instead, half-awake, I brooded on the phenomenon of fear, on how the regular wailing of sirens was breeding a curious contempt for the danger from the air, and how sluggishly a sleep-starved mind mobilised the body to react to a state of alert.

'Aren't you up yet, *Kind*? They're coming our way! Your

203

grandmother and I are going ahead. Hurry!' My mother stood fully dressed in the door, blankets over one arm, a suitcase in the other.

A series of thumps and waves of angry flak-fire renewed my sense of danger. I jumped out of bed and dressed as quickly as if someone were timing me with a stop-watch. On my way out I took a quick look through the kitchen window which, facing the inner courtyard, had so far escaped the impact of direct shock waves, and now revealed a sky in which, illuminated by search beams and target-markers, arrow-shaped formations of silver specs were moving sedately towards the inner city.

I grabbed my suitcase, raced into the cellar and once again joined a community of tenants whom I otherwise only met on the staircase or at the dustbin in the back yard.

There is no small talk at this hour. Some sit with their eyes shut, others stare vacantly at the concrete floor or through each other. But soon the thuds are getting heavier, the whistling time shorter, and now heads are straining towards the ceiling and faces express an intensity as if someone were counting aloud the seconds between a flash of lightning and the first clap of thunder, in order to determine the distance and the direction of a storm. The children stop fidgeting and draw closer to their mothers. The light from a forty-watt bulb flickers, the seconds are ticking away, one, two, three . . . I force my thoughts on to the blue dress which my mother is making for me out of an old drape. Should it have buttons down the front or the back? And what about a white collar? Silence. The whistling overhead has stopped, and we know it has stopped too early, and we know what this means. The cellar floor. Cold cheeks touch cold stone. My mother's arm is around me, my grandmother's skinny, trembling hand is in mine. Someone groans, 'Oh, my God!' and I understand how life can suddenly hang upon a silken thread. '*Vater unser . . .*' I pray, and stop. The Lord's Prayer is too long for the seconds that remain, but a mute outcry, a plea to be spared isn't: 'Please, God, please!' And now the light goes out and the ground quakes. A gargantuan force lifts us off the floor, dumps us again. Heads and bodies crash against each other in the dark, my eardrums stretch painfully. With no time to scream, I am ready to be absorbed by an infinite darkness or to step into a radiant light . . .

But only mortar crumbles from the walls and dust quickly fills the cellar. Hands and feet fumble around, people gasp for air, children find their voices.

The warden's time has come. 'Stay calm, everybody! I think number 16 across the road has been hit.'

Millions of dust particles are dancing in the beam of his torch.

And now, half blind and coughing, we do not wait for the all clear, but follow the beam and the warden's reassuring voice, holding on to each other's sleeves or coat tails, stumbling up the dust-clogged cellar staircase amid choking and spitting noises, and on through a narrow passage half-blocked with chunks of mortar. Lungs detect a draught of fresh air, and greedily we press on to its source, to the hallway where, complete with its frame and hinges, the main entrance door has been blasted inside, and the view across the street is laid bare: a mound of rubble and twisted steel steaming with dust in the light of a full gauze-veiled moon – the bizarre remains of number 16.

But the nightmare has not ended yet. Upstairs, the front windows are empty sockets and the rooms look vandalised. Above my divan bed, only centimetres from the 'Blue Boy', the wall has been hit by a piece of shrapnel, and mortar is oozing from the hole as if from a burst sack of sand.

The candle in my hand throws wobbling shadows as I see a window plank resting on a cloud of soft, white down, where only an hour ago my head had lain. And I gasp at the long nails which have speared and disembowelled my pillow.

Too tired, too shaken for many words, the three of us clean up the worst of the mess and have some lukewarm mint tea from a flask. There is no electricity, the last of the water is dripping from the taps and the water in the toilet bowl has frozen up. The sun is rising like an opaque glass bubble by the time I drop back into bed, shivering, curling up like an unborn baby, my thoughts drifting across the road where it has grown quiet after the rescue team has stopped digging.

Once again I have reason to fold my hands.

I woke to broad daylight and to a feeling of having spent the night camping in the Arctic. And I knew that leaving my downy cover, and braving the temperature in the room in my night-dress, would amount to no less than an act of bravery.

Needless to say, I had no choice.

In the kitchen, my mother was stirring a yeast-and-herb mixture – a *wurst* substitute commonly referred to as '*Führer-paté*'. She wore gloves and, under her apron, what appeared to be her entire winter-wardrobe. I looked at her red-rimmed eyes, at the open newspaper on the table, at the two pages of boxed, black-edged obituaries headed: '*Sie gaben ihr Leben für Führer, Volk und Vaterland!*'[7]

Sunlight streamed through the window which, miraculously, had once again been spared.

I yawned a good morning, folded the paper and sat down at the kitchen table. 'What a night!'

My mother stroked my hair. 'We've been lucky, another fifty metres . . . !'

I shivered. 'I'd give anything for a hot drink.'

'I'm afraid the gas and electricity are still off,' my mother said, 'and the water isn't back either. I had enough left to fill the kettle for some coffee, if I can get the stove[8] going. We're running out of briquettes, and the next allocation isn't due until next week.' She sighed. 'If only the gas would come on. I'd hoped to cook a soup from *Wurstbrühe*,[9] and the potatoes *Frau* Lemke gave me in exchange for my cigarette ration.'

'I'll get some firewood later,' I said. 'There's plenty lying around in the ruins.'

'Don't you go near them!' my mother said, 'it's far too dangerous.'

I shrugged my shoulders.

'*Ach*, aren't we living dangerously as it is?'

My mother's thoughts continued on their erratic course. 'Don't wake your grandmother – I worry about her, she's growing terribly thin.' Then, inspecting the ration cards, 'Will you go to the baker first, the Tuesday batch ought to be ready for sale. And,' pointing to the newspaper, '*Herr* Mahnke brought it up this morning, he says he'll be back later to nail the window boards back in the front rooms.'

'*Der gute Herr* Mahnke!' I mocked. I could not stand the janitor who, according to staircase whispers, was the most powerful man in the block. Solidly built, and always reeking of unwashed shirts and armpits, his round face was dominated by

---

[7] 'They gave their lives for the Führer, the people and the fatherland!'

[8] A small cylindrical iron stove, usually installed in living rooms during the war for cooking and heating.

[9] Sausage stock sold by butchers during the war.

pale-blue eyes in which, whatever the time of day, the pupils seemed to be swimming in a sea of milky aqua. And then there were his hands, fleshy shovels which, I was sure, had not seen a nailbrush for months.

In addition to his normal duties as Party member, air-raid warden and NS *Blockleiter*,[10] *Herr* Mahnke – better known as 'snooper Mahnke' – was appointed to enforce blackout regulations, and to check up on room occupancy and the sound political ambience of each household on his sovereign tenement territory. He was a man to be treated with outward respect, caution and the motto '*Feind hört mit*'[11] in mind.

'We are really quite indebted to him,' my mother said, referring to the morning, shortly after my arrival, when he had appeared in his official capacity to note down the number of rooms and occupants of the flat.

'Please let us keep our spare room,' my mother had pleaded. 'My daughter has come to live with us, and my husband might come back any day. He was called up in Silesia just before I left . . . Volkssturm . . . at his age . . . he's fifty-five!'

Herr Mahnke had assumed a pompous stance. '*Ja, ja, geht in Ordnung*,[12] *Frau* Börner. Just make sure your daughter registers for work. We need every pair of hands if we want to win the war! Did you mention a cup of *Bohnenkaffee*?'

Delighted, he had accepted a cup of astronomically-priced ground coffee of black-market origin. No *muckefuck* for *Herr* Mahnke! Oh no! After all, he fixed the window boards and would not enter the spare room in his list, and yes, it was wise to keep on the right side of such a man.

I also remembered the morning when, sitting at the kitchen table and taking his time over a glass of my mother's emergency brandy – offered in expiation of a blackout offence – he had not been able to take his eyes off me. His voice had been thick.

'A fine daughter you have here, *Frau* Börner!'

My mother had put on her most resolute face. 'Drink up, *Herr* Mahnke! There's a good chap. You must have got your breath back by now. Ranke's round the corner might have some turnips today, so we'd better try and get in the queue.'

[10] Lowest rank of Party leader, in charge of forty to sixty households.
[11] 'The enemy is listening.'
[12] 'Yes, yes, all right!'

With the friendliest, firmest smile she could muster, she had complimented him out of the door.

'Don't forget the *Volksopfer*,[13] *liebe Frau* Börner!' he reminded her, before the door closed on him.

I leafed through the *Völkische Beobachter*. It contained a strange, often bizarre hodgepodge of information, which in turn shocked, scared, assuaged, bored, buoyed up hopes or elevated the reader to a loftier plane – information which in one column might be conveyed by kettledrum, in another by the harp: 'Hannibal at the Gates of Berlin' – 'Soviet bestialities' – 'Goethe in Weimar' – 'The battle in Pomerania' – How to rejuvenate your skin in spring' – 'Blood orgies in the East' – 'How to care for your hair' – 'Gruesome scenes in a convent' – 'Recipe for cookies without fat and eggs' – 'Eisenhower's hordes terrorise German population' – 'Serving suggestions for nettles as a vegetable' – 'German women declared fair game' – 'The human face in Greek sculpture' – 'US raids on German cities' – 'Research into Dutch dialects' – 'Directions on how to use a *Panzerfaust*'[14] – Concert fixtures – A boxed advertisement for toothpaste that would last longer and clean brighter – A Swiss bank's statement of account – An urgent appeal to donate clothes, shoes, eating utensils, uniforms, expendable curtains and carpets to the *Volksopfer* – A poem sent in by a German boy soldier: 'Your smile, mother, / no longer reaches me / across the night; / for the one I was, / I am no longer. / Since I went to war, mother, / I have become a man . . .'

I threw the paper back on the table. What was one to believe? Where was one to draw the line between fact and fiction, between hope and passive acceptance? Oh, well, perhaps the coffee was ready now. But how could the lukewarm liquid, which tasted of bark, take the edge off a morning like this?

I switched on the radio. A song floated through the kitchen: '*Kauf dir einen bunten Luftballon . . .*'[15]

My father rang as I returned with a loaf of bread, a bucket of water drawn from the standpipe and a rucksack filled with

13 People's donation scheme.
14 Hand-operated antitank bazooka.
15 'Buy yourself a coloured balloon.'

pieces of wood which had once been drawing-room furniture.

'Are you all right?' he enquired. 'It's been a bad night.'

I related our lucky escape. My father, at the other end, held his breath for a moment, then turned practical again.

'Have you registered yet?' he asked.

'Yes, I told them both my parents lived in Berlin. So they didn't list me as a refugee, and I got resident's status and a ration card.'

'Good! What about university? Try and matriculate if you can. But act quickly, or they'll call you up for factory work now that you've registered. You've done your labour service, you've got a medical certificate. Mind you, there are rumours that even more classes will be scrapped.'

Underground trains and trams into the city were operating shuttle services between damaged sections of lines. After three changes and a brisk walk I arrived at the university, where I produced my Aryan passport, labour book and medical and *Abitur* certificates, and filled in an enrolment form for *Germanistik* and *Anglistik*.[16]

'Some departments are still working,' a grey-haired clerk explained. 'But what with the new call-ups and the overnight losses among academic staff . . . you never know who'll turn up in the morning. Many art classes have been suspended and the fate of the rest is hanging in the balance. You'll hear from us.'

On my way home, the underground train stopped at Nollendorf-platz.

'*Alles aussteigen!*'[17] the loudspeaker blared.

A man looked at his watch. '*Amis*,' he said. 'Right on time!'

Time passed slowly on the crowded platform. Shifting from one foot to the other, I studied morale-boosting posters and prewar advertisements for Sarotti and Palm cigars. In the nervous silence which betrayed the anxiety of people caught in an air raid away from home, strangers remained strangers, detonations and flak fire no more than baffled sounds.

An hour later, at my destination, I emerged to the sight of heavy rescue vehicles racing past. I recognised the familiar smell of pulverised mortar. I started running. A hundred metres, fifty,

[16] German and English studies.
[17] 'All alight!'

a corner. Then I saw the huge crater in the middle of the road, the ripped-off, honeycombed façade of our house which despite the beating it had taken still boldly overlooked the remains of number 16 opposite.

Breathlessly, I broke through the cordon and made for the side entrance of the house, but strong arms pulled me back.

'Sorry, no one's allowed in there yet. Do you live here, young lady?'

A uniformed man was in command.

'My mother, my grandmother!' I cried.

'Nobody's hurt inside, but we told the tenants to stay in the cellar until all their back rooms have been declared safe. There are men in there now, checking for structural damage. Your people were lucky, the way the blast was dissipated!'

As I stood waiting, I began to take in dispassionately what, in its senseless damage, was not entirely without comic aspects: for with their street-face neatly cut off, the rooms of four floors were gaping at the onlooker. In the living room, where I had slept since my arrival a week ago, my bed, a bookcase and two armchairs appeared not to have moved a centimetre, whereas an upright lamp, a casual table and a settee had vanished, and part of the carpet was hanging draped over the room's jagged edge. I noticed with childish delight that the 'Blue Boy' was still hanging, if obliquely, on the far wall, just as if someone had dusted the picture over-zealously without bothering to put it straight again. My grandmother's room presented an even more grotesque sight. A chest of drawers had been held back by a radiator panel and an array of pipes, while her wardrobe, its doors standing wide open, displayed a neat row of clothes on hangers, and her bed looked no more dishevelled than after a night's sleep. On the third floor, a washing line pegged with pink underwear and sober longjohns already frozen stiff stretched from one wall to another. How could anyone live with such wallpaper, I wondered, and watched with a curious detachment a hideous candelabra swaying gently from the ceiling like a garden swing. My eyes came to rest on a piano stool perched on a heap of rubble, while the piano from which it had been separated still hugged a third-floor wall. The grandfather clock in the far corner of a first-floor living room added the final tragi-comic touch by sonorously chiming out the afternoon hour.

I pointed to the towering mass of bricks, joists and timber opposite.

'I see they've started digging again.'

'Yes, we've heard knocking sounds – someone is still alive down there!'

Later, back in the mutilated half of the flat, and reunited with my mother and grandmother, I roped myself to a bed sheet and, with the aid of a broom and my grandmother's walking stick, retrieved clothing and bedding from the two front rooms. I also managed to unhook the 'Blue Boy' from the wall, although the glass broke in the process, and by venturing into my grandmother's room as far as I dared fished out some of her treasured belongings, among them a box with photographs, a curling iron and her favourite hat – the one, she said, she used to wear before the war when strolling along the elegant Kurfürstendamm with my grandfather.

Then we locked the doors which led into space and into an early dusk.

The telephone was still working. Unaccountably, water started dripping from the taps, while a lucky find of stearin candles, which the previous tenant had left in a drawer together with last Christmas's tinsel, provided light.

A telephone call confirmed that my father was all right, and I told him about another lucky escape and what I hoped had been an official matriculation. My father reacted promptly.

'I'll try and get you a room in the students' hostel on Kaiserdamm,' he said. 'It'll give your mother and grandmother more room to move. I'll get back to you in the morning.'

That night my grandmother and I bedded down in my mother's room, which felt like being back in a dormitory. My grandmother snored, my mother shifted restlessly in her bed. My own makeshift bed on the floor was cold and hard, and when sleep finally came, it brought uneasy dreams.

The siren went off in the early hours of the morning, but for the first time, drunk with sleep as I was, I did not try to interpret the whistling of the bombs, but dozed off in the cellar despite the pandemonium outside.

'You can move into the hostel tomorrow,' my father told me over the phone next morning. 'Nice room, nice place, all female students.'

211

That same morning I received an official letter.

'From the *Parteileitung*,'[18] I exclaimed. 'They didn't waste any time!'

'How is it that they can still send letters while we are only allowed to mail postcards?' my grandmother asked, dipping a bread crust into her ersatz coffee to ease the pressure of her ill-fitting dentures.

'What do they want?' my mother inquired with a worried look.

'*Liebe Volksgenossin!*' I read out in a ponderous voice. 'As an enrolled student . . . you are required under . . .'

I slammed the letter on the table. 'Well, that's it! No university for me! I'm to report for work at Borsig as a machine operator. Monday, seven o'clock. Oh well, I suppose I knew I wouldn't make the first semester!'

'A shame, *Kind*!' my grandmother cried. 'I don't like it at all, you working in a factory at a machine, side by side with all those foreign people – and the dirt!'

'What I want to know is how they found out so quickly. And look at the date – are they using pigeon post?'

I phoned and told my father. He muttered something under his breath and told me to sit tight, not to worry and not to report for work on Monday.

'There is an excellent college of languages in Dresden. I know the director. I'll try and get you in there. Just pretend you didn't receive the letter. Enemy bombers won't touch Dresden . . . all that baroque and rococo . . . they wouldn't dare to harm it! You'll be safer there. Give me a few hours. I'll be back to you before noon.'

Then, oh gift from heaven, the gas came on, long enough to cook a hotpot with the week's meat ration and turn a meal into a feast.

My father phoned again. 'Listen! Everything's organised. You're in! I've also arranged a travel permit for you. There'll be a train around ten tomorrow morning. I've checked. Do you remember where the fat flower vendor used to stand at Anhalter Bahnhof? I'll meet you there at nine.'

During the night, enemy bombers picked Berlin's southeastern rail exit for their target, thus continuing the recent zigzag course

---

[18] Local party headquarters.

of my life, a life in which – many months later – I would see more than a mere chain of events, more than pure coincidence.

I was still in bed when my father rang.

'I've just heard there won't be any trains down to Dresden for at least twenty-four hours. The line's been hit hard, it's on the news. It means you'll leave a day later. As long as you get out of Berlin!'

It was the 15th of February.

For once Berliners enjoyed a night of uninterrupted sleep – which my grandmother, in an unusual outburst of grim humour, attributed to a magnanimous gesture by the enemy. At breakfast, our spirits were notably higher; I thought the coffee tasted less of bark, the jam less of turnips, the bread less sour, and I kept a few breadcrumbs for the sparrows on the balcony. Outside, in tune with the sudden uplift of morale, the temperature had risen a degree or two.

I was alone in the kitchen when I switched on the radio for the news – and held my breath: Dresden was no more. In a holocaust said to defy the imagination, the whole inner city was reported to have disappeared during the night under a blanket of bombs and phosphorus. Casualties were estimated at several hundred thousand . . . I turned the radio off. I felt sick.

My mother returned. 'You look pale, child,' she said. 'What was on the news?'

I told her, and she rushed over to me and took me in her arms.

'Oh, my God!' she cried. 'If you had left yesterday you would have been there . . . your first night!' She looked for a chair to sit down, searched for a handkerchief, started sobbing. 'Sometimes I think I can't take any more.'

I was aching for some far-away picture-postcard retreat, for the scent of a hot summer garden, for the peace of a sleepy, sun-soaked lake . . .

My father phoned. His voice was small and solemn.

'I expect you've heard about Dresden. What a tragedy! And to think that I . . . Let me speak to your mother.'

My mother listened intently, argued and finally ended the conversation on a note of agreement, before handing the receiver back to me.

'Listen,' my father said, 'the general situation has changed drastically during the last twenty-four hours. Russian troops have crossed the river Oder, rumours put them even as close as

213

Straussberg. The *Oberkommando*, however, has made it clear that the Bunker is getting ready to mastermind the defence of Berlin. I told your mother I can wangle travel permits out of Berlin for the three of you. It'll be your last chance. Go to Tangermünde and stay with your cousin's relatives until everything is over. Your mother doesn't want to leave, I'm afraid. It's that new husband of hers, she thinks he might come back any day now. We can't force her, but I want you to go, for if and when the Russians get here – and I have no doubt that they will – all hell will be let loose. You are old enough to realise what will happen ... to the women, I mean. I'll get somebody to bring over the permits.'

'And you, *Vati*?' I asked.

'I've just received my call-up to the air force.'

My outcry was matched by my father's laugh.

'Yes, fancy, at my age, and with my poor eyesight! And I haven't held a rifle in my hand since the last war!'

The thought of my elegant father dressed in a second- or third-hand uniform, eating *Kohlsuppe* out of a mess tin and cleaning his gold-rimmed spectacles with a monogrammed handkerchief every time he got ready to pull the trigger or to shoot a *Panzerfaust* had something of the tragicomic about it.

'When are you leaving?' I asked.

'I have only twenty-four hours to wrap up business and to get you out of Berlin. And now, *mein liebes Kind*, look after yourself and your grandmother. I wish I could have spared you the war, but it was not in my power. God be with you!'

'And with you, *Vati*!'

The line clicked. I went into the bathroom and cried.

In response to the urgency of the situation, the parting from my mother was brief, and in her tight lips and brave smile which tried to hold back tears I realised that for all I knew I might be seeing her for the last time. And as her arms folded around me, I suddenly saw the gate of the Home opening wide, and I thrust at my mother in a single moment all the love that had been shut away with me on that soul-benumbing day in September many years before – the love which I had been withholding from her ever since.

CHAPTER 19

Last Train out of Berlin

A loudspeaker blares out information. An empty train steams
into the station where, with rising hostility, a massive crowd
starts moving towards the edge of the platform. Even before the
train has come to a halt and the doors have been fully opened,
humanity is billowing forward like some tough resinous substance released under pressure. In the pushing and shoving, in
the elbowing and wrestling towards one of the coveted doors,
lies the raw violence of mass hysteria, fired by hatred for those
who are taller and fitter, who will win a seat or standing room,
and by envy of the lucky ones who will be sluiced through the
doors with little effort of their own. Strangers, who only
minutes earlier had exchanged jokes and pleasantries with each
other, suddenly turn into arch-enemies. People are screaming,
cursing, are separated from their family and from suitcases.

'Willy, where are you?'

'Keep your bloody elbow out of my face, woman!'

One woman looks as if she has fainted, but with no room to
fall, she is being carried forward like flotsam on the crest of the
human wave.

Holding our suitcases against the back of a man in front, I
managed to create a pouch in which to shelter my grandmother,
like a kangaroo its young. But the moment the man reaches the
coach door, and propels himself up the steps, we are catapulted
forward. Suitcases crash against metal, my grandmother, finding
herself on the steps on all fours, tries in vain to straighten up and
climb them in a manner befitting a lady of her age and station.
Behind her, the crowd watches her limp efforts and their
frustration mounts.

'Do you need a lift, *Mütterchen*?'

A man's voice, with its wry Berlin humour, saves the situation, temporarily holds back the tide. Someone laughs. Hands the size of crane ladles shoot forward, get hold of the old lady's buttocks and deposit her into the carriage.

All seats have been taken. People are sitting ten or more to a compartment designed for eight, with more standing wedged in between the resentful knees of strangers. The chances of someone giving up his seat for my grandmother are nil. But a firm-chinned SS man materialises, and in no time room is made for the old lady. As she squeezes her featherweight in between two women, blissfully immune to the hostile glances of her neighbours, I tense my muscles in defence of my standing patch.

Within minutes the air in the tightly-packed compartment grows stuffy. Someone opens the window just as the train starts moving – not reckoning with the frenzy of those left behind on the platform, who in their desperate bid to scramble through the window push and elbow each other for a hold. As the train gathers speed, heads, hands and bodies drop away.

Time passed slowly. The train crawled along like rolling stock, and more than once it stopped on open track. In the compartment, a woman with a peacetime girth unpacked *Blutwurst* sandwiches, oblivious of her two hollow-cheeked neighbours who stared hard and swallowed saliva. Other passengers, suddenly discovering an edge to their own appetites, attacked more modest victuals. My grandmother produced two apples, but while I greedily dug my teeth into mine, she spread a table-napkin over her lap and carefully peeled and cut hers into bite-sized pieces with a dainty fruit-knife.

Hours later, passengers not sitting in the immediate vicinity of the WC were trapped. With the corridor completely choked up, anyone desperate to relieve himself was unable to do so, and efforts to form a human conveyor belt, and heave a young woman to the end of the corridor failed. Imprisoned in our compartment, many of us started shifting uneasily in our seats or from one leg to the other, and it was not long before the air grew foetid and a pool of urine formed under the seat of a woman who tried to escape embarrassment by pretending to be asleep. Not so an elderly man. Fortunate enough to be sitting by the window, he fetched an empty bottle from his haversack and, using his coat as a screen, relieved himself without blinking an eyelid, then emptied it out of the window. Such an unseemly action, however, did not raise a single eyebrow in the compartment, for shared human misery was understood and tolerated.

I wished I had not had that second cup of coffee for breakfast, but just as I was wondering how much longer I would be able to last out, the train screeched to a halt and we were ordered to alight instantly without our luggage and seek shelter from an imminent air attack.

Miraculously, there were no casualties in the ensuing panic. I lifted my grandmother from the train and steered her towards a nearby group of trees. Other passengers threw themselves into ditches or moulded their bodies into a furrow of the adjoining field.

It was all over in a few seconds – two whining, deafening dives out of the low-hanging clouds, two enemy fighter-planes strafing the train and rising back into the sky with the speed of swallows.

'Tommies!' a man said, 'and not one of our *Messerschmitts* in sight!'

And now, without waiting for the air to grow calm again, people began to relieve themselves, hundreds of them, on the spot, standing up or squatting, dispensing with embarrassment and the rituals of propriety.

On our way back to the train we passed a dead woman, and we glanced at the bullet holes in the flanks of coaches, at their spider-webbed windows, reacting unemotionally and as if long drained of indignation. We had seen much worse: all that mattered was that we had escaped again.

In orderly fashion, and without undue haste, we reboarded the train and resumed our former seats or standing positions as if by some unwritten law. But now, as soon as the train started moving, a sudden spirit of camaraderie developed. People offered their seats to those who had been standing for hours, and a flask of hot coffee made the round to the accompaniment of jokes and smiles.

'What I wouldn't give for *Bratkartoffeln mit Speck* and a *Schultheiss*!'[1] a man sighed.

Someone in the corridor played a tune on the mouth organ: '*Es geht alles vorüber . . .*'[2]

---

[1] Bacon-fried potatoes with a Berlin-brewed beer.
[2] 'Everything passes . . .'

Half an hour later the train stopped again – this time coming, unscheduled, to the end of the line. Where once a viaduct had spanned a valley, there was now a gigantic gap bounded by the lacerated, crumbling brickwork of side piers, tangled steel bracings and rail ends projecting into the air or twisted like pipe-cleaners.

'Tommies!' repeated the expert. 'Precision bombing – they're damned good at it! I still remember the day they bombed the Möhnedamm . . .'

'All alight!' Rail personnel pointed to the other side of the valley. 'You'll have to make your own way across. A shuttle train will pick you up from there . . . later . . . sometime.'

Weighed down by the two suitcases, and keeping my grandmother in tow, I headed towards the floor of the valley, where a narrow, sluggish stream, frozen in places, was partly obscured by trees. The going was rough. Neither path nor stepping stones eased the descent on this sun-exposed side, and thawed patches of bracken and grass proved slippery for many of the older folk.

The air had grown noticeably milder, and although some dark clouds warned of wintry showers, and the flat, purple-tipped catkins were still tightly closed, I thought the valley smelled of the first stirrings of spring.

'You're doing very well!' I said to my grandmother, seeing how bravely her stiff joints were coping. And there was a moment of comedy, when her skidding threatened to accelerate into an avalanche, which was only just checked in time by a gorse bush. Burdened as I was with two suitcases, reaching the bottom of the valley was no picnic for me either, and I was frequently tempted to use my luggage as a sledge.

'Let's rest for a bit,' I said as soon as we were safely across the stream and some boggy ground.

A keen wind, blowing a flurry of snow across the valley, reminded me that it was still early in the year, and that the late February sunshine held only delusions of spring.

The last of the daylight saw us safely into Tangermünde.

CHAPTER 20

War Comes to Tangermünde

The small mediaeval town stood high on a plateau on the western banks of the river Elbe, overlooked by the tall Stephans-kirche. On its eastern approaches, a steep riverside rampart and several fortified towers greeted the traveller with an air of haughtiness and defiance, and it did not require much imagination to see how, throughout the centuries, this impressive bastion must have deterred prospective aggressors from the East, long before they came to the swirling waters of its broad river-moat.

At the turn of the century industry had come to the town, bringing harbour installations and a railway line. Gradually the predominantly rural population had formed a sizeable proletariat with strong left-wing sentiments, and even the Third Reich's inquisitorial methods had not been able to eradicate this 'red blot' on the country's political map. All the same, Tangermünde still had a sleepy, picturesque charm. In the Old Town, one might easily imagine oneself to be back in the Middle Ages, walking through narrow, cobbled lanes, past slanting, timber-framed houses graced with rosettes, coats of arms or Latin inscriptions, and doors whose lavish engravings still bore witness to former patrician wealth.

Nowhere, however, was history more evident than in the splendid fifteenth-century *Rathaus* in which much of the town's history had been sealed and chronicled, and in the vaulted council-chambers of which a chapter of my life was to be written.

Weasel-faced *Tante* Bertha lived in the New Town in a tree-lined street where a row of small brick villas with front and back gardens faced low, rough-cast, terraced houses. From the start her tight lips and narrowed eyes made it clear that the two refugees from Berlin had been forced upon her against her will, and when she showed us to our attic room, she needed no words to tell us that, family or not, we had better make our presence in the house as little felt as possible.

A doctor's widow of uncertain age, *Tante* Bertha wore her hair knotted into a tight bun, and while her prim physiognomy matched her buttoned-up manners, her clothes reflected the dust-free sobriety of her rooms. Like many Tangermünders blessed with farming relatives or friends, she was still finding the war pretty tolerable in terms of butter, bacon, and eggs, yet despite this distinct advantage it was as difficult to make her part with a single egg or a dot of butter as with a smile.

On the other hand, she was an accomplished pianist, and for her mellifluous interpretations of Schumann and her spirited renditions of Chopin she seemed to draw upon emotions which dried up the moment the keyboard fell silent. She also read the Bible, did petit point and played the organ on Sundays.

Her daughter Hilda, my junior by two years, and in appearance as mousy as her mother, openly resented the invasion of the household by two 'strangers' and successfully copied her mother in keeping us at arms' length.

As soon as we had registered at the town hall, *Tante* Bertha had no alternative but to concede the use of the kitchen range for certain hours a day, and to allow her distant relatives to warm themselves in the kitchen or at the living-room stove. She was, however, under no obligation to share with us the richer fare in her cooking pots. Not surprisingly, her uncharitable attitude – whereby an occasional apple or slice of cake seemed a magnanimous gift, which my grandmother and I accepted with the humility of those forced to live on 1400 calories a day – was not conducive to friendly relations.

Two days after my visit to the town hall, an official letter from local Party headquarters ordered me to report for work at the nearby Heinkel factory the following morning: 'An an enrolled student . . . you are required under . . .'

It was still dark when I rose at 5 a.m. Rain was drumming on the roof, and in the draught from the window the candle threw restless shadows against the whitewashed walls.

My grandmother called from the depth of her featherbed, 'Make sure you're wearing warm underpants. There are bound to be a lot of cold draughts in a factory!'

220

It was still dark when I stepped out into the unlit street where the rain was changing into sleet. My footsteps echoed on the wet pavement, and I frequently turned and looked over my shoulder. Then there came other steps, heavier, hurried ones, and as I approached the factory forecourt, a couple of elderly workmen overtook me, touched their caps, wished me 'good morning' and clocked in at 5.59 a.m. sharp.

'The floor manager wants to see you first thing, *Fräulein*,' the gatekeeper informed me. Two armed SS guards, lounging against his cubicle, grinned and said, '*Heil* Hitler!'

Inside the huge shop-floor, the noise of machinery starting up bombarded my ears. I passed the lean figures of men and women in overalls, looked into faces blunted from the absence of smiles. I picked up shreds of Dutch and French conversation and, here and there, words in an unfamiliar language. German foremen strolled about, checked machines and their attendants, or unscrewed coffee flasks.

A thin, balding man came up to me and shook my hand.

'*G'Morgen! Fräulein* Gärtner? My name is Borgmann, floor supervisor. Now, let me put you in the picture. We need a machine operator down here, but my colleagues in the design office are crying out for an assistant. Their young man was called up yesterday. Can you draw?'

'I always got good marks at school,' I replied, 'and I once worked at a drawing board. I like sketching buildings and objects, and I'm good at flowers . . .'

Herr Borgmann smiled. 'No need for floral drawings here, my girl!' He told me to wait and disappeared in the jungle of machines.

I studied the one nearest to me. Craning my neck, I took in its full height, then backed away from the gurgling steel bowels which protruded from its shiny belly, and from an array of levers and push buttons which required the full attention of the operator. Behind the brute's armour-plated chest I could hear its lungs heaving rhythmically, like the bellows of an organ, and every time it exhaled it whistled before puffing tiny jets of steam through its clenched teeth. Bulging from their sockets, its eyes, one red and one green, signalled messages, and every time the red one flashed, the *monstrum horrendum* opened its fangs and spat out oddly shaped steel objects.

It was the first production machine I had ever seen.

Herr Borgmann was back with a chair, a pencil and a drawing pad. 'Here,' he said, 'try and draw our friend to a 1:20 scale. Do you think you can do it?'

With my eye for dimensions and detail, I set about transposing the monster onto paper as true to scale as possible. Twenty minutes later my examiner was back. He studied my effort and patted me on the back.

'Well done, girl! I see your place is at the drawing board. Report to *Herr* Meyer, our senior design engineer, the lucky bastard! Up the stairs, first right. Good girl! See you around.'

Herr Meyer proved to be less cryptic, and his gentle manners and tone of voice suggested that by temperament and inclination he might be better suited to playing the violin in a chamber orchestra, or teaching the classics to an attentive *Oberprima*. He outlined my duties.

'You will be doing simple work-drawings and tracings, developing a part on the drawing board through its machining stages. To be precise: if the production of a particular part involves work on five different machines you will need five separate drawings, one for each operator. Do you understand?'

I nodded emphatically.

'We work ten hours a day,' Dr Meyer continued. 'Sometimes more, with thirty minutes for lunch. There are two canteens, one for foreign labour, the other for German staff. Food is lousy, not enough to keep body and soul together. Turnips and cabbage mostly, and sometimes they throw in a pig's knuckle. And it's worse for them.' He pointed in the direction of the shop floor. 'Many have been with us for years . . . Dutch, Belgians, French, we even have some Poles and Czechs. As you can imagine, they're getting pretty restless . . .'

Two men in white dust-coats entered the room, but Dr Meyer did not lower his voice.

'. . . and God help us if they spring loose one day! But here, meet your two other colleagues.'

I shook hands, and within the hour I knew their shoe sizes and the reason for their *Verwendungsuntauglichkeit*,[1] which marked them unfit even for the quiet pace of an orderly room, and which included one amputated trench foot, awarded with the Iron Cross First Class, and a history of tuberculosis, not to mention

[1] Unfitness for further military service.

such afflictions as a case of shell-ruptured eardrums and a hernia.

I soon settled into my new job, aiming for neatness and accuracy in my drawings, and adding punctuality, good will and a ready smile. Before a week had passed I found myself not only accepted as a fully-fledged member of the design team, but labelled 'politically *bona fide*'. As a result, talk flourished freely between the drawing boards, of a kind which would stop dead at the door or in the presence of others. Keeping their ears close to the radio, open to canteen intelligence and an undisclosed executive source, the three men seemed indeed well informed about the state of the nation. Through them I learned that on 14 April a heavy air raid had destroyed nearly the entire *Altstadt*[2] of Potsdam, and that less than a week later, on the Führer's birthday – while Russian troops were standing at the gates of Berlin and half the country was in enemy hands – all ten-year-olds in its unoccupied territory had been mustered in a defiant *Weltuntergangsstimmung*,[3] to pledge allegiance to their leader, Adolf Hitler.

As April wore on, the mood and behaviour of the foreign workforce changed dramatically. An operator's recalcitrant mien, jeering remarks delivered boldly but too cunningly for retribution, or delaying tactics skilfully practised in a climate of diminishing fear, reflected the dwindling distance between American troops and Tangermünde with the precision of a sensitive instrument. The air on the shop floor reeked of malicious joy: the women walked with rolling hips and heads held high, the men stood idly around in groups, and in rebellious postures, only returning to their machines or benches at gun-point. Belatedly management increased canteen portions.

Arriving at the plant one morning late in April, I found the gates closed. No SS guard was in sight. A blond Dutchman, with whom I had sometimes exchanged a few words on my way to the canteen, detached himself from a group of loitering fellow-workmen and approached me from within the gate, a rifle in his hand.

'Go home, *Mädchen! Alles zu Ende!* Guards *kaputt! Deutschland kaputt!*'

His smile did not invite me to linger.

[2] Old Town.
[3] An 'end-of-the-world' mood.

In the course of the morning even the last optimists in town had to admit that the country was in its death throes.

American troops were reported to have formed a bridgehead up-river near the city of Magdeburg, while disintegrating German army units, fleeing from a terminal Russian thrust under a blanket of heavy artillery fire, were heading towards Tangermünde in an effort to put the river between themselves and the horror of a Siberian prison camp. Whether for reasons of strategy or prestige, the race was on between American tanks and Russian infantry for the coveted Tangermünde bridge, making the town a target and the river a buffer zone.

And Tangermünders – from children to octogenarians – held their breath.

For days the local food supply had broken down. Ration cards were no longer honoured, bakers, grocers and butchers were pleading empty shelves and store rooms. As a result, many stomachs were rumbling, and the prospect of empty cooking-pots merely aggravated the sense of panic.

Not surprisingly, nobody could recall, later on, how the stampede towards Meyer's sugar refinery and chocolate factory had started, and nobody cared to remember their own part in the disintegration of law and order. Perhaps it was the fact that police and Party officials had discarded their uniforms; perhaps a rumour that – with the end in sight – stocks were for the taking, which had spread like a bushfire among frustrated shoppers, among housewives opening their windows for a breath of spring before the looming thunderstorm, and among men who had found office doors and factory gates closed that morning.

Within minutes a crowd forms, swelling, surging and charging towards the factory. An army of men and women turns into an angry mob, and their powerful charge forces open gates and warehouse doors. Finding no opposition, refugees reinforced by formerly law-abiding, stoical locals pounce on the priceless stores. Need and greed overlap, the uncertainty of the future invites mass hysteria. Discipline, for years dutifully practised in shop queues, is forgotten at the sight of goods which have either been strictly rationed or completely absent from the average consumer's table since the beginning of the war. Cases are being smashed, cartons ripped, sacks slashed open. Hundreds of hands shovel sugar and cocoa into bags or snatch tins of sweetened condensed milk and chocolate from shelves, defending their loot as viciously as if it were gold nuggets. With bags and baskets full, they cram more into their pockets. Sugar and cocoa run from torn sacks, paper bags burst open and spill their contents on the floor. The air thickens with cocoa dust, tins roll in between legs, wood splinters, people are panting. In the scuffle straps and fabric tear, handles are swept out of hands and treasured acquisitions scattered and trampled underfoot.

I squeeze my way through the crowd, stuffing my coat pockets with tins of milk and bars of chocolate, wishing I had been carrying a shopping bag when I was swept away by the human tidal wave.

Back at the house I store my modest haul in the attic room away from *Tante* Bertha's censorious eyes, and then I spoon up the sweet, sticky cream like honey, and break off small pieces of chocolate, keeping each long enough in my mouth to melt and so prolong the exquisite experience. I watch my grandmother adding the rich milk to her ersatz coffee, and her face light up as she takes her first sip.

We smile at each other. I lick my fingers. Spring sunshine is flooding the room.

Tante Bertha called from downstairs.

'Marianne, there is someone for you at the gate!'

Gisela, a typist at the *Bürgermeister*'s office and my friend, stood beside a heavily loaded bicycle. She looked pale and frightened.

I liked Gisela. Being roughly of my own age, and likened by many to Lilian Harvey, the film actress, she had befriended me on my first visit to the town hall, and we had since spent many Sundays chatting, playing draughts, walking beside the river or building castles in the air in the manner of nineteen-year-olds to whom the war had denied most of the fringe benefits of adolescence and young adulthood.

With her slim good looks, which in any garrison town would have drawn keen wolf whistles, Gisela had always struck me as being utterly wasted behind a typewriter and among files and wire trays.

'What on earth are you doing here?' I asked. 'Your bike looks like a pack horse!'

225

Gisela kept her voice low. 'I've heard at the office that a company of Negro soldiers is moving towards the town and could be here by nightfall. I have no idea where the rumour is coming from, but it's all over town, and the men say the women shouldn't take any chances, because the first thing the blacks will do is to rape them . . . sort of blacken pure Aryan blood, if you know what I mean! I'm going to spend the night in a field. It's not too cold. Will you join me?'

'Give me a minute!' I said.

'Bring a spade along!'

'What on earth for?'

'Well, we'll have to dig ourselves in, won't we? . . . to remain undetected.'

I ran off to tell my grandmother of our plan, and asked Hilda to lend me her bicycle. 'Don't you come back with a flat tyre!' she whined.

I packed a tin of milk, a few bars of chocolate and as much bedding as I thought fit for a night in the open. *Tante* Bertha said, '*Blödsinn!*'[4] when I gave her my own version of how the Negro hordes were expected to run wild, but rather than take any chances she asked her daughter to build herself a hiding place in the cellar behind a stack of wood. Gisela and I waved goodbye to my grandmother at the attic window and rode off as if we were on a cycling tour.

Apart from a few nervous ripples, the town was as calm as a lake minutes before a storm breaks. We cycled along at a leisurely pace and, once out of town, turned into a country lane which meandered through fields clothed with the yellowish-green tints of spring. The sun was about to set, the wind – which had nothing of its seasonal brusqueness – held the sweet, tangy scents of sprouting meadows and breathing soil. To all appearances, it was a peaceful, pastoral scene, yet it was marred by the sound of distant thunder which echoed from every point of the horizon like a gigantic peripheral storm, the eye of which was steadily narrowing.

Having stored our bikes in a disused barn, we dug two shallow trenches the size of coffins well away from the lane and lined them with remnants of hay. It was dusk when, wrapping ourselves in our eiderdowns, and keeping chocolate and tinned

[4] 'Rubbish!'

milk well within arm's reach, we called it a day and went 'to bed'.

'It feels like lying in an open grave,' Gisela said.

Her comparison did not appeal to me, for I thought it marvellously exciting to bed down under the open sky, waiting for the stars to come out and, until sleep came, to be wanting for nothing.

'I don't mind,' I replied. 'I just love watching the sky at night. It always reminds me of the planetarium my father used to take me to as a child.'

'Aren't you afraid?' Gisela asked.

'What, of the dark?'

'No, I mean of the *Amis*, of Negroes, of being raped?'

'Of course! But what's the point of letting your imagination run riot? Besides, if you've never sat in a dentist's chair before, how can you shudder at the drill touching a nerve. Right now all I want is for the war to end, to see my parents again and to stop feeling constantly hungry.'

'And I want my Franzl back, my fiancé. We're going to get married as soon as he comes home, and have lots of children. I can't wait for the day when I can turn my back on all those town hall files!'

The straw rustled as I turned towards her trench.

'Did you and your Franzl ever . . . I mean . . . did you and he . . . ?'

'Did we make love together?' Gisela volunteered. 'Yes, a few times, just before he left to join the army. My mother would have killed me had she known.'

'What was it . . . I mean, what is it like?'

'What's it like?' Gisela echoed, and in reply heaved a sigh which seemed to stretch back to town, and which left everything to my imagination.

'You know,' she went on, 'the mere thought of soldiers touching me, whether black or white ones, makes me want to puke. Fancy, legs in dirty boots forcing your thighs open, skin smelling of sweat and grease, unwashed, impatient hands fumbling around . . . I think I'd want to die if I got raped.'

I uttered appropriate sounds of revulsion, and we wished each other good night. Disturbed, and feeling the weight of Gisela's projected images upon me, I fixed my thoughts on loftier things, by communing with the sky in which I could make out the first stars and a rising moon.

227

'*Lieber Gott*,' I prayed, 'please don't let me get raped!'

I woke around midnight to an orange-tinted sky in which white flashes and red trailing stars mimicked a silent firework display.

I roused Gisela.

'They're bombing Magdeburg.'

Gisela sounded awed. 'Isn't it weird, what with no sound coming over?'

'It's too far for that. It also depends on the direction of the wind and the type of bombs,' I explained. Now I was the expert.

'I've never seen anything like this! What's the red glow?'

'Incendiaries. They usually follow them up with bombs which explode and spread the fire. I've seen it all before ... many nights.'

We spoke no more, each of us remaining alone with her thoughts and the noiseless spectacle which had lifted the night for miles around, and which – by the time we finally went back to sleep – left only a red, dome-shaped glow on the horizon to tell of the agony of a city.

Rooks, picking noisily at the sweet spillage on milk tins and chocolate paper, woke me shortly after dawn. Amused, I left the birds to their morning raid, but when one of them climbed onto Gisela's quilt and, having picked a hole, began to pluck down from it, I shooed the intruders away.

Gisela's head emerged from her trench.

'We had visitors,' I said, pointing to the birds which had moved off to a respectable distance.

Gisela yawned.

I glanced around. 'I can't see any troop movements on the main road ... no life at all. I feel we ought to go back. If the *Amis* are coming, and if there's going to be fighting, we don't want to be caught in the middle of an open field.'

We picked up our bikes and cycled back to town, as undetected and unmolested as we had come.

'You're a sport!' Gisela said when we parted.

I shook my friend's hand. 'So are you! Take care! I'll see you when everything is over. We must take our bikes out again!'

There came the sound of two heavy explosions from the direction of the river.

'All's been quiet,' said my grandmother, who looked as if she had not closed an eye during the night, 'but we'd better start moving into the cellar all the same. *Tante* Bertha has just buried her silver in the back garden.'

I met my aunt on the staircase. She was carrying a pair of bed sheets.

'Any sign of the enemy?' she asked.

'We didn't see a soul.'

'Hm, in that case I'd better wait before hanging my white flags out of the windows. One can't be sure – that dumb *Ortsgruppenleiter* or some fanatic might string people up on the nearest lamp post, if they are too eager to surrender.' It was the longest speech my aunt had made since our arrival.

The street remained empty all morning. By midday, a dark growling sound, which could easily have been mistaken for a heavy barge chugging upstream towards the harbour, was rolling towards the town from the northwest. The time had come to prepare for the impact with an enemy from whom – rumours aside – no one quite knew what to expect.

'I just hope our troops won't want to defend us!'

Hilda, not yet in hiding, edged forward on her chair.

'I've heard *Herr* Seeler talking to someone across the road. He said they've blown up the bridge, and that *Werwölfe*[5] have taken up positions on the Neustädter tower and in various houses, and they have orders to shoot *Panzerfäuste* at enemy tanks!'

'God help us!' a scornful *Tante* Bertha exclaimed. 'Those goddam Hitler Youths will be the death of us yet! Some, I hear, are hardly out of their nappies, and I'm sure they'll all wet their trousers before shooting a *Panzerfaust*.'

'I don't think so, mother,' Hilda dared to argue. '*Herr* Seeler from next door said they are very keen and patriotic, and will go on fighting to the very end.'

It was not long before we identified a sinister sound with the movement of tanks over cobblestones, a signal for *Tante* Bertha to race upstairs and hang out her sheets from the front windows. By the time she returned the walls of the cellar were shaking.

'What a racket!' she shouted. 'It's enough to deafen anyone!'

[5] Underground ambush movement consisting mainly of Hitler Youths and young SS men.

I ventured to the cracked window – a mere peephole – which allowed a dwarf's eye view of the street. The first tanks were moving up, cautiously, threateningly, their star-marked broadsides looming only metres away from the window, a grey mass of steel which showed no concern for blossoming lime-trees or fences. And with them there came greenish uniforms, big buttocks and broad shoulders, men who jumped from tanks and moved like leopards, who crouched in doorways, covered comrades or aimed bursts of automatic fire towards sites of resistance. Watching for snipers, white and black faces stared tensely from under green-netted helmets, jaws constantly masticating. With a crushing sound, a tank mounted the pavement and mowed down part of *Tante* Bertha's garden fence, to take up a firing position by the gate, its long gun trained on some target down the road. And now shells whizzed, machine-guns clattered, mortar fell from the ceiling, empty cartridges and steel fragments clicked on to the paved forecourt. My eardrums ached.

Plugging my ears with my fingers, I stood mesmerised, yet for some reason totally unafraid, a mere observer recording, from a cellar-window perspective, the last phase of a war which had come right into our front garden.

Tante Bertha tried to raise her voice above the pandemonium. '*Diese verdammten Werwölfe!*'[6] It was the first time I had heard her swearing.

'There you are, mother!' Hilda shouted back, '*Herr* Seeler was right.'

'Come back from the window. I beg you!' my grandmother's lips and sign language intimated.

Tante Bertha, about whom, ironically, everything was brown this morning – her dress, her cardigan, the blotches on her face, not to speak of the straggly hair which had escaped from her bun – handed her daughter a white, homemade flag and told her to hide in the corner behind the pile of wood.

'That it should come to this!' she wailed, once the decibel level outside allowed for conversation again. And, straightening her shoulders, 'Well, I for one never voted for Adolf Hitler!'

By the afternoon the fighting had grown sporadic. A breathless

[6] 'Those damned werewolves!'

Herr Seeler stormed into the cellar.

'Have you heard? Our troops have stopped shooting? The bridge is down, they say, and our infantry cut off on the other side. Thousands of men are trying to swim or cross the river on rafts, so as not to fall into Russian hands. The town is teeming with American tanks and soldiers. By the way, quite a few houses have been shelled, and some are on fire. And now those bloody werewolves are prolonging the agony! They're sniping from towers, windows and cellars. *Was für eine Scheisse!* Excuse the expression, *liebe Frau Nachbarin.*'

'I wish someone would tell them that we have already lost the war,' *Tante* Bertha said. 'What are they hoping for? A posthumous award for bravery? I thought when we hung out our sheets we made it abundantly clear that we didn't want to be defended.'

'Quite so,' *Herr* Seeler concurred. 'By the way, there's a rumour that Niemann's baked some bread last night.'

'Yesterday they said they had no flour left!' *Tante* Bertha argued.

'Ah, but you didn't really believe them, did you? Mind you, how we'll get to it is another matter. Anyway, it's all over now.'

He lifted his fist and turned to go.

'Yes, *Herr* Seeler, it's all over now,' *Tante* Bertha said, ignoring the man's unequivocal salute.

My grandmother, however, added her own question.

'Is it?'

'I'll go and see whether Niemann's have got any bread,' I said. 'I'm absolutely starving!'

Tante Bertha sounded angry. 'Don't be a fool, Marianne! You mustn't go outside yet. The ideas you have!'

It's all right for you! I thought. You've had your belly full every day. And I saw you munching something only a short while ago.

My grandmother frowned.

'Please don't go, *Kind*, it's still too dangerous.'

But something had fused in my mind. I saw bread, smelled bread, felt my teeth tearing into a hefty chunk. Grabbing Hilda's flag, I ran upstairs, heedless of the restraining voices behind me.

The street appears to be quiet. The tank in the front garden has long moved on, leaving behind squashed wire fencing and a flattened, tread-marked bed of tulips. Holding the flag high over

231

my head, I chase across the road into the nearest doorway and assess my chances of reaching the corner.

The cobbled, formerly serene street, in which the only aggressive thing had been the strong perfume of freshly-burst lime blossoms, reveals its scars and litter: a burning house, a blazing tank, two sprawling bodies; a helmet lying upside down, a pavement mottled with debris, metal and dismembered branches – a street still groaning, still echoing shots, still dangerous. But as hunger rudely superimposes images of fresh bread, I tense myself and, running and squatting, make my way down the road in the same way as I had just seen the first batch of American soldiers trying to avoid a possible ambush. I turn the corner, and am thrown back by heat and smoke. The baker's house is on fire, and with it his shop and the rumoured supply of bread. I am about to retrace my steps, when all hell is let loose. A sharp bark, a whining sound, an exchange of fire, an explosion. The blast slaps my face. Somewhere, someone is howling. Shrapnel and empty cartridges chip into masonry above my elbow. I crouch far into the corner of a doorway, still not registering any fear, still as observant as if I had stepped out of my mortal shell. But now a bulky shadow darts into my dubious refuge, and my eyes clamp down on an American uniform, on a face covered with sweat and dirt and caked blood. Steel-canopied eyes are staring at me, and a finger is hooked over a trigger.

My white flag dances in front of the barrel.

'Scram!' the soldier hisses, and now more friendly, 'Go inside, girl!' His gun changes direction, points to the spot from where, only seconds ago, shots have been fired. As more greenish men materialise and form a rearguard, my soldier runs and crouches, takes aim and cleans out a sniper's nest.

I start back, inching my way along house fronts, flitting from the cover of one door to another. In the process I trip over the body of a young soldier, over incredibly blue eyes riveted to the sky. For one brutal moment I think of a mother's heartbreak, then a machine-gun goes tuck-tuck-tuck, and is answered in turn. Bullets are zipping around, shouts, incomprehensible in their hoarseness and foreignness, but carrying an unmistakable message, throw me to the ground. A sudden silence. Seconds dropping like hailstones into the street. And I do not wait for the lull to be shattered again, but make a daring sprint home, my

232

flag raised high over my head as if it were a cross. It's the hundred metres all over again, only this time my prize is neither a cup nor a seat on the last refugee truck, but my life.

'That was very foolish of you, Marianne!' *Tante* Bertha scolded, when I got back to the cellar and had given the flag back to Hilda. 'You could have got yourself killed! They don't give out medals for foolhardiness, you know.'

'Thank God, you're back!' my grandmother said quietly. 'The things you're getting up to. I was worried sick!'

'Sorry!' I said. 'By the way, there isn't any bread, Niemann's house is burning like a torch.'

And now qualms caught up with me, and I realised that while to an onlooker my suicidal excursion might have smacked of daredevilry, a primordial need for food had inhibited any rational thinking by belittling, if not totally ignoring, the risks involved.

Outside, armoured cars stacked with battle-ready infantry were rolling past, followed by jeeps in which broad-chested men sat with the ease of authority or with arms folded in conqueror style. Heavy trucks and transporters brought up the rear. Vehicles roared and jolted, cursing their cobbled path. A street was trembling, a whole town was trembling. What now?

An hour had passed when the doorbell rang, and kept on ringing as if it were jammed. At the same time, fists hammered against the door, wood shook under the kick of a boot.

'*Ja, ja,*' *Tante* Bertha cried, already halfway up the stairs, '*einen Augenblick, ich kann doch nicht fliegen!*'[7]

Heavy steps pounded through the house. Too agitated to speak, *Tante* Bertha returned in the wake of two giants armed with machine-pistols. They looked cautiously around.

'*Deutsche Soldaten? Waffen?*'[8] they bawled.

'*Keine Soldaten und keine Waffen!*'[9] *Tante* Bertha replied, firmly pushing her way past the greenish hulks and suddenly growing very tall and broad in front of the log screen.

Casually, the tip of a barrel moved her aside and dislodged the stack of wood. The soldier grinned when he caught sight of

[7] '. . . one moment, I can't fly!'
[8] 'German soldiers? Weapons?'
[9] 'No soldiers, no weapons!'

Hilda huddled in a nest of logs, her mouth puckering, the white flag trembling impotently in her hand.

'No need to be afraid,' he informed her. 'We don't harm women and children. D'you understand?'

More logs crashed to the ground. Hilda started crying. *Tante* Bertha, spitting fear and fury, edged forward to the crumbling pile of wood.

The soldier looked at me. 'D'you speak English, girl?'

I nodded. 'Yes, a little.'

'Tell them what I said.'

I translated. The soldier pulled out two strips of chewing gum and thrust them into my hand. A minute later, the intruders had left the house.

Once daylight had gone, an eerie, somewhat unreal silence descended upon the street, a silence still shaking, still not trustworthy enough to tempt people out of their cellars. I licked the last milk from a tin and fell asleep on a bed of potato sacking.

PART THREE

CHAPTER 21

'Please translate, Miss Gärtner'

I was the first to wake. I stretched my stiff limbs and crept upstairs and into the back garden. I took a deep breath, then another and another, clearing my lungs not only of the musty smell of the cellar but, symbolically, of every particle of dust and smoke, if not of the whole stench of the war years.

The crisp air, in which the scents of spring had reasserted themselves, was filled with a delicious stillness which was accentuated, rather than torn apart, by a thrush calling from a gable. In their first bloom, the mauve candles of lilac trees held the promise of fragrance. Forsythias, standing in their own yellow cloud, a blossoming cherry tree and a bed of staunch tulips added more colour to the garden tableau.

As I watched a pair of lemon-tinted butterflies dancing ecstatically from one cup of nectar to another, a wealth of feeling sprang up inside me. How good it was to be alive! How good to have senses which responded to the delights of a fine May morning, and to a calm which – set against the rising sun in the east – had both the joyous and the solemn quality of church-bells ringing in peace.

Tante Bertha expressed her satisfaction that her brief involvement in the war had ended. At breakfast, caught by a sudden tide of magnanimity, she offered her two lodgers a cup of ground coffee and a slice of buttered bread. She also promised she would heat some water, and I had visions of washing my hair and laundering some clothes.

But the termination of local hostilities, and the resumption of a near-normal household routine, were not to be celebrated yet. Within the hour, Tangermünde's entire population was ordered to leave town and seek shelter in surrounding villages. Scattered

237

German units on the eastern banks of the Elbe – so the new masters claimed – were going to shell the town.

'Our troops wouldn't do that!' *Tante* Bertha cried indignantly and refused to go. But she had no choice. American soldiers combed every house and sped up evacuation. Given half an hour to pack, and with five kilometres to walk to the nearest village, people grabbed what they could carry and locked their houses firmly behind them. While *Tante* Bertha and Hilda went off to stay with farming relatives, my grandmother and I joined a stream of evacuees, and by evening we had settled down in a crowded barn.

'Oh well,' the old lady said, blowing her nose with a lace handkerchief, 'I suppose there is a first time for everything,' and was soon fast asleep.

In the morning we washed ourselves under the yard pump and looked around for something to eat, but the doors of the farmhouse remained closed, as did the ears of the farmer's wife to requests for food.

The sun stood high when an American jeep drove into the yard and an officer demanded to be let into the house. Minutes later he emerged with a parcel shaped like a violin.

'A leg of beef!' a man said and licked his lips.

'Pork more likely,' another one corrected him. 'I can tell.'

Pointing to the silent audience of evacuees, the officer gave the farmer a clipped order.

'OK?' he shouted.

'OK!' the farmer replied sullenly, and for emphasis nodded his head like a puppet.

It was not long before we were crowding around a huge vat filled with a soup made of water, flour, and cabbage leaves, which offended the taste buds, but soothed the stomach. Those who had been wise enough to pack a cup or spoon were first to take their fill, while others began searching for something that would double up as a scoop, or pleaded with their neighbours for the loan of their eating utensil. Others stayed behind in the barn, furtively slicing into bread and sausage.

The days passed sluggishly. Jealously guarding their suitcases with which they had staked off their sleeping space in the barn, people's eyes often wandered in the direction of Tangermünde, while their ears waited in vain for the sound of exploding shells.

238

The pump handle was screeching, water was splashing into a trough, a queue had formed for the morning wash. Children were noisily objecting to cold water and combs frisking through straw-tousled hair. Suddenly a farmhouse window was flung open wide and funereal music blared across the yard. Men and women stood transfixed, the pump handle came to rest, the children fell silent. I dried my face with a handkerchief, my grandmother – in the final act of her mini-toilette – picked strands of hay from her coat. There followed a roll of drums.

'*Aus dem Führerhauptquartier wird gemeldet . . .*'[1]

A steely voice informed the nation that the Führer, Adolf Hitler, had died for Germany, fighting with his last breath against Bolshevism.

It was the first of May, a day still remembered by many for its maypoles, dancing and merriment.

No one cried, no one cheered, and those who felt like mourning or rejoicing kept their emotions well in check. '*Der Führer ist tot!*[2] it echoed round the yard, and people looked as stunned and as incredulous as if someone had suggested that a new Christ had risen.

'So what?' an old man asked in a Saxonian dialect. 'At least the war will soon be over now.'

With this message in mind, business at the pump resumed.

More days went by with nothing to offer but watery soup and a bed of straw amid the smell of manure and makeshift latrines. The pump handle was never still. Boredom, uncertainty and irritation at the lack of privacy and elbowroom at night led to friction. People began to question the wisdom of staying away from their homes any longer. To pass the time, I took my grandmother for walks through the fields where we kept our eyes open for any activities in the sky or on the ground. But not a single shell, bomb or gunshot pierced the rural peace.

At last, one fine, memorable morning, we learned of the unconditional surrender of the German army.

'The war is over!' everybody cried, and at the long-awaited announcement the news of the Führer's death immediately paled into insignificance. Strangers embraced, men and women

[1] 'It is reported from the Führer's headquarters . . .'
[2] 'The Führer is dead!'

sucked in the air as if the farmyard held damask perfume.

But now impatience got the upper hand.

'If the war is over, what the hell are we doing out here?' people asked. 'Have the *Amis* forgotten us? Come, everybody! Let's go home!'

Postwar euphoria was, however, soon to turn sour, for on their return householders found their homes ransacked and every locked cupboard and drawer forced open. In what was rumoured to have been a strategical looting and fitting-out spree engineered by the new American town commandant, thousands of former forced labourers had been allowed to appropriate clothes, shoes, bedding and valuables – in short, whatever their suitcases would hold or their eyes fancied.

According to the first batch of evacuees returning from rural banishment, the foreigners had been seen marching exuberantly into their new Displaced Persons camp, the women wearing lipstick, rouge, high heels and even – despite the warm sunshine – furs, which they stroked provocatively, while the men, all spick-and-span in their appropriated outfits and with several watches ticking on their wrists, were bowed down under the weight of their booty. Many had smelled of *Schnaps*; many had shouted abuse at German bystanders.

Tante Bertha was beside herself. She blamed 'all those fools' who had supported Hitler; she blamed the American commandant for having turned a blind eye to the looting, if not for having organised it; she cursed the irony of the war which had claimed a share of her belongings the moment it was officially over.

All the clocks in the house, with the exception of a grandfather clock, had gone. A heap of splintered sideboard drawers revealed the anger of the thieves at not finding any table silver. The piano stood open, the larder had been raided. In the living room, a picture had been cut out of its frame; an ebony paper-knife, a bone-laced tablecloth and a Persian rug were no longer in place. Bric-à-brac and toiletries had disappeared as well as, for some strange reason, the sheet music for a Bach fugue and a framed photograph of *Tante* Bertha's deceased husband in the garb of his pre-1933 students' association.

Not surprisingly, *Tante* Bertha's dull, old-fashioned clothes had found no takers; nor had her shoes, which would not have

240

flattered younger legs. Hilda lamented the loss of clothes, shoes and other items, among them her first bra. In their bedrooms, mother and daughter stared incredulously at their naked bedsteads.

In our attic room, my grandmother and I took stock of our own losses.

'They've taken my only decent dress and my Sunday shoes, and oh, my silver Games trophy from Italy!' I wailed. Yet somehow the sense of loss did not hurt as much as I would have expected, and I remembered the liverish-looking lady from Berlin: 'Every time it is getting easier!'

My grandmother picked up the looters' rejects from the floor, folded each item neatly and put it back into the empty drawers.

'Thank God, they've left me most of my underwear,' she said. 'And here's my warm nightdress . . . my corset . . . my set of perming tongs!'

The old lady sat down on her creaky bed and folded her hands.

'I'm glad we still have our bedding.'

'I'm sure they couldn't carry any more.'

'One can't blame them really,' my grandmother went on. 'All those years living in a camp and working for us, their enemy! They're bound to hate us. Ransacking our houses – perhaps it was the best, the most harmless way to settle their account with us. After all, how easy it must be to be carried away by revenge. Better to find they have been and gone.'

I looked affectionately at my grandmother. This dear, frail lady, I decided, had a lot more common sense than one gave her credit for.

On the second day of Year Zero, which marked the beginning of the postwar era, a jeep screeched to a halt in front of the house. A giant white-helmeted Negro soldier got out and rolled his way towards the door. The bell rang peremptorily. Three times.

Tante Bertha called me downstairs.

'He's asking for you, Marianne.' She took up a chaperone's position behind me, her face rigid with disapproval.

'*Fräulein* Gärtner?'

'Yes,' I said, staring at the black chubby face with the restless mandibles, and at a baton which performed on his thigh as if it were a tambourine.

241

'They want you down at the town hall ... to act as an interpreter ... now! Commandant's orders!'

'What, me?' I burst out. 'There must be a mistake!'

'You are *Fräulein* Gärtner from Berlin, aren't you?'

The giant stood hand on hip. His jaws were grinding away. 'Come on, ma'am, let's get going!'

I combed my hair, grabbed a cardigan and climbed into the jeep.

'*Pass auf!*'[3] *Tante* Bertha called from the door.

As we drove off, I noticed curtains moving in several windows, and eyes watching, taking in the outrageous spectacle of me, a German girl sitting beside a coloured American sergeant, without tearful protest or seeming to be under a visible threat of violence.

I climbed the broad staircase to the council chambers as if the hangman were waiting for me, and in the pit of my stomach there was the same sensation I had experienced as a schoolgirl every time I had been summoned to the headmaster's office for some misdemeanour.

'Wait here!' the sergeant said, showing me into a small room adjacent to the Commandant's office.

And there, coming in through a side door, was Gisela. She looked thin, pinched and pale, and her prettiness was further blotted by dark rings under her eyes.

We shook hands like two long-lost friends.

'I hope you don't mind,' Gisela said, 'but I recommended you for the post of interpreter and secretary. They're looking for someone who speaks English and who hasn't been a member of the Nazi Party, someone young and – don't laugh – intelligent, and not tainted by Nazism, as they call it. And it must be someone who doesn't hate them, and who has enough integrity to deal with bribery attempts by townsfolk – you know, I scratch your back, you scratch mine. I thought of you. In fact you were the only one who might know enough English and who fitted the rest of the bill.'

'You flatter me,' I said. 'I have only school English ... and I seem to have forgotten everything. I couldn't possibly cope. Just listen how they speak! Their diction bears no resemblance to the English we were taught at school! It would make *Frau* Weber, our

[3] 'Be on your guard!'

242

English teacher, squirm! I can only understand every third word.'

'I assure you, the way things are going up here at the moment, every third word is miles better than our present gibberish and gesticulating.'

'My God, I feel awful! Where's the loo?'

Gisela playfully boxed my shoulder. 'Come on, where's that spirit of yours? The major has practically combed the town, but those who have a reasonable command of English have either been national socialists or have otherwise *Dreck am Stecken*.[4] Others are too senile or too hostile to the Americans, and of the old communist guard no one knows any English. You were the obvious choice – young, clean political slate ... I say, you weren't in the Party, were you?'

'No.'

'Thank God for that!'

'But I was in the Hitler Youth.'

'Ah, but that doesn't count, they say – unless you have been some big shot. By the way, I hope you can type.'

'With two fingers.'

'It'll have to do. You'll learn fast.'

Gisela winced and her hand went to the right side of her abdomen. 'Please take the job, Marianne. I'm afraid I only have a smattering of English, and I've not been feeling too well lately. Besides, the major is trying to set up an administration, and already there has been no end of misunderstandings. A return to law and order is what the *Amis* want, and to organise food supplies. There are hundreds of displaced persons to take care of. A daunting task! But I must go. They've started screening former staff. See you soon, and good luck!'

As I waved Gisela out of the door, I wondered whether I ought to have thanked her for having such a high opinion of my character and linguistic ability, or whether I should resent being propelled into the spotlight where, wedged between my compatriots and my new lords and masters, I would have to survive on a limited command of English and two-finger typing.

The major and new ruler of Tangermünde was seated behind his desk in a large, fan-vaulted room of monastic severity. Everything about him seemed to be square – his close-cropped head,

[4] Skeletons in the cupboard.

his chin and shoulders, even his chest, on which a row of ribbons commanded instant respect. Blue eyes, narrowed to inquisitorial slits, scanned my face, toured the outline of my breasts and the gentle swing of my hips. But not a single muscle moved in his face, no lewd flicker escaped from under his eyelids, and his lips remained set in a thin line. He consulted some papers on his desk and squeezed deeper into his armchair, the tall, carved back of which had all the dignity of a chair of state.

'You are Marianne Gärtner?' he asked.

'I am.' My mouth was dry, and I was wondering how to address my prospective employer. '*Herr* Major', 'Mr Major' – somehow it didn't sound right. It was not the sort of thing they had taught us at school.

The major looked up. 'Sit down, *Fräulein!*' And now his questions came like a round of shots.

'How old are you? Have you been a member of the Nazi Party? Of the Hitler Youth? Rank and position held? What did you do before you came to Tangermünde? Where are your parents? Name of father . . .?'

I listened to the strange tongue as an ornithologist might strain his ears to identify the call of a rare bird. I desperately searched my memory for words and carefully lined them up to make the briefest of replies.

'Have you got a fiancé or a boyfriend?' the major continued.

'No.'

'Can you type?'

'A little.' I hoped the major would not want me to demonstrate my two-finger skill.

'Have you read anything by George Eliot?'

I shook my head.

'English novelist. She wrote *The Mill on the Floss*. Great book, you must read it sometime!'

I said I would, wondering at the same time what to make of the word 'floss' and of the major referring to the author as 'she', if his Christian name was George!

'Would you like to work as my interpreter and secretary?' the major asked, not waiting for an answer. 'Good! You will be paid in Reichsmark by the town council. Mind you, hours will be irregular while I am in this chair, but if I require your services beyond the curfew, you will be taken home.'

'What is curfew?' I asked.

244

The major rummaged in his desk drawer and produced a small dictionary. 'Here, take it! I have another one.'

'Thank you. When do I start?'

'Oh, right now! Please tell the *Bürgermeister*[5] to come in with his men. We have a hell of an agenda this morning. Make a note: curfew, sewage, treatment of water, requisition of quarters, nonfraternisation, emergency food supplies, repair to electricity sub-station ... It'll be a long session. Are you hungry?'

'I'm starving!'

The major opened a carton. 'Here, have some cookies!'

'Biscuits,' I corrected.

My new boss smiled for the first time.

'OK, biscuits. I see you'll have to teach me proper English.'

I helped myself.

'Not just one, girl! Here, take a handful, there ... that's it! The corporal will bring you a couple of sandwiches and a cup of coffee. We start in fifteen minutes. OK?' He picked up the phone and drawled an order.

In the adjacent room I take possession of a desk, typewriter, pens and paper, two wire trays, a telephone and three empty files. An official unit stamp completes the desk array, flatters me with the trust it conveys, the status it confers.

I gulp down a cup of coffee, tuck heartily into delicious corned beef sandwiches made from the whitest of bread. Racing through the dictionary, I jot down the German word for agenda, curfew, sewage, requisition, fraternisation, before American officers, followed by four German civilians with drawn-in shoulder blades, file through my room into the major's office. A small, jovial-faced man in his Sunday suit detaches himself and shakes my hand.

'Funk is the name, I am the new *Bürgermeister*. Welcome to the town hall!'

Equipped with pen and paper, I take my seat at the conference table.

My hands are clammy. I seem to be back in the Berlin cellar, listening to the whistling of the bombs, counting ...

The major lights a cigar, his bland-looking aides cigarettes,

[5] Mayor.

and while the American party busy themselves with papers and maps, their German conference partners, who seem very small in their seats, greedily inhale wafts of Virginia tobacco and Lucky Strike.

The major opens the meeting. His eyes are fixed on me. And now he is a drill sergeant and I am one of the ranks who has miserably disgraced the honour of the platoon. He catapults his first demand across the table.

'Tell the *Bürgermeister* . . . !'

'Please, tell the *Herr Kommandant* . . . !'

The two parties address themselves to me in turn. American fists slam on the table, German faces look strained. The major issues curt orders, sets up rules, does not argue. He is in sole charge, the master of Tangermünde, and as such he makes it clear that he will not tolerate arguments from, or stubbornness in, its citizens, nor any obsequious attempts to bargain for relaxed conditions, and when *Herr* Funk dares to appeal to the 'fairness' of the *Herr Kommandant* in his treatment of the local population, the major suddenly assumes a martial posture.

'Fairness?' he repeats, visibly controlling his urge to shout. 'You are asking for fairness? What about the Jews, the millions of slave labourers you Germans abducted, the armies of innocent people murdered in the occupied countries? Did your butchers, your SS executioners and tormentors, *Herr Bürgermeister*, ever show fairness to them?'

For a moment the room is dead quiet. The Germans stare into their laps or study the exquisitely arched ceiling, the major stubs out his cigar . . .

Like learning to ride a bicycle, the first half-hour was a matter of knocks and bruises. Faltering attempts to understand US military jargon, or to translate words normally not found in any school book, ended in my embarrassed plea to have certain sentences repeated or rephrased. However, as the hours went by I found that my compulsory linguistic exercise was extending my vocabulary and building up a stock of useful phrases, thereby increasing my confidence and contributing to an easier atmosphere around the table.

At the end of this first marathon meeting, the major patted me on the back.

'Well done, girl! You're learning fast. Now, will you type this standing order and these two drafts. My driver will take you home when you are finished.'

Back at the house that night, and for many nights to come, I looked up in my dictionary whatever unknown words and phrases I had come across in the course of the day and compiled them into my own glossary of recurring terms and US military slang. I often stayed up late, until my candle had burnt down, fired by a singleness of purpose which I had not known before. But the more I learnt about the intricacies of the language, and of the different shades of meaning conveyed by a certain choice of words, the more I realised that responsibility had been hung round my neck like a heavy chain of office. For it was not only imperative that I understood and translated correctly, but that I was able to manipulate words sensitively, in order to strike the right key and the right meaning. Just as the outcome of a dialogue, or the success or failure of a conference, hinged to a considerable extent on the range of my vocabulary and linguistic versatility, so did the relationship between the major and the *Bürgermeister*, and – in a wider sense – between American troops and German civilians. Yet while such dependence scared me, I knew that only by steadily sharpening and polishing the tools of my enforced trade, would I achieve the kind of confidence which would allow me to square my shoulders and approach every conference session with a good measure of sangfroid.

A week passed without a major catastrophe resulting from my getting lost in the maze of American idioms, unintelligible drawls or GI slang, or in translating the *Bürgermeister*'s gentle but long-winded remonstrations. On the contrary: the gulf between those giving and receiving orders seemed to have narrowed slightly; my legs no longer felt like lead when I climbed the stairs to my office, and I now used four fingers for typing.

I had also learnt to resist attractive offers from attractive GIs.

Shortly after I had started work at the town hall, an army clerk, who looked as if he had stepped straight out of a picture of 'Sunset in the Bay of Naples', brought me a cup of coffee and a doughnut.

'Joe is the name, short for Giovanni,' he informed me, his dark eyes flashing, his hand running through the buds of jet-black curls. Boldly he rested a buttock on my desk. 'What are you

doing after work, baby? D'you want some cigarettes . . . chocolate . . . a tin of beef?' He smiled a Mediterranean smile, and I
would not have been surprised if he had produced a guitar and
serenaded me.

A week of similar approaches by other GIs and noncommiss-
ioned officers had taught me to ignore any offer which might risk
my reputation, interfere with my work or violate nonfraternising
rules. In the end, the men would leave good-humouredly, winking
or throwing a kiss, or just saying, 'Never mind, baby, you're OK!'

The major was out one morning, my 'in' tray was empty, all
movement to and from my office had temporarily ceased. The
keys of my typewriter were glistening in the sunshine which
streamed through the high, curtainless window. For the first time
since the end of the war I relaxed – and remembered Gisela. I
thought of the Sunday ahead, of green fields and quiet country
lanes, of cowslips, bird song and wide skies . . .

'Where is Gisela?' I asked a German clerk in the registry.

'Gisela?' The man raised his eyebrows. 'Haven't you heard?'

'Heard what?'

'She's dead!'

'What?' I shouted, seeing my friend cycling through the fields
with me and, more recently, pleading with me and wincing with
pain.

'Peritonitis. She didn't have a chance, what with no drugs. Poor
girl!'

I was conscious of an acute sense of loss. Gisela, my friend, with
whom I had shared many a laugh, and who had manoeuvred me
into the town hall with a politician's powers of persuasion –
Gisela dead?

I was aghast. During the war years I had learnt to accept that a
person could be here today and gone tomorrow, and that death,
gregarious and unselective as it was, would strike without asking
how long its victim had lived, nor how many dreams a man or
woman was still harbouring. Now, weeks after the end of the war,
Gisela's death did not make an iota of sense.

'She was gone within three days,' the clerk added, but his voice
barely reached me.

As the days went by, my English improved at the same pace as the
amount of office paperwork increased. Local citizens, it seemed,

could not undertake anything without a chit authorising the bearer, and while the Americans were content to retain one copy of all certificates, travel passes and memos, German council files requested a record of even the most trivial action and regulation in quintuplicate.

In my capacity as interpreter I was also getting out and about a lot, being whirled by jeep to factories, estates and outlying farmsteads, to warehouses, harbour installations, the prison or the hospital. I had become a familiar sight in town at the side of the major and his aide – exposed not only to the contemptuous stares of many Tangermünders who might have thought of themselves as 'decent' Germans, but to slanderous talk, not always behind my back. 'That's her ... she works for the Americans ... they say she sleeps with the *Kommandant*! Of course, she's not a local girl ... !'

And they would know 'for certain' that for prostituting my services to the major, interpreting, secretarial or otherwise, I was being amply rewarded with butter and eggs and chocolate and nylons, and those lovely American tins of beef. Surely, so their faces implied as I ran their gauntlet, I was no less than a collaborator, someone not worthy of their spit!

I felt naked and defenceless. Yet although I was perched between two stools, my loyalties divided, my services seemed – ironically – to be as indispensable to the German population as they were to the administrators of Tangermünde. And the same people who pilloried me for working for the enemy brought their business to my office, and might well come crawling and slobbering and smiling sweetly in an attempt to extract favours from me, such as a certificate, a signature or an official stamp. And they might curse me under their breath on the way to the door if I refused to bypass the major's orders or military regulations, or declined to add my own weight to a request for a special permit or the exemption from a certain rule, or pointed out that I could not possibly recommend the applicant to the *Herr Kommandant* as 'well deserving', 'politically clean' or 'genuinely motivated' if I had never set eyes on him before!

The nature of my involvement often made me a buffer-stop for wounded national pride and smouldering hostility on one hand, and for battle-hardened resentments and attempts to impose immediate postwar measures on the other. From my two-way observation post I was privileged to see my tireless boss as more

249

than a former enemy and present autocratic ruler, his men as more than tall, well-fed bullies or tentative fraternisers who walked like wildcats, drove through the town as if they owned it and indulged in something as un-German as chewing gum! But despite the sharp-tongued gossip, the bootlickers, the self-confessed communists and the unreformed Third Reich Teutons I met many men and women who did not fit the American image of the '*böse Deutsche*'.[6]

The provision of food featured high on the major's daily agenda, and to secure supplies, he began to explore local resources, ordering the handing over of all hoarded stock. Civilian rations were fixed at 1000 calories a head, far below subsistence level and without any guarantee that such a level could be maintained.

While some local inhabitants, like *Tante* Bertha, managed to supplement their diet through the generosity of farming friends and relatives, many people in town were starving, and in particular the thousands of refugees.

By now too weak to climb the steep stairs to the garret, my grandmother spent most of the day in bed; at work I often felt light-headed after a long interpreting session. But a few cookies, a doughnut, a corned-beef sandwich or a bar of chocolate left on my desk by some kindly benefactor staved off fainting spells.

'*Fräulein* Gärtner!'
At the end of his third week in office, the major called me into his room. He did not indulge in Christian name intimacy nor in the terms of endearment which seemed to flow so effortlessly from his men's lips, and which always made me feel like a dressed-up doll.
'Let me introduce you to your new boss.'
A dark-haired captain with a prominent nose and a bluish, smoothly-shaven chin came forward and shook my hand. His smile drew my attention to rows of ultra-white teeth.
'Hi, Marianne!'
'My unit and I have been posted,' the major explained, 'and the captain here will take over tomorrow. You'll be working for him in the same way as you did for me, and I trust you'll give him the same loyal service.'

[6] 'Bad German.'

I assured the two officers that I would. The captain looked me up and down like a film producer assessing a would-be starlet.

'See you tomorrow then!' the captain said and winked at me.

At a loss for a suitable conversational phrase, I smiled thinly and turned to the major.

'I have some urgent papers for you to sign, sir.'

The major smiled. 'OK, let's have them!'

Leaving the door slightly ajar, I went to pick up various documents from my desk. The men's voices drifted through the door, shreds of conversation, mutilated sentences, half understood, and all referring to takeover procedure. During a pause, the captain dropped military formality.

'Pretty girl! What's she like? Has she been screened?'

The major's reply was inaudible.

'Is she . . . do you think she's an easy lay?' the captain asked.

I returned, and the two officers remained silent while I waited for the major's signature. As soon as I was back at my desk, with the door firmly shut behind me, I consulted my dictionary for the German word 'lay' as used in conjunction with 'easy'. I had no doubt that the captain had referred to me, but the dictionary did not disclose any meaning that would make sense, and I decided to make the stubborn phrase the subject of my evening study.

Before he left the town hall that night, the major shook my hand. 'Thank you for all your help, Miss Gärtner,' he said. 'You've made my task infinitely lighter. Here, please accept this as a token of my gratitude. I hope you enjoy it.'

I looked at the major's copy of *The Mill on the Floss*.

The new *Kommandant*, by his own admission a former shoe salesman from California and a bachelor, ruled over Tangermünde for less than two weeks. He did so with élan and with a Hollywood smile which he only dropped when lashing out at hagglers and obsequious *Bürgers*. In his capacity as company commander he had also to attend to any urgent military business that might arise.

'Although the war is over' – so he explained his dual role – 'we still have an operational role to play. There are still pockets of German *Wehrmacht* around who have not surrendered, and werewolves are still roaming all over Germany.'

It was not long before the captain's eyes grew more daring,

251

and his hand might stray over mine or a sentence be charged with innuendoes.

One morning he dismissed his driver, requisitioned a black Opel, and sallied forth on an official visit to the neighbouring town of Stendal with me in the passenger seat.

There was not a single cloud in the sky and nothing timid about the early June sunshine. Whistling 'Yankee doodle dandy', followed by 'I'm in the mood for love', the captain looked at his watch and, once out of town, turned off the main road into a country lane. We had not been driving for long when, at the sight of a lush meadow bordered by hedges and fields of young wheat shoots, he stopped the car and got out.

'What a lovely day!' he said. 'Let's take half an hour off and sit in the sun.'

I did not move.

'Come on, baby!'

'The ground is still too damp,' I said, lamely.

'You can sit on my jacket.'

'I'd rather not.'

The captain warbled 'OK' and, still smiling, climbed back into his seat. An arm went round my shoulder, half-open lips advanced towards mine, a hand cupped my breast.

'Do you know that I'm in love with you?' he asked.

I remained rigid and silent.

'May I kiss you?'

Stammering something in hideous English, I recoiled from his threatening masculinity.

'Please let me love you,' the captain pleaded.

This time I had my answer ready. 'I'm sorry, I don't . . . I . . . not until I'm married. It's the way I was brought up.'

'Then will you marry me?' the voice persisted. Lips brushed my cheek and sought my mouth, fingers shot up my thigh, crept under the elastic of my panties as under barbed wire. I felt my nipples peaking and the vice of my thighs wait for permission to loosen. I wriggled free and jumped out of the car.

'I'm walking back!' I cried, embarrassed, sulking. Suddenly, the engine roared, the car reversed, the passenger door was held open and within minutes we were back on the main road. The captain's foot stood hard on the accelerator. He was no longer whistling and his smile took at least five kilometres to reappear.

By the end of the second week, the captain had not only

252

promised me blue Californian skies, but nylons, giant steaks and a wedding ring. Yet he always gave priority to military and administrative duties, and I respected him for it. For only I knew that behind his uniform, behind his urbanity and his suave, glossy looks, he was pouting like a child who desperately wants an ice cream and knows it cannot have one, but will not give up trying.

I felt a great sense of relief when I learned of the captain's marching orders, and more than an itch of curiosity at the news of a planned British takeover of Tangermünde.

On his last morning in the town hall, deciding not to be cheated out of at least a symbol of revenge, the captain pinned me against the wall and kissed me, before playing his trump card by speaking to me in flawless German for the rest of the day. And nothing short of a disaster could have wiped the mischievous smile from his face.

The morning sun had reached my desk, filling the room with a blinding brightness which made me screw up my eyes. Fascinated I watched a bumblebee flinging itself against the windowpane in its search for a way out.

I wished that I too could escape, if only to savour the scented air and pastel shades of the first postwar summer. And I wished I could have at least one meal a day which would not leave me hungry, one long night of sleep unmolested by the mad potpourri of English words in my head.

The arrival of a young British officer put a stop to such wishful thinking.

CHAPTER 22

A Scottish Interlude

Tall and slim, he held a baton in the vice of his armpit and stood as erect as if he were taking a parade. Dark, wavy hair accentuated a high forehead, a small moustache lent the unlined face not only years but a dapper masculinity.

'*Fräulein* Gärtner?'

I stood up and took the proffered hand.

'I'm the new officer in charge of the town's administration. I understand you will be acting as my secretary and interpreter.'

I liked what I saw: a face revealing intelligence and just a trace of that haughtiness which, in its full bloom, I had seen on the baron's face, and which I had come to associate with class and good breeding.

'Will you call the mayor and tell him that I wish to see him, the chief of police and the head of transport in my office in half an hour!'

An authoritative, clipped voice, which seemed to pretend to be at ease giving orders, but which, to my galloping imagination, could not conceal a warmth and a sonority more suited to reciting romantic poetry and to candlelight dialogue.

Yes, he was very attractive, very imperious, very 'English', my new boss.

'*Fräulein* Gärtner!' The voice called me back to attention. I was still smiling, for somehow the room seemed suddenly larger, and I no longer resented June unfolding itself outside without me.

In his inaugural address to the *Bürgermeister* and his key men, the new captain explained that he was a soldier who had been actively involved in the fighting, and that as deputy to the company commander he would be running the town's affairs until the arrival of a military government representative. It

254

would, therefore, be his responsibility to oversee the work of the *Herr Bürgermeister* and his staff, to preserve law and order, and to organise the collection and distribution of food supplies.

'I am here to work and to achieve quick, tangible results,' he said, and no one doubted his intentions.

It did not take him long to come to grips with his new task and with the Tangermünder mentality. Like his predecessors, he did not suffer fools and wranglers gladly, and if necessary he assumed a lordly stance with those who refused to accept his authority or the simple fact that Germany had lost the war. Without the blink of an eyelid he gave orders, requisitioned, delegated, confiscated. Yet he also listened patiently to arguments and proposals likely to promote his own policies or to solve the question of how to feed and hold in check the edgy mass of displaced persons waiting for repatriation.

It was no mean task for a junior captain.

'Priority number one: food supplies!' he announced on his second morning in office. He rolled up his sleeves and studied an area map. Within the hour he had commandeered a fleet of private vehicles, organised petrol, and detailed army drivers to pick up whatever foodstuffs farmers would yield under pressure. With myself in tow, he then set out to talk to farmers about the needs of the townspeople as well as their own problems.

Growing bolder during such rounds, I would beg farmers' wives for a few eggs and some butter, and I didn't have to ask twice for an apple or a glass of milk. Strengthened by the welcome addition to her own diet, my grandmother left her bed again, had a modest meal waiting for me in the evening and listened with renewed interest to my account of the day's exciting events.

'You're so very English!' I said to the captain shortly after he had established himself as the town's new administrator, associating his polite and reserved manners with everything that was English and upper-class. In reply, he roared with very middle-class laughter.

'I'm not English,' he retorted. 'I was born and bred in Scotland, and I'm with a Scottish regiment. We Scots don't like to be called "English"!'

I opened my dictionary. 'Tell me,' I said, 'do you play the . . . bagpipes? Do you wear a . . . kilt at home?'

The captain looked highly amused.

'No, I don't play the bagpipes; yes, I sometimes wear a kilt. I can see I'll have to tell you something about Scotland and the Scots when we have an hour to ourselves. Now, there's urgent work to be done!'

I was intrigued.

'Are you a Scot, too?' I asked the stocky corporal with the ruddy complexion when he brought my afternoon cup of tea.

'Aye,' he said, 'I'm a Glaswegian.'

'A what?'

'I come from Glasgow.'

'What is Scotland like?'

'How much do you know?'

'Very little, I'm afraid. Let me think: bagpipes, kilts, castles, sheep, James Watt, Mary Stuart, tartans, lots of rain, mountains . . . how am I doing?'

'Oh, fine.'

' . . . and I read something about a monster in a lake.'

The corporal tipped his cap back and grinned. 'Och, that'd be Nessie. Mind you, between you and me, nobody's ever seen more than a ripple on the loch. But we know it's there all the same. Here, let me tell you something about Scotland . . .'

I often felt the captain's eyes on me and, in his manners, sensed a struggle to override nonfraternisation rules, whatever preformed notions or prejudices he might have brought with him to Tangermünde.

'There's something about you,' he said one day, 'something different, something . . .' and he searched my face for that elusive quality to which he could not put a name.

Inevitably, the moment arrived when, sitting beside each other in the back of a chauffeur-driven Horch, proximity, with its strange flux and counter-flux, created an ambience which cancelled out all pretences.

'May I call you Marianne?' the captain asked, and took hold of my hand.

Next morning I found on my desk a poem dedicated to me. Written in French in the style of traditional romantic poetry, it closed with the words '*Je t'aime*'. It was unsigned, but a grammatical mistake, spotted immediately, after years of swotting French irregular verbs, suggested the writer's identity.

I reacted predictably. Flattered, attracted not only by his looks and a smart, brass-pipped uniform, but by the depths of his affection, I drifted, a breeze in my sails, towards his open arms.

'Today is my birthday,' I said. 'My grandmother has baked a strawberry cake. I was wondering whether you'd care to come along. Two people don't exactly make up a party!'

'I'd love to come,' the captain replied. 'But you know that I'm not supposed to even shake the hand of a German. All social intercourse is banned, let alone a private visit to a German *Fräulein*'s house! To be caught "fraternising" is considered a crime and a court martial offence.'

But I would not be disheartened.

'Six o'clock all right?' I asked, smiling – and I did not wait for an answer.

And the captain came.

I met him at the door. My grandmother, unable to remember her school English, said '*Guten Abend*' and offered an embarrassed smile. *Tante* Bertha and Hilda, refusing to shake hands with the former enemy, nodded a cool greeting and mercifully withdrew.

My grandmother served a plate of modest-looking sandwiches and a luscious strawberry flan.

'*Der erste Kuchen seit langer Zeit!*'[1] she said, and I translated, unashamedly pointing out what dietary sacrifices were involved in baking a cake at a time like this.

The sun was setting when the captain and I found ourselves alone on the veranda. Through the latticework, rose-tinted light had formed rhomboid shapes on the white table-cloth. *L'heure bleue* had set in, the hour in which perception increases and thoughts and feelings are heightened in the fading light. The balmy air, heavy with the perfume of roses and sweet peas, made us languid and reluctant to talk, and soon our silence had a delicious sense of sharing which knew no geographical or military barriers. Inside the house, *Tante* Bertha unwittingly matched our mood by playing Schumann's 'Träumerei'.

The captain, who so far had been sitting at an unobjectionable distance from me, visibly relaxed and edged nearer.

[1] 'The first cake for a long time!'

'Tell me about yourself, Marianne, about your family. Is that your grandmother playing the piano?'

'You go first!' I begged. 'Tell me about yourself.'

'Well,' the captain began, 'I'm twenty-two years old. I volunteered for the army as soon as they would have me – about the time of Dunkirk. Most of the time I was in the thick of the fighting. But to start from the beginning . . .'

Later, when the shadows were closing all around us, and my grandmother had put in her third chaperone's appearance, the captain whispered, 'We could go on to a river barge from here . . . there's a consignment of French cognac on board . . . whole crates of it and no trace of the skipper. We requisitioned the lot yesterday. Perhaps we could open a bottle and drink a toast to your birthday . . . and I would like to drink . . . to us?'

In the harbour, lanterns threw dancing specks on the black water in which a full moon was reflected as a distorted, bobbing shape. We sat down on the foredeck of the barge. Glasses clinked.

'Here's tae us,' the captain said, and I had my first taste of French cognac. And we linked arms, took another sip and kissed, thus sealing our friendship the German way.

'It seems strange,' I said, 'if not faintly treasonable, to be drinking *Brüderschaft*[2] with a former enemy, taught as we were to hate and despise the English. The war is hardly over.'

'It isn't any different for me,' the captain admitted. 'But then you make it so easy for me to love my former enemy.'

There was peace in his arms. But not for long. I felt his heart beating wildly, his manhood urging, daring, exploring, when the image of a German uniform, a frozen blood-splattered body blanketed by snow, wedged itself between us.

'Please take me home, Alastair,' I said, disentangling myself. It was the first time I had used his Christian name. 'I think the war is still too much with me. There's been so little time to adjust. Everything is moving, constantly changing, and people are stepping in and out of my life as if it were a tram. I, too, have changed. It seems only yesterday that I stupidly risked my life for a loaf of bread!'

[2] A way of sealing a close friendship and agreeing to use the intimate 'du'.

'I understand,' said the captain, and pressed my hand. 'Anyway, it's time I took you home.'

Business at the town hall went on as usual.

While clearing the town of former politically active Nazis it was noted in official quarters that never before had so many Tangermünders professed to be socialists, and so few to have had knowledge of crimes committed under the blessing of the swastika flag. On the credit side, the occupiers were encountering less hostility in their dealings with Germans, '*Ja, ja, die Engländer sind ganz in Ordnung!*'[3] many people said, perhaps remembering the evening, shortly after the battalion's takeover, when the kilted band of the Scottish Highland Light Infantry had scored high with the large crowd assembled in the market square, which had enthusiastically applauded the men in their colourful attire and smart bearing. And, watching the pipers and drummers marching and counter-marching, playing reels, marches and strathspeys, a long-forgotten if not wholly unfamiliar fairground mood had gripped the town.

Some people, of course, were still walking stiffly with giant chips on their shoulders, and some grew bolder and did not mince their words. Staring at my ruffled summer skirt one day, under which my belly was blown up with cabbage and the watery soups of the last two years, a German policeman asked me whether I was pregnant by the *Herr Kommandant*, and he looked around at his colleagues, waiting for them to cheer his audacious remark.

There was other local news.

In the villa of the highly respected *Herr* Meyer, proprietor of the sugar refinery and chocolate factory, an unknown villain – suspected of being a former *Zwangsarbeiter*[4] with years of bottled-up revenge notions – had thrown an inkwell against a silk-covered wall and slashed a life-sized family portrait. An unofficial opinion poll confirmed that Tangermünde preferred British to American rule, but then – so someone wrily pointed out – the Americans had not had a pipe band playing in 'skirts'!

Although the nonfraternisation rules were still strictly

[3] 'Yes, yes, the English are quite all right!'
[4] Forced labourer.

enforced, life was steadily assuming a degree of normality, except that permits, passes, questionnaires and application forms were now part of our routine. But while the amount of paperwork seemed to increase in direct proportion to such normality, the private *entente* between the captain and me was working smoothly for the benefit of the town.

Late June was splashing its colours into gardens and over the countryside when my duties brought me into contact with Red Army officers. Right from the start, I saw in the presence of Russian uniforms in British-run Tangermünde a sinister threat, and the first such meeting, although it ended on a hilarious note, did nothing to temper this presentiment.

It started off innocently enough. The leader of a Russian group of displaced persons who had been working at *Herr* Meyer's chocolate factory until the German surrender, and were still camping on the premises, asked the captain to speed up their repatriation by arranging a passage across the Elbe.

The captain reported the matter to his superior who, in turn, took it up with the British High Command. A few days later a Russian staff car drew up outside the British officers' mess and a jolly-looking Russian colonel, accompanied by a Czech interpreter, was welcomed by the company commander, who introduced the captain and me. Whisky was produced. Would the colonel care to try the vodka of Scotland?

The Russian beamed and nodded his consent. A double was poured for him.

'Water?'

'*Njet!*' He waved the suggestion aside like an insult and emptied his glass in a single draught. When, with due haste, this had been replenished, he raised it and uttered what sounded like a set of expletives. The interpreter explained.

'He drinks to the glorious Russian army and its companions-in-arms!'

The colonel signified that he was ready for another double.

'He drinks to Stalin, Roosevelt and Churchill!'

There was another refill, another toast.

'He drinks damnation to Hitler and all the fascist dogs!'

It was obvious that to the interpreter this was no more than an ordinary toasting session.

For hours we sat around a shiny rosewood table which

260

someone with a grudge against the German owner of the villa had savagely scratched in places. Whisky was still flowing freely. By the time the negotiators had agreed to a mutually acceptable procedure, the Russian was drunk and very raucous. After lunch, staggering out into the garden for a breath of air, he veered towards a goldfish pond, blind to the beauty of blazing perennials through which his boots left a trail of vandalism. He must have tripped, for a mighty splash explained his sudden disappearance, and the sound of thrashing water his attempts to find his feet on the pool's slimy bottom. In the process, several goldfish were swept out on to the patio, and it took four mess waiters to rescue a cursing, much sobered-up colonel and carry him to his car. I tried hard not to giggle at the Russian's soaked authority, in contrast to the Czech interpreter who remained cool and unruffled, perhaps because it was his frequent lot to witness such minor mishaps.

Not until the next incident, however, did I realise that the tail end of the war had only just reached Tangermünde.

It was nearly midday when a Russian officer, accompanied by two aides, arrived at the town hall. He carried a silver-tipped baton, and the combination of an imposing build, a lavishly decorated chest and a pompous stance instantly reminded me of Hermann Göring. But there was nothing risible about his massive shoulder boards, his gold-trimmed hat and his air of senior rank.

'*Komendant!*' he bawled at me, and the room began to shrink.

'This way,' I said, and the weighty visitor strode into the captain's office as if he were Stalin himself.

Not expecting such an important-looking and obviously very superior officer, the captain jumped to his feet and saluted snappily. I withdrew, but before long was called in again.

'The colonel here does not speak any English,' the captain informed me, 'but he says he has a fair command of German. Will you interpret please! But before we start, Miss Gärtner, I must have your promise that nothing you hear in the course of this meeting will leave the room. We must be absolutely sure of that. A panic among the civilian population must be avoided at all costs.'

This then is the beginning of the drama, I thought. There had been vague rumours in town lately that something might be afoot, an 'arrangement' between the Russians and the Western

Powers, rumours too preposterous to be taken at face value, yet too frightening in their implications to be dismissed altogether.

The four men stared at me. Conscious of the high confidentiality of the subject to be discussed, I realised that this would set me further apart from my own people among whom I lived and whose fate I ultimately shared.

'Yes, I promise,' I said, and so became privy to a concession by the Western Allies to their former partner-in-arms: a sizeable chunk of German territory west of the river Elbe, at present occupied by British and American Forces, was to be ceded to the Soviets, including Tangermünde.

Fear raced through my body, reaching my toes and my fingertips – the fear of men reported to have brutishly raped German women, to have used WC bowls to wash potatoes and, furious at seeing them disappear on pulling the cord, to have machine-gunned them – men who in many instances, it was known, had defiled houses with their excrement, or who had thought nothing of using even the sacred insides of grand pianos as pissoirs.

'*Fräulein* Gärtner!' The captain woke me from my nightmare. 'I was saying that we would want the stock of refined sugar . . .'

I translated.

An hour later, turning to go, the Russian colonel casually acknowledged the captain's parade ground salute with a wave of two fingers.

'Will you be staying on, *milaya*?'[5] one of his aides asked me, and his leer made me button up my blouse.

'*Auf Wiedersehen!*' said the other, and his eyes unbuttoned it again.

Long after they were gone, I could still hear the men's heavy boots slap the stone stairs.

'What is to become of me?' I asked the captain. 'Did you see the way they looked at me? They literally undressed me! Please, I don't want to stay when they take over!'

The captain stood up and folded his arms around me.

'There's more bad news, Marianne,' he said gravely. 'I received my marching orders this morning. You see, the war isn't

---

[5] Darling.

quite over in some parts of the world. I shall be leaving Tangermünde with my company at dawn tomorrow. A military government major will be in charge until the takeover. Remember, don't talk to anyone about this, not even to your grandmother! Act normally, as if nothing is going to happen. People will be watching you, and if the plan became known, it might trigger off a general exodus. Anyway, the town is already sealed off.'

My chest felt tight.

'Don't worry,' he continued, 'I'm going to make out an exit permit for you and your grandmother. You would have to be ready at short notice.'

He held me as if contemplating desertion.

'How very dear you are to me,' he said finally, before planting a kiss on my cheeks. 'You know, there's an English song which was very popular during the war: "We'll meet again / don't know where / don't know when . . ." – and so shall we, I'm sure, in a better place, in a better future . . .'

It was late when the captain drove me home through the curfew and through a sudden blanket of summer rain. I stood at the kerb, he saluted, and the car shot forward, wheels bouncing over the wet cobblestones; and I felt the rain running down my cheeks.

It was still raining when I arrived for work next morning. I introduced myself to the major, a mild-mannered, soft-spoken man with whitish hair, who smoked a pipe. As I left his room I had already forgotten what he looked like.

On my desk I found two envelopes addressed to me. One contained a document authorising my grandmother and me to leave town, and signed, 'Lt General Robertson'. For good measure it bore an official army stamp. The second envelope yielded a sheet of paper with two borrowed lines from Verlaine:

> *Il pleure dans mon coeur*
> *Comme il pleut sur la ville . . .*

As the drama unfolded, and more Red Army officers paid furtive visits to the town hall, the people of Tangermünde held their breath, watching the stage and waiting for the actors to give away a clue that would reveal its ending. And I had to watch myself, in case an anxious expression, a hurried pace, or any deviation from my usual routine confirmed their suspicions that a new zonal frontier had been drawn up. Although I was seething with unease, and was only too conscious of the weight of privileged knowledge, I did not share my burden with anyone.

Inevitably, the morning arrived which opened the curtain on the last act of the drama.

'This is it!' the major told me. 'The takeover is to be at midnight. I need not remind you of the importance of maintaining secrecy.'

'For what it's worth, major, will this get me out of town?' I asked. 'I don't want to stay on . . . please . . . I am scared!'

The major merely glanced at the bogus pass.

'You won't need this. I've seen my predecessors' reports on you, and I'm satisfied that you have discharged your duties loyally and with excellence at all times, and this in a climate which you couldn't have found easy at your age. I'm arranging for you and your grandmother to be picked up by car this evening. You will be taken to Lüneburg in the British Zone. Seven o'clock sharp! You must leave quietly and avoid any fuss. Also, I'm afraid you may only take a few personal things – we mustn't raise suspicion. Now, go home, girl! Thank you and good luck!'

'I won't come with you, *Kind*, as much as I hate to stay behind,' said my grandmother. 'I hope to go back to Berlin one day . . . It's where I belong. But you must go! I absolutely insist! The thought of you being . . . Please go!'

It was still daylight when a green Opel quietly drew up at the house. My grandmother accompanied me to the gate and, making a valiant effort not to cry, sealed her farewell with a red rose.

'Here, take this, my *Kind*, and may God be with you!'

As I climbed into the limousine, hastily opened curtains and windows brought out the watchers. A few minutes later news of my departure spread through the town like a dry heathland blaze. In less than an hour, many people would leave their homes and push on west with loaded bicycles, prams or handcarts, only to be turned back by British troops at the town's boundary. At midnight, the curtain would fall; at dawn, boots would smack the streets, and tanks, jeeps, *panje* carts and horses bring in the

264

enemy from the East, complete with commissar, hammer and sickle and another brand of modern barbarism – an enemy who, for the first time in history, would not be intimidated by the town's ramparts, towers and battlements, nor by the lack of a bridge across the river. It would not be long before the silence of fear would be broken by screams, not long before the welcoming cheers of those lining the streets, wearing red armbands or rusty Communist badges, would die away. Tangermünde would have been handed over on a plate . . .

As the car moved off I saw the lonely figure of my grandmother at the gate, waving a lace handkerchief. Something was hurting awfully inside me, perhaps a presentiment that I would never see her again.

By the time the town's last steeple and tower had disappeared from view, I was still holding the fragrant rose like a burning candle.

CHAPTER 23

'Celles sont des poules!'

At last I turned and looked at the two female passengers in the back seat, at pale, podgy faces long past the bloom of twenty-year-olds, on which heavy rouge stood like feverish blots and lipstick screamed garish messages.

'*Guten Tag!*' I said, and introduced myself.

Eyes narrowed, curiously glanced at me from under mascaraed lashes.

'*Nous ne comprenons pas, nous sommes Belges!*' one of them said.

'Oh, you're Belgians!' I cried, and fell into halting French. But the two women remained silent. The driver grinned and turned to me.

'They understand German all right, miss, they're from the DPs camp. The blonde is called Fifi, the dark-haired girl Marlène. Everyone knows them! I am to take the three of you to Lüneburg. There's a place where you can stay for a couple of nights. You, miss, are to report to the British resident officer for a job in the morning. All right?'

'All right,' I replied, and gave my attention to the passing countryside.

The small garret room, which had stored the day's heat, was uncomfortably close despite the open roof hatch. Fifi, in a hurry to enjoy the cooling comfort of nudity, kicked off her shoes and freed her choking waist from a lace-up corset and her formidable bust from its bra. Marlène's proportions were less Rubenesque. Tall and slim, she stripped in ten seconds flat and paraded her high-peaked breasts and dark pubic jungle in front of me and the mirror, perhaps taking pleasure in exhibiting her naked flesh, perhaps wanting to mock, or shock my own bashfulness, before

266

she spreadeagled on her bed, crying, '*Merde! Quelle chaleur!*'

The two girls smoked and chatted until long after midnight. I did not understand a single word they said, but between their beds and mine a concrete wall seemed to separate more than two languages.

'You can start right away!' the British officer in charge of the military government office told me. 'I'm afraid this is all I can offer you at the moment. The lady who's been manning the reception desk is off sick.'

I thanked him and accepted the job. Someone showed me into a glassed-off cubicle where light, space and air were at a premium, and I began to hand out questionnaires to German applicants and record the name and type of business of any would-be caller.

The hours passed at a painful speed as the undemanding nature of my new job became clear to me. At the end of the day I had not spoken more than ten words of English; I was desperately bored, hungry and very tired.

When I got back to the garret room, Fifi and Marlène looked as if they had spent half the day in front of the mirror.

'Do you want to come along with us tonight?' Fifi asked me in German, generously dousing herself with a musky perfume. 'We're invited to dinner at the Belgian officers' mess . . . a lovely chateau . . . friends of ours! They said you should come, too. A car will pick us up, and there'll be gorgeous food . . .'

My empty stomach contracted at the mention of food.

'Thank you!' I said. 'I'll come.'

Meaningful glances passed between the pair.

A pleasant drive through a soft, rolling landscape of purple heather, juniper trees and silver birches, freckled with grazing moorland sheep, took us to a stately mansion whose façade suggested a decade of neglect, while its park and gardens retained but an echo of their former landscaped splendour.

Weeds had heavily invaded the gravel paths, unclipped box hedges had reverted to their natural shapes, a grimy fountain held no water but the decaying leaves of several seasons. Where once a green sheet of cropped lawns had provided a pleasing vista, Belgian military vehicles now parked at random; in formerly terraced flowerbeds cabbages, potatoes and other vegetables sprouted unashamedly, surrounded by broken sculptures on crumbling pedestals.

Our hosts came to meet us on the grand staircase. The party was on.

'*Bonjour, mademoiselle! Enchanté!*' I pass through a lane of smart uniforms, flashing eyes and handshakes. My feet sink into the hall carpet, a mirror throws back my image, and I am pleased with what I see. Fifi and Marlène begin their spiel, Fifi by putting her hips into a provocative roll and sticking out her chest at the men each of whom she addresses as '*mon chéri*'; Marlène, her lips glowing, her tits unencumbered by a bra, by exuding *femme fatale* smiles. I am sipping something sweet and potent, while around me – babbling like a brook, yet remaining low enough to suggest the presence of royalty – conversation is full of flattery and flowers of speech, and so charmingly French.

At last the dining room. A huge round table, crisp white linen, candles, silver and crystal. I sit between two officers who vie with one another for charm and table conversation. But their elegant small-talk does not reach me, for I am recording the nearby clatter of plates and tinkling of glasses, the popping of corks. My fork poised, my mouth watering, I devour the sight of the *hors d'oeuvre* a waiter has placed before me. When did I last have a hot meal? Two days ago, three? Mercifully, someone says, '*Bon appétit!*', and now silver is dancing in the soft light, and I spear my first tasty morsel.

One course follows another, dishes I have never eaten before. '*Cuisine belgique!*' my partner on the right informs me, and I accept a second helping of the tenderest meat. The wine soon relaxes me and brings a sense of wellbeing. By the time the fresh blueberry tarts and whipped cream proclaim the culinary finale, and liqueurs make the round, my school French has acquired greater fluency, my shyness given way to a spontaneous gaiety.

After dinner, there is dancing in the great hall. '*Mademoiselle?*' A proffered arm. I whirl around with changing partners, smiling, blissfully happy and equating the whole experience with a filmland dream.

Just before midnight, Fifi and Marlène steal out of the hall, in their tow three officers clutching bottles and glasses. I decide it is time to go back to town, but my request for transport is met with puzzled expressions and a sudden failure to understand my French. When I intimate with a polite yawn that I am tired, an officer shows me to a boudoir-type room which is taken up almost entirely by a voluptuous double bed and soft cushions, wall-length mirrors, silken fabrics and pink lights.

'We expected you to stay the night,' he explains. 'You will find everything you need in here.'

A signet-ringed finger strokes his black moustache. His smile flickers, his eyes, assessing the situation like a general before a battle, question the wisdom of putting a foot in the door, calculate the chances of mounting an attack.

'*Bonne nuit, monsieur!*' I say, and with a show of determination shut the door and turn the key in the lock twice.

I soon realise, however, that a locked door does not necessarily lull one into a sound sleep, for long after the music downstairs has stopped, and the corridors have grown quiet, I hear bare feet padding to my door. The handle is turned, discreet knocks and low voices coo for admission, while only a few paces beyond I lie in bed in a flimsy black nightgown, the eiderdown pulled up to my chin and my insides as petrified of my stealthy wooers as a child of the bogeyman.

In the morning, freshly bathed and eau-de-toiletted, I went to the breakfast room. It was still early and I was alone with the sideboard which beckoned with steaming hot coffee, crisp baguettes and croissants, butter and pots of golden honey. I heaved a sigh of delight and went to load my plate.

I was musing about the sense of wellbeing provided by a contented stomach, when a driver put his head round the door. '*Mademoiselle*, the car is waiting to take you ladies back.'

Fifi and Marlène looked pretty seedy under their make-up, but were otherwise in high spirits. Flanked by noisy French badinage and officers in open-neck shirts, they made sure of their *grande sortie*.

'*Au revoir, mes amis!*' they cried, flinging kisses into the air.

Feeling a bit like a spoilsport, but intent on leaving like a courteous house guest, I offered my hosts a smile and a '*mille mercis*'.

Throughout the drive back to town, Fifi and Marlène – whose outsized yawns suggested they would take straight to their beds – pointedly ignored my presence in the front seat. I knew I would not be asked to dine at the chateau again. But I did not mind, for I felt like a chicken which had escaped hands eager to pluck its feathers.

'*Pourquoi fréquentes-tu ces femmes pareilles, une jeune fille comme toi?*' the Belgian driver asked me when he had dropped off the couple, before taking me to my new place of work. And hammering the point home, '*Celles sont des poules! Poules! Comprends?*'

'Do you like your job, Miss Gärtner?' asked the colonel, the head of a British AMGOT[1] detachment.

A week had gone by, a week of sitting in my tiny receptionist's cubicle for eight hours a day, of nights in which I had the garret room to myself until sunrise, when Fifi and Marlène, returning from their latest party errand, filled the crowded space with giggles and spicy French talk, and fouled it up with perfume, the smell of unwashed bodies and breath reeking of alcohol and Gauloises. By the time I got back from work, they would be all dolled up again, ready for another night shift and for the hooting signal which picked them up.

With their company in such obvious demand, they could of course not be expected to waste energy on making their beds or tidying up a room that looked permanently burgled, nor to squander words on '*la Boche*', as they now lovingly referred to me.

'Are you happy with us?' the colonel rephrased his question.

I cautiously looked at the man behind the desk who spoke such beautiful, uncluttered English and whom – were it not for his uniform with its crown and pip, and the associations with war, power and life-or-death decisionmaking these conveyed – I could have taken for a man of the cloth, an academic or an aristocrat.

'Well,' I began, 'I am grateful of course to have been given a job, but the work doesn't really stretch my brain. And I'm not happy sharing a small room.'

The colonel's mouth hinted at a smile. 'I understand,' he said. 'In fact that is why I was wondering whether you would care to accompany this detachment to a new posting in a town called Gandersheim – a very nice place I hear. We shall require a German there, to run a public liaison office – someone who can speak English and whom we can trust implicitly. Arrangements would be made for you to rent a room in a local inn. Do you drive?'

[1] Allied Military Government.

270

'No, sir.'

'Well, you would have to take some driving lessons, in order to commute between your office and our headquarters, which will be a few miles out of town on some country estate. A car and petrol will be no problem, and it won't involve you in any expenses.'

I needed no time to think and accepted the post on the spot.

'Well, that's settled then,' the colonel said. 'The company is leaving the day after tomorrow, at ten o'clock sharp. You won't mind riding in the front of a truck?'

'No, sir!'

'Right! You'll be receiving further instructions.' I was dismissed. As I left the room I felt like shouting 'yippee'.

CHAPTER 24

Gandersheim: A Beginning

The long column of trucks and jeeps wound its way through the narrow streets, past twisting side lanes and quaint, timber-framed houses with carved gables and flaming flower-boxes, which looked as if they had been borrowed from the *Meistersinger*'s traditional stage décor. The war, as far as I could see, seemed to have spared medieval Gandersheim. As its sleepy mood suggested, no bombs had wreaked havoc here, and no troops had raged in the ecstasy of victory. At its southeastern end, visible only as a bluish hue, rose the hills of the Harz Mountains, while close to its northern gates, bathed in pink light, gently-wooded slopes and meadows formed the town's back garden.

The truck stopped in the centre of the market square, to allow me to alight.

'The farmhouse inn should be just up the road,' said the young lieutenant with whom I shared the driver's cab. 'There'll be a room for you. Someone will pick you up in the morning and take you to the colonel's office.'

As the tail end of the truck disappeared it grew quiet in the square which was dominated by a majestic two-steeple minster hugged by equally regal trees. Close by stood an abbey, its ochre-coloured west wing aglow in the setting sun, and the town hall with its slate-grey, rose-tinted roof which towered over its gargoyles, oriel and dormer windows.

A group of old men, seated around a well and sucking on their pipes, studied me with the imperturbability of their age. Two children playing hopscotch looked at me as if I were Father Christmas. A horse and cart. A mongrel dog. I picked up my suitcase and walked towards the inn. I passed a butcher's shop with an empty display-window, a dairy with a sun-bleached

272

Libby cardboard cow, a café with no sign of custom, dirty lace curtains and wilting pot plants in the window.

I was hungry and tired. I was apprehensive about a new start in life, and a future which – whether or not it was predestined – would mainly depend on my efforts to give it light and meaning.

An unsmiling innkeeper showed me into a small room with two windows, one of which faced a farm-cum-backyard, the other a sewer-like trench separating the far end of the building from the jungle of someone's back garden. A bed, an earthen-ware jug and bowl on a stand, a metal bucket and a rickety wardrobe, table and chair made up the furnishing.

'This is it!' he said. 'The rent is thirty marks a month, including breakfast, payable in advance. You won't get another room in town. Too many bombed-out people from Brunswick and Hanover, too many refugees from the East!' The marginal politeness and a hint of contempt in his voice suggested that in his opinion any girl willing to work for the occupying forces could only be a whore or someone capable of high treason, and that such a girl, even if under the protective wing of the British military and paying her rent regularly, would be no more than tolerated under his roof.

I hesitated.

'Take it or leave it!' He stifled a yawn.

'I'll take it!'

It was a strange place in which I had come to stay. I was the only lodger apart from a middle-aged man who moved as furtively as a black marketeer and dressed like an undertaker. In fact, everything was black about *Herr* Schuster, even his eyes and his sparse, oily hair which he wore with a meticulous side parting. I would not have been surprised if his finger nails had been in mourning, too. He seldom smiled, but if and when he did his face belied the presence of mirth. My dislike of him was intense and physical, so much so that whenever I passed him in the narrow corridor my skin broke out in goosepimples and on the screen of my imagination there flashed images of a modern Rasputin, if not of a Mephisto incarnate.

Herr Schuster, who occupied a large room opposite mine, was evasive about the kind of postwar career he pursued. One thing, however, was certain: he enjoyed special privileges out of reach of the common *Bürger* and average consumer, and his devotion to Wagnerian opera – the weighty strains of which burst forth every evening from his gramophone – firmly secured his status in the inn as an intellectual.

Apart from ersatz coffee and a slap of ersatz jam, my breakfast consisted of what I could afford on my ration card, which was a slice of bread and, every third day, a penny-sized knob of butter. It was undecorously served at the kitchen table, among pots of lard and mixed pickles, amidst vociferous family arguments, and only inches away from *Herr* Schuster's breakfast tray which boasted such infinitely richer fare as homemade *Wurst* and slabs of butter, not to mention ground coffee, the aroma of which lingered in my nostrils long afterwards.

The hostelry was remarkable for its variety of smells, whether seasonal or permanent. Depending on the temperature and the direction of the wind, the corridors reeked of manure in summer, of rising damp and rotting wood in winter, and all the year round of cabbage, pigsty and the sour beer served in the taproom, while at regular intervals, when the shaft-and-pit privy was drained, the revolting stench of sewage wafted into the kitchen as well as my room.

And there was the back yard for sounds. Crammed as it was with sheds, junked up with broken cart-wheels, troughs, tubs and rusting machinery, it not only failed to offer an inspiring view from my window, but was alive at night with rats and cats, in daytime with chattering geese, hungry pigs and the din of metal buckets, axes, hammers and cantankerous female voices.

It was the place where I had come to live. It was my new home.

The atom bomb had been dropped over Hiroshima and Nagasaki; Japan had surrendered. In Gandersheim, the curfew had been lifted, nonfraternisation rules had been relaxed. In a room of the *Landratsamt*[1] and former abbey I had been installed as public liaison officer – a post which I soon found to be as demanding and as double-edged as my previous job.

From the moment I opened my door for business, and for many weeks to come, householders and tradesmen, smallholders and owners of large estates, professional people and local dignitaries filed through my office, pleading their cases humbly,

[1] District Council offices.

adroitly or verbosely, bowing and scraping towards my desk or approaching me with the self-assurance of their age and station. All too often, under the umbrella of a tempting smile, a petitioner would offer me the contents of his briefcase in return for a speedy or sympathetic handling of his application, challenge my integrity by producing a dress-length of material, a chunk of cheese, a tablet of peacetime soap, a pair of nylons – bribes which I politely rejected, increasingly astonished at my remaining so incorruptible, or reacting so stupidly, in the face of my own needs.

But while I was enthroned behind my desk in the pale bloom of my twenty years, the holder of military government trust, application forms and a rubber stamp, once again envy began to spread, and rumours about my possible fringe benefits and loose morals to isolate me. For the appointment of one so young and inexperienced was considered to be no less than an insult to the brave *Bürger* of the town. Why, I was not even a local girl! Admittedly, my English was good, and to all intents and purposes I appeared to be quite efficient, but . . .

I spent much of my free time in the surrounding countryside, which by now was liberally splashed with autumn colours. I brightened up my room with flowers and, in the evenings, left my door ajar to listen to grand opera escaping from *Herr* Schuster's room. I read Ernst Wiechert's *Das einfache Leben*[2] like a bible, battled through Rilke's wise and comforting rhetoric on the subject of loneliness in *Briefe an einen jungen Dichter*[3] and, whenever overcome by self-pity, cried tears of empathy over Klabund's lines *Ich bin so alleine / wer weint, wenn ich weine / wenn ich lache, wer lacht?*[4] Sometimes I prayed, sometimes I felt like venturing back to Berlin across the zonal frontier. Yet in my lonely turmoil there were always moments when hunger seemed but a temporary evil, solitariness but a calm, beautiful lake on a warm summer day.

When the first autumn mists began to descend from the hills, I turned to more practical and realistic leisure activities. By now

[2] The simple life.
[3] Letters to a young poet.
[4] I am so alone / who cries when I am crying / when I am laughing / who laughs with me?

desperate for some extra food, I climbed roadside apple-trees or sneaked into an orchard in the last light of day, where, easing the thief's task, a ladder might stand propped up against a plum or pear tree. And there was the Clausberg, with bramble bushes waiting to be raided, and late bilberries to be picked.

The monthly butter ration now stood at 125 grammes, the meat entitlement at 150 grammes. There were no eggs, and half a litre of skimmed milk and one doughy loaf of maize bread had to last a week. For lunch at the inn I would order a plate of cabbage, swedes or turnips, cooked in stockpot style and garnished – in exchange for hefty meat coupons – with shreds of pork fibre. My evening meal, which I took in my room, seldom consisted of more than a slice of bread spread with beetroot jam during the week, with the remainder of my butter ration and some variation on the *wurst* on Sundays.

I avoided my image in the mirror, the pale face and dark-ringed eyes, the swollen belly which made me look pregnant. One day a doctor diagnosed malnutrition and hunger oedema, but then, so he pointed out, millions were suffering from the same symptoms, and as he was unable to prescribe eggs, butter and milk, I was to preserve my strength as best I could, gather herbs for infusion and . . . why not ask my British bosses for some food?

Instead, I walked miles at the weekends, begging farmers to sell me some butter or cheese. More often than not the pilgrimage would turn out to be a waste of time and energy, but whenever a trip had yielded a section of German Brie or a quarter pound of butter, I would feast in my room that same evening and polish the lot off in one go.

Plying a flourishing bartering trade, and accused by sarcastic tongues of having no more containers in which to bank their Reichsmarks, no more socks in which to stuff their notes, farmers now fixed their own prices. A Persian rug might go for a pound of butter, *wurst* or bacon, a gold watch or jewellery for potatoes or home-slaughtered meat. Everything was offered, but not everything accepted, as farmhouses began to overflow with precious carpets, pictures of rutting stags, silver and cuckoo clocks. Yet although farmers were despised as the unspoken dictators of the bartering business, hunger still brought people from towns and cities to their doors, offering their last valuables, while others, with nothing to exchange, stooped to begging – as I did.

It was a time which taught me a few hard facts about my fellow-beings. Traditional class distinctions, which before the war had segregated people with money, title, rank or position from those less privileged, now no longer existed. Indeed, a new stratum of society had emerged, encompassing farmers, butchers, grocers and anyone with hoarded or undelivered produce – a breed of *Volksgenossen* accepting offers from the highest bidder. They, and the new army of black marketeers, together with their shady, unscrupulous middlemen, the full-stomach operators, the exploiters of the hungry, the despair of the have-nots, now stood firmly as the true rulers of the zonal economy.

I also learned that the costs of war had not been evenly distributed. Like many small towns and villages in the Western zones, the war had bypassed Gandersheim, as the eye of a hurricane might spare a house or a patch of land on its freak path. True, I had met some nice people there, but mostly among those who had lost everything in Pomerania, Silesia, East Prussia or in the cities – people with kind hearts and voices, who, like myself, were longing for new roots and a home, while searching desperately for a formula by which to live out in the cold meanwhile.

'We are outsiders in the eyes of the locals,' they would say. 'They don't accept us because we are making them feel uncomfortable.' And they recounted how, on arrival, they had found doors and windows shut, and eyes peeping from behind net curtains as if the newcomers were gypsies or vagrants. Charity, they felt, certainly began at home in this town!

But they had done more to the local people than ruffle their consciences. With their lean features, their worn clothes and their individual horror stories, the homeless had brought disquiet into the peaceful community, for here, in the first light of Germany's postwar dawn, the war seemed to be merely a nasty word which many locals would have liked to sweep under their carpets. The town did not have any scars to act as a visible reminder. No bullets had chipped off masonry, no shells had blasted holes into houses, no bombs had razed streets. Not even a window, they said, had cracked! How many among them, I asked myself, had ever gone hungry or shivered in winter? How many had ever come face to face with the knowledge that the next moment might be their last? And I had yet to meet those

277

Christian *Bürgers* who practised the 'love thy neighbour' bidding of the church they attended on Sundays.

Soon after I had taken up my job, a course of driving lessons was arranged for me, and it was not long before I passed my test. I did so with flying colours, which was perhaps not surprising since my performance on the road was not unduly disturbed by traffic other than a single military vehicle driving in low gear, and a cart being pulled across a road junction. The colonel handed me the keys to a requisitioned Opel, and I now visited him on set days in his headquarters – the estate of a former high-ranking German officer.

I was sitting in his office one day, waiting for him to approve or reject applications and sign permits, when a concealed door opened in the wooden panelling and Fifi appeared. With the air of one who has the right to move around freely, she rolled her hips about the room, casting heavily-mascaraed glances at the man behind the desk, and looking pointedly through me, while pretending to dust and tidy where, to all appearances, nothing needed dusting or tidying.

'Here you are!' said the colonel, returning some documents to me. 'As I was saying, the special regulations do not apply in cases where . . .' Although visibly distracted and embarrassed by Fifi's provocative behaviour, he did not ban her from the room, but continued with the business in hand with the presence of mind befitting an officer and gentleman. And ending the meeting: 'Ask the kitchen to give you a cup of tea, Miss Gärtner!'

As I was closing the door behind me, I knew I was leaving Fifi in control once again.

I stormed out of the inn into a stiff October wind which held the threat of an early winter. Proceeding at a fast pace through town, and crossing the footbridge over the swollen stream, I took the path which led up the Clausberg, the town's own backyard hill. Here, out in the open, the wind blew unchecked, forking through trees and sweeping over the browning meadows like a birch broom. Now and again, a squally rain shower cleansed my face of tears, before the next gust of wind blasted it dry, and the cycle started all over again.

Although I shivered in my thin coat, I welcomed the inclement weather as something that reflected, and in some way balanced, my state of mind. Two letters, the first sign of life from my father and mother, and the first mail since postal services had been resumed within the zones, had brought me out on this hill – as if by distancing myself from news of a family tragedy, and events that could well have frayed or severed my lifeline, I could restore my perspective.

'The neighbours found them and helped us to bury them.' My mother's account of the murder of her sister and brother-in-law in Berlin had been an emotional one, and just one out of many similar stories that were emerging of drunken, trigger-happy Russian soldiers on the rampage, out for rape and the victor's spoils, bawling, firing rounds into the air, kicking in the door of a suburban villa, finally staggering away, leaving behind a trail of splintered chairs, broken glass, a vandalised grand piano and – two bodies. Perhaps my uncle had resisted, perhaps he had made a courageous attempt to protect his wife, whose dress was found to be torn. No one would ever know. No one but their next-of-kin would ever care in a climate which suggested that where millions had died a few lives more or less hardly mattered. A Russian officer, to whom my mother had conveyed her outrage, had phrased his sentiments equally brutally and with the logic of the time: 'German soldiers did the same in Russia!'

To add to my mother's grief, there was still no news from the man I called Uncle Max. 'Perhaps he is a prisoner-of-war,' my mother wrote. 'Perhaps he is not allowed to write.'

My grandmother had enclosed a few shaky lines. 'The scenes after you left Tangermünde, *mein Kind*. Terrible! People tried to leave town, but they were turned back. And then Russian troops arrived and dreadful things happened. A woman from across the road threw herself out of the window. I am glad to say, though, *Tante* Bertha and I remained unmolested, and Hilda was safe inside her stack of wood in the cellar. But how I thanked our Maker that you had left in time!'

My father's letter carried a Hamburg stamp. Discharged from a British POW camp, and sentenced by a de-nazification court to earn his living and his ration coupons locally as a labourer, he was working in a tree nursery, planting saplings, weeding and turning compost. He lived in an unheated, sparsely furnished box-like room with a roof hatch for a window, the picture of an ice-clad mountain on the wall and a hand-painted porcelain chamber pot under the bed. Yet the frugality of his new life, rather than bending his spirit, seemed to be fostering a philosophical attitude.

'My back may feel broken in the evening, but I have a roof over my head, and a plate of hot soup for lunch from a mobile kitchen. It is more than some people have. Perhaps we all have to pay in some way or other not only for what we did, but for what we were too blind to see, too complacent or too cowardly not to do.'

My father, the former suave, well-dressed sales director with an expense account, had landed on his feet. But would he ever learn to walk again?

The long letter, written on poor quality paper, had finally, reluctantly, revealed news that had caught my breath. The source had been a reliable one: a survivor of the Dresden inferno, a man who clearly remembered the sight of the devastated language college – the heap of rubble, the gaping hole where the students' shelter had been, the dust screen behind which no living soul could have survived.

'It would have been your first night there, had you been able to make it to Dresden that day,' my father wrote; nor did he spare me more unsettling information authenticated by an enclosed newspaper clipping: according to a Berlin correspondent, Russian soldiers entering the city in the wake of their fighting élite had forced their way into the university's students' hostel where, a few weeks earlier, my father had arranged accommodation for me. The toll of the rape victims, and of those trying to escape 'a fate worse than death' had been high: eight female students and the warden were reported to have committed suicide by hanging themselves or jumping from windows.

'Words cannot express what I feel,' my father had ended his letter; 'all I know is that someone high above has been shunting you around several times onto safer tracks.'

I turned back. The wind was pushing me, lifting me downhill over the sodden path, and I felt like shouting into the wind, and against the grey roof tops in the distance, 'I am alive!'

I had been in my post two months when the colonel announced that British policy aimed to re-establish local German government, and that as part of such policy he had appointed a *Stadtdirektor*[5] to form his own local council and deal with the

[5] Town clerk.

day-to-day affairs of the town. As a result, most regrettably, my services would no longer be required. Perhaps I would care to move to a smaller, neighbouring town and set up a similar office there?

I politely declined the offer, and instead outlined my plan for opening up a translation office in Gandersheim. After all, many people required translations nowadays, and too few of them spoke or wrote English.

'A splendid idea!' the colonel cried. 'Let me know if you need my assistance. I shall ask the *Stadtdirektor* to give any such venture his fullest support.'

I received a glowing testimonial, a handshake – and was dismissed. Fifi, sipping a drink in an armchair, her silk-stockinged legs crossed, and revealing strips of white thigh, speared me on my way out with a good-riddance smile.

Rumours that I was going to start a translation bureau in town, to which the *Herr Kommandant* had given his blessings, helped me in my search for suitable premises. Within a week I had rented a small shop room, found a second-hand typewriter and gratefully accepted from the new *Stadtdirektor* the loan of a desk and two chairs from town hall offices. I hung the picture of a sunflower on the wall, stuck a huge notice in the shop window and fed my first sheet of paper into the typewriter.

I did not have to advertise for custom, for the news that I was open for business spread through town as if by loudspeaker, and soon my first clients were knocking at my door. I was confident. I had a dictionary; I had, through hard study, acquired a sizeable vocabulary; and although I still battled with English syntax and juggled with synonyms, my translation had reached an acceptable standard – as standards went at the time.

In due course, an official board of examiners – appointed to check on dubious translators going into lucrative business – put my translating skill to the test. I passed and, no less proudly than if I had gained an academic degree, framed my diploma and hung it up on the wall where customers could not possibly fail to notice such proof of excellence – a document which seemed to guarantee a professional competence which, I knew instinctively, I had not attained by a long way.

I often worked or studied late, depending on my stock of candles, for electricity was still coming on for short periods only.

I opened my first bank account, and it was not long before I was asked by the editor of the *Braunschweigische Zeitung* to translate certain articles for the British censor. Suddenly people began to greet me in the street, the men even lifting their hats – a sign of respect, as someone remarked wryly, usually reserved for councillors, the butcher and the bank manager!

Now that I no longer had an official reputation to protect, I felt free to accept in payment what no longer constituted a bribe, but boosted my diet; and if occasionally a tin of corned beef from some undisclosed military or black market source landed on my desk I asked no questions, but devoured its contents that same evening.

November was unchanging in its mood, with low-hanging grey skies, strong winds and prolonged periods of rain forming a bleak and mournful background to *Totensonntag*,[6] *Heldengedenktag*[7] and *Buss-und-Bettag*.[8]

Appropriately, the town was soaked in tristesse, being daily reminded of the sombre nature of the month by the sight of wreaths, bouquets of white chrysanthemums and whole households making solemn-faced pilgrimages to the cemetery. The church was full every Sunday, and broadcast requiems and Bruckner symphonies added their own funereal note.

Winter arrived when the first candle was lit on Advent wreaths. I had a small stove installed in my one-room office, and in the evenings, while the frost renewed itself, or blizzards were sweeping down from the hills, I would sit close to it, working, studying, reading a novel or just listening to the cosy crackling and spitting of the burning log, my thoughts not barred by any frontiers.

Nonfraternisation rules were lifted. As a result, keen socialising ensued between members of the British garrison and German *Fräuleins*, and at Saturday night dances at the corporals' and sergeants' mess fraternisation was practised to the strains of 'In the Mood' and other hot or sentimental rhythms played by Will

---

[6] Sunday on which Protestants commemorate their dead.
[7] National Day of Mourning (Remembrance Day).
[8] Day of Prayer and Repentance (Wednesday).

Glahé and his band. In the interval, anxiously awaited by the guests, who dug heartily into sandwiches and freshly baked *Streusselkuchen*, the men would try to solve language problems with the aid of a pint or two, and make sure they reserved the last dance with the lady of their choice. For after the dance, and before barrack gates closed, there were no rules making it an offence to continue fraternisation in dark alleys or hallways, whether in whispered broken English or German, or in silence.

Not surprisingly, the image of the '*böse Engländer*'[9] soon ceased to exist in the minds of German *Fräuleins*, while the soldiers' own notions of their former enemies were no doubt corrupted by shapely legs, a pretty face or the sheer power of romance.

Officers, on the other hand, were still bound by the rules under which communication with German females, other than in an official capacity, was an offence, and so continued to exhibit in public an air of aloofness coupled with impeccable parade ground manners. It was, therefore, considered a momentous occasion when the *Stadtdirektor* was asked by the British garrison commander to make up a list of 'nice young ladies' to grace the officers' Christmas dance.

After thorough vetting – as though they were applying for membership of an exclusive club – a number of local *Fräuleins* deemed 'suitable' to dance in the arms of British officers received personally delivered invitation cards.

I was one of them.

On the night of the dance, I washed my hair, applied some lipstick and rubbed my cheeks until they glowed like Italian apples. I dressed up my 'Sunday blue' with a ribbon and a dainty gold chain, and I hoped no one would notice the ladder in my only pair of nylons, or take offence at the sight of my rustic-looking shoes which I feared, might not look too happy on a dance floor.

At the door of the *Kaisersaal*, the splendid hall of the former abbey, the German guests were received like members of a foreign delegation. Officers in smart dress uniforms came forward and picked their partner for the evening according to some undisclosed system. To my delight, my escort turned out to

[9] 'Bad Englishman.'

be a blue-eyed captain in his thirties, who wore his incredible good looks with the same ease as his rows of medal ribbons.

Drinks. Vermouth for me, whisky for the captain. Drawing-room conversation. A band striking up. A bow. 'May I have this dance, please?' A Viennese waltz at regulation arms' length loosens up limbs and tongues. A foxtrot. A slow waltz. And now smiles come easier, faces and bodies inch closer to each other. Fraternisation officer-style is under way.

Seated at a ringside table, the garrison commander and his guests are watching the spectacle on the gleaming parquet floor with approving eyes. The light from the crystal chandeliers envelops the dancers, softens the stern expressions of abbesses and princesses in their gold frames on the wall . . .

At half-time, pyramids of cake and snow-white sandwiches are placed on each table. My heart and stomach leap at the sight, my eyes assume the size of saucers.

The captain smiles. 'I'll get us some coffee, excuse me for a moment.' Visibly enjoying himself, he adds, 'Don't wait, help yourself!'

I do not wait. And when I'm sure no one is looking, I open my handbag and, in a very unladylike manner, stuff it full of sandwiches and cake. Something to eat tomorrow, I keep thinking. Tomorrow is Sunday. I shall have a feast in my room!

The first postwar Christmas differed little from Christmas 1944 in that without proper heating the cold was just as cruel and – for those without sizeable savings, barterable goods, farming friends or their own backyard husbandry – hunger just as acute. Whatever quality of life still existed, was jealously guarded, and for some it was little more than a matter of hanging on.

Indeed, apart from a few extra candles and a loaf of stodgy maize bread, there was little but hope to kindle the Christmas spirit. But the woods around were full of fir and spruce, and there was no limit to the amount of unassuming, yet welcome, items which, converted or restyled, carved, stuffed, sewn, stitched or glued together, could be made into Christmas gifts.

Shop queues, invariably a barometer of public opinion and a reliable source of information, revealed how some housewives had managed to bake some of their traditional Christmas biscuits – and emphasised the value of the mark in relation to under-the-counter and black-market goods.

'I've saved up the ingredients for my Pretzels over three months!'

'I paid two hundred marks for half a pound of butter!'

'That's less than I paid for a pound of sugar!'

'My husband had to part with five hundred marks for a pound of coffee!'

'I know somebody who knows somebody who can get you an egg for fifty!'

At a Christmas party staged by British soldiers, refugee children were treated to cake and cocoa and a friendly grin from Father Christmas, before being presented with chocolates and toys – a gesture of goodwill which probably did much more than bring smiles to young faces.

Christmas Eve was a cold, clear night which promised a further drop in temperature, and the streets were covered with a fine layer of snow. Long stretches of pavement, turned by children into slides, threatened unsteady legs, and on my way to the carol service I passed groups of elderly people who, weary of slipping, waddled to the minster and its ringing bells like a flock of penguins.

The church was packed. A notice pointed out that candles and a box of briquettes had been graciously donated by the British garrison commander.

'While ten million people are still seeking each other,' the minister began, 'while we are living in the shadow of millions of graves, let us listen to the Christmas story as to a message that might bring new hope and light into our lives. And it came to pass . . .'

Carols, uplifted by the strains of the organ. I heartily joined in the singing, feeling part of a body of people undivided, if only for an hour, by sentiments or by cultural, social or dialectal barriers. Here, shoulder to shoulder, local-born residents were sitting next to refugees; threadbare coats touched furs or warm winter wraps; pale, pinched faces bent over hymn books, or faced the pulpit, alongside those which the war years and postwar hunger had scarcely touched.

'Peace on earth and goodwill to all men.'

285

My thoughts strayed back to former Christmas Eves, to bounteous gifts, roast goose stuffed with sweet chestnuts, star-shaped almond cookies and trees touching the ceiling.

Where, I wondered, should I start to thank the Almighty? I had survived. I had done so with neither my body nor my spirit broken. And humbly, I saw such graces for what they were.

The iron stove thawed my limbs. I lit a candle, read my Christmas mail and held a fir branch into the fire, so that the room took on its resinous smell. I breathed hard against the frozen windowpane until, through a melted patch the size of a porthole, I could see the quiet street.

I wished it were snowing. I like snow. Lots of it. Snow to hood roofs and cap lanterns, to dress up trees and smooth a harsh urban winter scene, to crunch under one's feet or to muffle one's steps. And how I loved snow in the mountains!

Pictures came racing back. The Riesengebirge.[10] Christmas Eve with my father in a soft-carpeted hotel. A fleet of waiters. *Baumkuchen* melting on my tongue. My first taste of champagne. 'Only half a glass, waiter, my daughter is only fourteen!' Tramping through the glistening snow to a tiny, timber church embedded on the mountainside. Bells ringing like glass chimes, snow sighing under the boots of midnight pilgrims, stars shining as brightly as they must have done once over the nativity scene . . .

More flashes of memory: Christmas in the Erzgebirge[11] in the third year of the war. Being one of a party of young skiers rounding off the night's celebration by swishing downhill through the powdery snow to the village, each holding a burning torch. The girls glowing and daring from hot rum punch, the young local mountain-soldiers, on short home leave, laughing and singing and showing off their wizardry on the slope with elegant stems and parallel turns, not counting the hours to their departure, nor the miles back to the front.

I wrapped myself in a blanket and pulled my chair closer to the stove. A cup of hot, sweet British army ration tea. A baked apple. Filtering through the ceiling were Christmas music, family voices, the pitter-patter of small, excited feet.

[10] Sudeten mountains.
[11] Saxonian and Bohemian mountains.

CHAPTER 25

Spring Calls with Many Voices

The winter was long and cold. When the frost finally released its grip, and the days grew longer, young and old emerged from a state of physical and mental hibernation with a strange uplift of spirits. Nobody could recall later what had triggered off the town's arousal. Was it the first green shoots, the smell of spring soil? Or the café, where the radio was tuned in to swing music, and where behind washed curtains and fresh pot plants patrons ordered ersatz coffee and cake, albeit noticeably short of butter, eggs and sugar? Or the huge noticeboard in the market square, every centimetre of which was covered with do-it-yourself posters, scribbled advertisements and Wanted in Exchange notices – evidence that the townspeople were trying to rid themselves of end-of-war paralysis? Here an amateur drama group announced the performance of Klabund's *Der Kreidekreis* on an improvised stage of the *Schützenhaus*,[1] tickets at the door; a milliner, claiming to have once fashioned hats for stars from stage and screen, offered to re-model ladies' hats, provided you brought your own felt; a former state-opera ballerina advertised ballet lessons, each pupil to bring a log or briquette to help heat the studio; tenor voices were wanted to form a choir, and an accordionist and a saxophone player for a dance. Items were offered in exchange: a pair of riding boots for a pound of nails, a diamond ring for a coat, the collected works of Schiller for writing paper, a tin of white paint for sheet metal.

The first manufacturing companies registered for business, as yet mainly operating like cottage industries, geared to the art of improvisation and to using whatever scrap material the new entrepreneurs could lay their hands on. They did not have to

[1] Riflemen's clubhouse.

look far for goods that had an obvious market, for the range was endless in a country in which industry had virtually come to a standstill, and was not only without steel, but without nails, needles, writing paper, light bulbs, shoe cream, soap and soap powder, thread, glass, glue, shampoo, shoe laces, to name but a few. Among the new products to prove the ingenuity of far-sighted manufacturers were cooking pots made from German army helmets which, hammered into shape and given a handle, found a waiting market.

Dressmakers advertised their services, and soon the first new spring frocks, made from drapes, curtains, quilt covers or a combination of two or three old dresses, appeared on the streets – creations which, inspired by the latest Paris fashions, turned brusquely away from the austere, functional German styles of the war years.

Desperate for a new dress, I sacrificed one of my two patterned duvet covers for a swinging, calf-length skirt and a narrow-waisted, low-neckline jacket. The dressmaker said it was *le dernier cri*, and a perfect Dior copy. She had seen pictures of the French couturier's spring line, and apparently all the women were going crazy over it. What a pity one couldn't buy new dress material, and that customers had to bring their own thread! The money she could make!

A reading fever had broken out in town. Lending libraries did brisk business, and the first new books – paperbacks printed on yellowish, brittle paper – found keen buyers.

'People are ravenous for new books,' a bookseller told me one day when, hoping to find a copy of the Forsyte Saga, I had been rummaging unsuccessfully among second-hand books that ranged from *Tarzan of the Apes* and Karl May's beloved adventure stories to the classics, from cheap romances to novels not long ago approved, or actively promoted, by the Reich's book censors. 'There's a market here, if ever there was one!' she cried. 'Writing unpublished between 1933 and 1945, new German writing, writing from abroad . . . A lot of people want to know what's been going on around them while they were fenced in.' Her eyes sparkled, her hands shot up in the air. 'It's marvellously exciting, like a curtain being raised from the rest of the world. The things we didn't know! The books we weren't allowed to read! The new mental perspectives! You have no idea, *Fräulein*, what kind of writing never reached our bookshelves! I should know. My family's been running one of the country's oldest publishing houses.'

I was fascinated by the bookseller's enthusiasm, and for the first time I heard about books that had been burned or blacklisted, about émigré writers who, watching the decline of Hitler's Germany from outside its spiked fence, had expressed in their essays, novels and poetry not only their sadness but, perhaps by way of catharsis, their love-hate relationship for the country they had fled, or which had ostracised their works. I also learnt about the merits of new writing emerging from the postwar cultural chaos, of writers analysing, accusing, satirising or weeping over the ruins of their country, or seeing the land of their fathers and forefathers rising again from the ashes as in some Faustian dream.

'Could you perhaps put my name down for one of the new novels?' I asked.

The bookseller entered my name on a list. 'With pleasure,' she said. 'Mind you, you'll have to bring in an old book or two in exchange – apart from paying for the new one. It's the paper, you see. One book for another, or about two pounds' worth of paper. That's the present policy.'

A chamber orchestra was to play eighteenth-century music in the abbey's *Kaisersaal*, to mark the German cultural dawn of 1946. Tickets for the memorable event went as fast as if the great Furtwängler himself were to conduct the Berlin Philharmonic, so I was delighted to receive one with the compliments of the *Herr Stadtdirektor*.

On the night, British officers in dress uniform occupied the front seats, and the new guard of local dignitaries and their wives the second. Many a dinner jacket smelt of mothballs, many a lady seemed to have dipped deep into her wardrobe, and I noticed not without a twinge of satisfaction more than one pair of eyes taking note of my duvet cover 'Dior' dress.

A hushed silence: then the sound of strings, flute and spinet dominated the hall, in which hundreds of candles supplied by an appreciative garrison commander helped to recreate a *Hofkonzert*[2] setting. Golden light was reflected in the long mirrors and gleaming parquet floor and caught in the crystal chandeliers, modelling the musicians' faces.

[2] Royal court musical evening.

A flute solo was played from a tall music-stand. And now Menzel's famous painting *Das Flötenkonzert*[3] comes alive, and I am back in Potsdam, back in Sans Souci, in a world of wigs and silk and lace, where I do not hear my feet crying out for a new pair of shoes, my stomach for bread for which I have run out of ration coupons.

A cultural event of a different kind was the reopening of the local cinema for the showing of a documentary film on concentration camps. Despite earlier rumours that the commander-in-chief of the British Army of the Rhine would make the viewing of the film mandatory for every German civilian in the zone over the age of sixteen, attendance had finally been left to the discretion of individual *Bürgers*, except in communities surrounding the Bergen-Belsen camp.

On the first night many locals responded to the challenge – perhaps out of curiosity, perhaps out of a sense of duty, perhaps even to be able to brag about the courage it took to go and view crimes that had been recorded for posterity.

Not surprisingly, the sentiments aroused by the film spilled over in the *gemütliche* ambience of the taproom-cum-restaurant of the inn, where, after a pint, tongues loosened, and the regulars in collars and ties, in carefully pressed suits fraying at the cuffs and turn-ups, facilely renounced old and articulated new convictions, conducting political postmortems and discussing the phenomena of Hitler and Nazism with the hindsight of armchair politicians. Sometimes, falling back into old habits, a speaker embroiled in a heated argument would glance cautiously over his shoulder. On Thursday evenings a table was reserved for the town's intellectual élite, who tackled the country's past and present problems on a higher plane, and were duly addressed by the innkeeper as '*Herr Doktor*', '*Herr Rechtsanwalt*' or whatever title their profession or position accorded them.

For me, the inn was a place of education, a veritable treasure chest of information.

One evening, shortly after the first showing of the controversial film, a card player, ignoring my presence at the neighbouring table, puffed a smoke screen around himself and his companions and voiced his views.

[3] Flute concert.

'The nerve of confronting us with such horrific scenes! Surely we had nothing to do with those atrocities, and we couldn't have prevented them even if we had known. I just can't believe that Germans could inflict such cruelties on human beings. It's mind-boggling!'

'But there were a lot of things we didn't know, eh?' argued another player. 'And you see what some people are capable of. Mind you, I get squeamish every time I have to kill a cockroach.'

The first speaker saw his cue. 'Strong meat, that film was! I had no idea what I was letting myself in for. Couldn't sleep last night. And I made the mistake of taking my wife along. She was sick all over my trousers. Your deal, Walter.'

The man called Walter took his time. 'I don't know,' he said, dealing each card as if counting out money. 'I think it will be difficult to live down what happened in those camps. The world won't forget, not for a long time, perhaps not for generations.'

'Come on, let's get on with the game.'

I did not see the film on Belsen, Auschwitz and Buchenwald, for the very thought of watching on screen what in the paper, even at a glance, had made nauseating reading, made me feel as if I were standing on a narrow ledge outside the top floor of a skyscraper.

When the film had played to empty houses for a week, it was taken off, and English and American films were shown to members of the British Forces on certain nights, officers and sergeants being allowed to bring one German guest each. On other nights, re-runs of selected German films and musicals made for full houses.

A British officer invited me to see *Waterloo Bridge*, my first English feature film. I did not understand everything that was said, but the bitter-sweet sentiments needed no translation, and Cadbury chocolate bars and fudgy sweets, generously supplied by my escort, saw to it that my own emotions did not run too high.

After the show, the officer insisted on seeing me home. 'The streets are dark, and there are too many other ranks about for a young lady like you.' He told me that he was leaving in a day or two to go back to civilian life: would I like some English books and newspapers?

'You must read, read, read,' he said. 'It's the best way to

expand your vocabulary. Submerge yourself completely in the language, until you dream in English. And now, may I practise my German on you?'

Emaciated, their uniforms in rags, their ashen faces still holding all the dust and misery of Siberian mines, the first prisoners-of-war returned from Russian camps, and a few to Gandersheim.

Walking on crutches or with the aid of a stick, they limped or shuffled down from the station, the visible reminder of everything people wanted desperately to forget: the war, and the defeat of the nation.

The trial at Nuremberg, by now well under way, was making daily headlines in the press and in the German newsreels. Hermann Göring and other former Nazi leaders were shown, crowding in the dock and expressing, in a straight-back, chin-raised *Preussische Haltung*, or in faces reflecting arrogance, defiance, resignation or infinite boredom, their own attitudes to the trial. Looking shrunken in their suits, or in uniforms bared of decorations and the insignia of rank, some of the former Reich leaders, renowned for their pompous manners, resembled punctured balloons, while Göring, the former *Reichsmarschall*, who had once invited the nation to call him 'Meyer'[4] if a single enemy aircraft ever flew over Berlin, looked as unimposing and nondescript as the name suggested.

In the inn's taproom *vox populi* continued to reign unrestrained.

'They should hang the lot! See what the bastards did to us, and to others!'

Others sounded more moderate. '*Ach*, let them have a fair trial, and let's get on with what they left us.'

The meadows had turned bright with spring flowers, and gardens resounded to the jaunty song of thrushes and bullfinches. The Gander, during most of the year a bubbling stream sneaking past the foot of the Clausberg, had risen over its banks. Spring was also evident at the inn, where there were no more morning tantrums in the kitchen, and the proprietor grinned at me whenever his wife's back was turned. Equally affected by the stirrings of the season, *Herr* Schuster commented favourably on

---

[4] The equivalent of 'Smith'.

my new dress and went out without hat and overcoat, sporting a gaily patterned tie.

I felt restless, possessed by strange and not so strange longings. I daydreamed of Italian sun, of biting into a juicy pork cutlet, of studying in the dignified library of a university, and of having a man's arms around me. I was also getting fed up with *Herr* Schuster, who had recently added Wagner's *Walküre* to his record collection, which made me wish he would break the lot and provide more light-hearted, spring-inspired music for my evening's listening.

Spring was at its peak when Eric erupted into my life with the force of a medium-sized earthquake.

For days, in a series of translations commissioned by the *Braunschweigische Zeitung* for the British censor, I had been working on a leader dealing with democracy, party politics, elections and voting procedure. Battling with political jargon, and aware of my own linguistic shortcomings, I was wondering how long it would be before the editor found someone in Brunswick capable of providing more accomplished translations. My head ached, my dictionary was a mass of dog-ears, the text in front of me seemed spiked with syntactical and grammatical difficulties.

There was a knock. A tall English soldier with corporal's stripes and eyes the colour of cornflowers entered the room, removed his cap and ran his fingers through his blond, curly hair. I looked at a face to which I took an instant liking.

The young man stared back at me as if he had expected a retired school teacher or ageing academic behind the desk, and certainly not a young woman who looked no older than twenty.

'Good morning!' he said. His eyes cruised over my face and strayed down to the point where my breasts peaked against my blouse.

'Good morning!' I replied. 'What can I do for you?'

Breaking off his visual journey, my visitor pulled a piece of paper out of his pocket.

'I wonder if you could translate this short letter for a chap in my platoon. He's taken up with a German girl, and now he's had an accident, they're flying him to a hospital in England tomorrow. He's jotted down a few lines . . . doesn't want her to think . . . She doesn't speak English, and he and I don't know any German.'

I read the letter.

'What are you doing with yourself this weekend?' the corporal asked when I had finished translating the simple message of love and farewell. 'We could go for a walk or to the pictures. It gets lonely in camp at weekends, and I don't fancy the mess every night.'

I stayed silent.

'My name is Eric. I was reading English and History at university when I was called up. The army wanted to commission me, but I said "No thank you".'

'You seem to have seen plenty of action,' I said, pointing to his medal ribbons.

He brushed lightly over them and grinned. 'Who knows – if I had accepted a commission, I might be a major now.' Picking up a ruler and wedging it under his arm, raising his chin high and narrowing his eyes, he pretended to take a company parade.

We laughed.

'Well, will you come out with me even though I don't have any pips?' Eric may have been a corporal, but he looked like a nordic prince. His eyes pleaded, persuaded, made the ground under me shake.

'All right, I will,' I said – and then I remembered with a shock that I would be sending off next morning a far from perfect translation. I saw my chance. 'Would you, if it's not too much trouble, check this text for me, please?'

Eric did not have to be asked twice. He pulled up a chair and read the draft of my translation, changing the construction of a sentence here, polishing a phrase there, and explaining points of syntax and grammar. Our arms touched, his face came within centimetres of mine, my concentration waned. Before long, my chest ached with sweet restraint.

The moment he had finished, I jumped up and exclaimed a touch too breezily, 'Thank you very much for your help!'

'May I pick you up at three on Saturday?' Eric asked, and from the door, 'Do you know any English poetry?'

Saturday obliged with the finest of spring weather.

Eric did not wait until we had left the town behind before he took my hand, and when we passed an elderly couple he held it still more firmly in protest at their disapproving stare. Taking our time, we climbed the grassy slope of the Clausberg, walking side by side in that strange unison of spirit which abhors compulsive and casual conversation, and which made me feel as if we had known each other for a long time.

The wooden seat, into which generations of young couples had carved hearts and initials, overlooked an undulating field of daffodils.

'Now for a lesson in English poetry,' said Eric, and he opened a small leatherbound book. ' "I wandered lonely as a cloud . . ." '

In the days to come, Eric made the English countryside come to life in my mind through the power of his narration and the medium of poetry. I thought it must indeed be very beautiful in spring, if in his thoughts from abroad a poet had once yearned 'to be in England / now that April's there'; and that England must be a great country to live in if one of her soldier-poets had gone so far as to call the spot where he might die 'a corner of some foreign field / that is for ever England'. And more than ever I was resolved to see for myself what this England was like, this country so beloved by her poets, and once so hated and besmirched by Nazi propaganda.

The war had spared Eric more than his life: front-line soldiering had not removed the gentleness from his hands nor made him deaf to poetry or blind to the beauty of a wild flower; combat and barrack-room life had not roughened his speech and manners. And here was I, once again walking with a spring in my step and finding the mere grip of a hand to contain all the sweetness of being young and in love. And more: by accompanying my mentor on trips beyond my own horizons, sharing the results of his tentative philosophical probings and his discovery of some of the things said to be hovering between men, earth and heaven, I found my mind racing towards what promised to be its intellectual sunrise.

A clear night, a bed of grass, a uniform jacket spread out under me. We are lying on our backs, star-gazing, drunk with each other's company, with the balmy air and the scents of June, which seems to have turned the whole countryside into a garden.

Reluctant as we are to spoil with words the magic of the hour, the space between us soon begins to vibrate, and my view of the sky is obliterated. Eric's body feels warm and young and eager, but although my own desire is reaching far out into the night the preachings of my elders are keeping my lap closed. All at once the

295

sky returns into my field of vision. A voice is at my ear: 'Why not, darling, why not?' And I think of those who, prisoners of their own gentility, had always shunned the word sex as if it would burn their lips or had connotations of working-class impropriety; of those who, waving warning forefingers, had etched the slogan in my mind, 'A decent girl doesn't do it before she is married!' And I tell the man beside me about the code I was brought up to respect, like millions of other girls of my generation.

'There's something else,' I said. 'You people are here today and gone tomorrow, like trains steaming past, and leaving nothing behind but puffs of thinning smoke.'

'But I love you,' he protested, 'and I would marry you if it were possible.'

July brought incessant rain and a change of battalion. Eric took his leave and promised he would write and return one day to marry me. I settled down to read an anthology of English poems and, in the evenings, leaving my door ajar, I listened with self-tormenting pleasure to *Herr* Schuster's latest record – the heart-rending love-duet of *Tristan und Isolde*.

The local cobbler and shoemaker passed sentence on my last pair of shoes. 'I'm afraid they're beyond repair, *Fräulein*, even if I had leather, proper waxed thread, and nails! But I can sell you a pair with wooden soles. I salvaged the material from a German army dump. Mind you, the uppers are a bit stiff . . .'

I squeezed my feet into clog-like contraptions and hobbled around the shop. 'They're far too small!' I cried.

'I'm afraid they don't come any larger. In fact this is the last pair, and there won't be any more for some time. At least they would keep your feet dry!'

Twenty-four hours later my feet were screaming with blisters and my gait was like that of an old Chinese woman whose feet had been bound in her youth.

As luck would have it, a former shoe salesman called Lebe-schön came to pick up a translation. His cheeks and waistline belied the lean diet of the postwar months, his suit showed no threadbare or mended patches and his own fine leather shoes obviously did not torture their wearer. He pulled out his wallet.

'How much do I owe you, *Fräulein*?'

In reply I took off my shoes and showed him my suffering feet.

Herr Lebeschön slapped his knees. 'Hm, I take your point. Your poor feet! A young lady like you oughtn't to have to walk around in footwear like that. Just leave it to me. I'll get you a decent pair of shoes. No problem for Uncle Egon. What size do you take? Any preference in colour or style?'

Herr Lebeschön was, of course, not the only crafty citizen to make a good living by procuring and bartering commodities which had long been unobtainable or in scarce supply.

At the inn one evening, a draught blew open *Herr* Schuster's door just as I stepped into the corridor, so giving me a full view of his room, and of crates and boxes stacked high in a corner. Caught uncorking a bottle, and humming the opening bars of the *Tannhäuser* overture, he shot forward and closed the door with the air of a man who has something to hide. The last thing I noticed were his suede shoes which looked as if they were brand-new. But hard as I tried, I was unable to find out more about the well-dressed, well-shod permanent resident from number two – who, judging by appearances, was not only a large-scale black-market operator, but lived in a room which reminded one of a warehouse, sounded like a Wagnerian set, and smelled of English cigarettes, alcohol and urine.

A country road. Fields long harvested and freshly ploughed. Bronze colours dancing in roadside trees. Bold breezes brushing through leaves, showering them to the ground like confetti. A swarm of rooks taking off as if to a given signal, moving through the sky like a flying carpet, its edges flapping, its shape changing with every manoeuvre.

I was trudging back to town, pondering over the success of my Sunday pilgrimage to the district dairy. *Herr* Werner, the proprietor and a former client of mine, a man as round as an Edam cheese and smelling of sour milk, had been generous: a section of Brie, a quarter pound of butter, a slab of *Weisskäse*. As a bonus he had spared me his usual protestations that production had to be accounted for down to the last gramme and litre.

I was quickening my steps at the thought of the treat ahead, when a British army jeep shot up from behind and braked hard. An officer opened the door invitingly.

'Would you like a lift back to town, *Fräulein*? It is still a good four miles to go.'

'Yes, please!'
It had all been so easy.

Paul entered my life at a crucial moment. With Eric long gone, and his occasional letters failing to evoke in me more than a weak echo of our short romance, I longed more than ever for someone to laugh and talk and stroke my loneliness away.

A captain in his late thirties, and a sculptor and stonemason in civilian life, Paul had the build of an athlete and the rugged features of a mountain shepherd. Yet he was soft-spoken and mild-mannered, a man of insight and perception who weighed his words and smiled readily. The war had called him away from work on an English cathedral, from a craft which I had always associated with man's effort to praise God, and to gain himself immortality in stone.

Detached from his unit in Hanover to set up a local PCLU,[5] he had taken quarters in a requisitioned house in Bahnhofstrasse, where he soon found himself a not altogether welcome presence in an all-German street.

'I feel like a thorn in their flesh,' he joked, for he was not impervious to the tight-lipped, scornful stares of his neighbours. I sympathised: had I not been subjected to the same?

Paul did not need to look at my ration card to realise that my stomach was in a constant state of rumbling. He arranged for his driver to deliver sandwiches to me in the mornings, and at the end of the second week he asked his batman to draw extra rations and set his table for two at the weekends. I voiced no objections, savouring rashers of bacon and eggs and strange little sausages and roast beef and chocolate pudding. But it was not just a comfortable stomach which endeared Paul to me. Thoughtful and kind-hearted, he combined paternal qualities with those of a friend; and when he finally opened his arms I flung myself into them, discarding the conventions of my upbringing without any excuses, regrets or twinges of guilt. The years of wagging index fingers had come to an end.

With their eyes here, there and everywhere, and particularly on my comings and goings, some people in town began to point at

[5] (Brit.) Pioneer and Civil Labour Unit.

me, and one day two stern-faced, gossiping matrons raised their voices when I passed.

'She's taken up with that tall Englishman in Bahnhofstrasse. *Frau* Kuhn says she saw her leaving his place at seven in the morning!'

'Did she really! Well, I bet my Sunday hat they won't have been telling each other fairy stories all night!'

'She wouldn't have been mending his socks either! Of course, she's from Berlin. They have no shame, those city girls!'

How were they to know of our quiet Saturday evenings together? Of hours spent in the silent harmony of a married couple, finding a pseudo-domestic bliss in reading or listening to the radio together, bending over a chess board or playing 'Lili Marlene' or *Wanderlieder* on the accordion before going to sleep in each other's arms as naturally, as unashamedly and inevitably as if we had worn wedding-rings? Nor did they see us walking in the hills on Sundays, putting as many kilometres as possible between us and those vituperative critics who had exchanged scurrilous talk for Sunday clothes and a devotional air.

'Would you like to come with me to a weekend shooting party?' Paul asked me one day. 'Wild boars, on a large estate. There'll be five of us, three subalterns, one sergeant and myself in charge. Our host is a German ex-officer and gentleman farmer, quite a jovial chap – owns hundreds of acres, half of it forest. He had to request the shoot officially, since Germans – even farmers – aren't allowed to keep firearms. Do come along. It should be good fun and the fresh air will do you good.'

'But I have no proper shoes,' I wailed, 'no proper clothes! And won't I feel out of place?'

Paul waved my arguments aside. 'My dear girl, you'll be my guest, and you'll pass scrutiny in whatever you're wearing and whatever company you're in. So don't worry! Here, try on one of my army pullovers. Splendid! Now all we need is a pair of boots. Jack!' he shouted.

The batman entered. 'Sir?'

'Can you get this young lady a pair of boots or wellingtons?'

'No problem, sir!'

It was to be a memorable weekend.

Paul showed me how to carry, hold and shoot a rifle. But given a chance to fire the first shot at what to me looked like a harmless, overgrown pig with a long snout and a cute ringlet tail, which had frozen to the spot in sheer fright, I aimed well above the creature's head, chipping the bark off a tree.

'You were lucky he didn't charge you, *Fräulein*!' said the gamekeeper and grinned. 'Wild boars can behave like bulls. And what with their tusks and your red headscarf . . .!'

At the end of the hunt our host counted the number of carcasses.

'A fine bag, gentlemen!' he said in nearly flawless English. 'They've been a plague. Without rifles, you see, we had to let them breed unchecked. They practically raided the fields last winter, and they damaged a lot of trees. Perhaps you'll come again?'

'It could be arranged,' said Paul. 'You organise the beaters, and we'll bring rifles and English beer.'

'Agreed!' The slim man in his sober forester's suit summoned his gamekeeper and pointed to the kill. 'Take care of them, Walter. One for the house, one for you, two for the British officers' mess, one for the men . . .' And turning to his guests, 'Now, gentlemen, let's walk back to the house and end the day in style. How does your old English hunting song go? "D'ye ken John Peel with his coat so grey . . ."?'

English voices rose tentatively, but much as they tried they could not get beyond the first few lines. A young lieutenant struck up a marching song, another offered to carry my rifle. Paul took my arm. The Scottish sergeant said, 'Now roll on some grub and booze!'

The note for the evening was set.

With my cheeks still glowing, and feeling ravenous from stalking for hours through the forest and across fields bared to a bracing October wind, I joined heartily in a meal of roast pork and crackling, fist-sized dumplings and red cabbage. A full-bodied red wine fired our spirits and triggered off some riotous singing round a spitting hearth. Finally, with my inhibitions gone, and Paul's arm around my shoulders, I allowed myself to be coaxed into singing, '*Sah ein Knab ein Röslein stehen*', a performance which, duly applauded, inspired the Naafi beer-happy sergeant to give a husky, nostalgic rendering of 'My heart lies in the Highlands'.

Next morning I woke to the scent of fresh pinewood. Sunshine filtered through the shutters. From the kitchen there rose a muted clatter of plates, the smell of ground coffee and freshly-baked rolls. Outside the window, birds were chirping away as if they owned the place. My eyes wandered through the sleeping landscape of Paul's face, and suddenly neither past nor future seemed to exist.

'Tell me something about your country!' I begged him one Sunday, when an early dusk and rain spluttering against the windows in Bahnhofstrasse had shrunk the world to the size of the room. I did not have to ask twice. Turning tourist guide, he took me on a double-decker bus ride through London, in a motor launch up the Thames, by rail to quaint towns, by car to thatched villages, by coach to Oxford. Stately buildings and graceful country gardens took shape in my mind, together with the sombre beauty of the Welsh hills, Wordsworth's lakes, the poetry of Kentish orchards. It was Oxford, however, which in his descriptive *tour de force* evoked the most vivid and haunting pictures in my mind: turrets and spires topping noble colleges; quadrangles set against the tranquillity of spring meadows; punts gliding noiselessly down the Cherwell past laughter and necking under trees; young men in vacant mood, lazing about on exquisite carpets of turf or, books by their side, resisting the temptations of less studious pursuits. Crowded bookshops, crowded Saturday dance halls. Long gowns, short gowns. A city steeped in history and tradition, teeming with cyclists. A place abounding with spring and summer beauty, vibrating with life in term-time and feigning sleep during vacations.

'I'd love to go to Oxford,' I said. 'How would I set about it?'

Paul's answer was blunt. 'I think it will be some time before Germans are allowed to visit Britain. So soon after the war, they're not exactly popular at home. It'll take time for public opinion to change.'

'I understand,' I said. 'But you'll see – I'll get there one day!'

'I'm sure you will, pet. With your determination everything is possible.'

The wettest, bleakest and most blusterous month of the year was drawing to a close when Paul received his posting orders. Calmly, like a man who had come to a decision after much deliberation, he braced me for the imminent end of our relationship.

'Cruel as it may sound, I feel my posting and my home leave have come just in time. If I were to stay on, Marianne, I might not have the strength to leave you. I have fallen in love with you.' He pulled me towards him. 'I've never made a secret of the fact that I'm a married man and the father of two children. Look at it from my point of view: my wife and I have been married for fifteen years, it's been a good marriage, and I love my children. Do you understand, pet, my old ties are too strong!'

My skin broke out in goosepimples. Once again, my mother disappeared behind a gate; once again, I was sitting on a white bed in a white room in white sunshine; I waved goodbye to Sebastian, Alistair and Eric, and I saw Paul gingerly stepping out of my life. The sensation of nakedness returned, of bare skin exposed to arctic temperatures, of a landscape alive with past and present fears – the angst of crossing a new threshold, of a bomb that might stop whistling, of rape, of a lonely room . . .

'Of course you must go,' I heard myself saying as firmly as a selfless screen heroine might bid her lover goodbye. And I realised that while Paul had chiselled his memories of his wife and children in stone, those he would be taking back had been traced in drifting sand.

There came the moment when I walked back to the inn alone, to a room I had come to hate and which in its shabbiness reminded me only too clearly of the life to which I would wake up the next morning.

As I curled up in bed that night, I decided to embark on one of the riskiest adventures of the second postwar year: I would try and make my way to Berlin for Christmas, to heap upon my mother my stored-up love and let her benefit from the resilience of my youth. But how was I to get across the zonal border? Who would be able to pinpoint a weak link in the tight Russian patrol chain? Who would know where to contact a guide able to find his way through the forest in the deep of the night?

There was only one man who might know.

Herr Schuster's face showed little surprise when I outlined my plan. He fetched a map and spread it on the hall table.

'Try and get a train south. There aren't many running yet – a third of the rail network no longer exists. Get off here, and walk a few kilometres to this village.' *Herr* Schuster's index finger travelled expertly across the southwestern approaches of the lower Harz Mountains. 'You'll probably find people already waiting in the village. You'll recognise them by their rucksacks and anxious faces. Wait for a guide to make you up into a group. They never take more than eight or ten people at a time and, of course, they'll charge you for their services. After all, it's their risk as well.'

'Is the frontier marked?' I enquired naively.

'It's a drawing-board line, *Mädchen*,' *Herr* Schuster explained with the patience of a schoolmaster. 'There's about a hundred metres of buffer space between the two zones. The British keep to their side, but the Russian patrols are unpredictable, not very particular at night about straying a little west. There have been many incidents. If you manage to make it across, keep low for a while, steer clear of the first village and give anything that smells, sounds or looks Russian a wide berth. Try and reach a railway station. They have a few single-track trains running over there – the idiots pulled up most of the parallel tracks after the war. Once you're past the first village you ought to be all right. Good luck!'

I thanked *Herr* Schuster and, wanting to leave an agreeable impression, pointed to his closed door behind which the room seemed to tremble with the lofty sounds of Wagner.

'What lovely music!'

'*Lohengrin*, prelude to the first act!' He looked pleased and instantly launched into an eloquent description of the Holy Grail motif.

There were six days to Christmas. An icy, easterly wind had been sweeping over the town for days, numbing all life in the normally busy market square and turning every pool of rain water into an icy rink. The sun had not yet risen, and the only early morning sounds in the street were the rattle of milk cans.

It was the hour at which I set out on my journey.

EPILOGUE

'England, here I come!'

Zu neuen Ufern lockt ein neuer Tag.
Goethe, *Faust*, I[1]

There have been many periods in my life which I can recall as vividly as if I were living through them again. Indeed, I shall never cease to be amazed at the mind's ability to recapture with uncanny precision colours, sounds, smells, a landscape, the tenor of a conversation, the pitch of an emotion. And there have been months or even years which would be almost entirely forgotten were it not for single incidents projecting like poplar trees from an otherwise flat landscape.

It is against such images that I remember the period between my failed attempt to cross the border in 1946 and the currency reform in June 1948, a momentous event which proved a milestone in the German economy and in most people's lives:

My grandmother had died – from starvation according to my mother, from the lack of a hospital bed, drugs and milk and butter, according to the doctors. My father had died, and although his physician spoke of cardiac arrest, I suspected that his spirit had finally broken. I had eventually managed to visit my mother in Berlin, smuggling myself across the border and back in goods wagons. At the inn, the hotly debated subject of German 'collective guilt' had made the voices of the regulars hoarse and the innkeeper's beer flow freely. *Herr* Schuster had taken himself and his business to more lucrative pastures, the local rifle club had re-opened without rifles, and a three-man band played polkas, tangos and waltzes for Saturday-night

[1] To new shores beckons another day.

dancing. I caught whooping cough, and over the period in question, suffered from scabies, boils, excessive thirst, anaemia, muscle cramps, diarrhoea and bleeding gums, while my translating business decreased as British military government transferred German business into the hands of German authorities.

On a Sunday towards the end of June 1948, heavy, rain-laden clouds had been casting a cheerless light on the town and the sullen faces of its inhabitants. Next morning, however, a perfect June day greeted the early risers, of which there were many. As uninhibited sunshine highlighted the many strange and wonderful sights that met their eyes, word of the overnight miracle raced through town.

Housewives, pensioners, children and refugees stared wide-eyed and open-mouthed at shop windows which, having been empty for years or stuffed with tatty signs, were suddenly flaunting their goods. In the shoemaker's window, ladies' and gents' shoes, in different sizes and colours, perched on makeshift supports; a dress shop displayed summer frocks and items of underwear, including such rarities as brassieres; in the butcher's window, fresh pot plants surrounded hefty chunks of bacon, *wurst* and tinned meat, while other traders offered equally coveted goods in return for Deutschmark – the new West German currency.

At the grocer's I pressed my nose against the window like a child mesmerised by a prewar Christmas toy display. Behind me, people gasped, each reacting to their own needs and dispositions.

'Do you see what I see?'

'Incredible! I keep pinching myself.'

'Fancy those bastards hoarding all that stuff while we were bloody starving and had nothing to wear! They should hang the lot!'

The atmosphere was explosive.

'If only they hadn't held on so long my wife might still be alive today,' croaked an old man whose suit looked two sizes too large.

A child summed up the overnight wonder: 'Mummy, is that real chocolate in there?'

But few window-shoppers bought any of the tempting goods they needed so badly. Every man and woman, regardless of age

308

and social station, now had the same amount of money in their pockets – forty Deutschmark, the per capita quota issued on Sunday in the three Western zones at local banks and town halls. The Reichsmark was no longer worth the paper it was printed on. With the stroke of a pen, and behind a screen of official secrecy, millionaires and paupers had been made equal in monetary terms overnight – at least until some financial genius had worked out a formula under which to convert assets.

As from today, the customer would be king again, shop-keepers would put on smiles and practise the art of persuasion: '*Guten Morgen, Frau* Müller, what shall it be today?' And weighing, looking at the scales, they would ask sweetly, 'A few grammes more, all right?'

Painters, joiners and plumbers, too, would descend from their Olympian heights and offer their services for good new money. Competition would be keen, any type of work being undertaken, any kind of job eagerly sought. How else was one to pay for food and rent and whatever might ease life or add a pinch of joy to it? And every new mark earned, saved or invested – or so the first economic visionaries among the crowd explained – would improve living standards and form the basis of new private capital.

But who, I reflected, would want to spend a single mark on a translation on this memorable Monday, or in the weeks to come?

As expected, I did not have a single customer for three weeks. One morning I found my office broken into and my typewriter stolen. I arranged for my desk and chairs to be returned to the town hall, took down the shop-window sign and calmly walked away, under my arm one valuable object the thieves had overlooked or spurned: my English dictionary. I did not look back. Somehow, it had been a painless operation, and one I was sure would leave no scars.

Next day I registered with the Civil Labour Unit.

'We have a vacancy for an English-speaking switchboard operator in an officers' leave centre. It'll be shift-work. All meals provided.'

I accepted.

I had been in my post for two weeks, and was working the Saturday late shift, when the English manager rang.

'Miss Gärtner, will you come up to my room. I'd like to dictate a letter.'

'I can't do shorthand, sir,' I said, wondering what letter could be so important that it could not wait until Monday and for his secretary. I did not like the manager. I did not like his dark hair, which looked lacquered, nor his eyes, which looked hungry. I did not like the napoleonic pose he assumed in his dealings with staff, and once I had heard him speak like a kitchen hand to a waiter who had incurred his displeasure.

'The manager wants me to take a letter, *Herr* Martin,' I told the concierge, whose regal presence in the reception area conferred grand hotel status on the centre.

Herr Martin's bushy eyebrows shot up. He glanced at his watch. 'Hm, does he? Well, off you go then, but keep your wits about you!'

I knocked feebly against the door.

The manager was sipping a drink on the edge of his bed. His shirt was open and his shoes were off. The room was throbbing to a trumpet solo, accompanied by saxophone and percussion instruments. The record sounded scratched.

'Sit down, *Fräulein*! No, not there, come and sit next to me!'

I moved a chair towards the bed. It seemed a reasonable compromise.

'Like a drink?' he asked and picked up the phone. 'Jack, get me two Bloody Marys!'

'The letter, sir.'

'Ah, yes, the letter. Come, tell me something about yourself.'

While I was giving the sketchiest account of my life, he loosened his belt. I watched a cigarette dangling from his mouth and waited for the moment when the stub of ash would drop and burn a hole in the eiderdown.

'I'm a trumpeter by profession,' he confessed. 'Used to play in a big band until the war. London, Blackpool, all the big spots. Gawd, what a bloody marvellous time the boys and I had!'

A waiter entered with two cocktails and silently withdrew.

'Here's to you, *Fräulein*!' The manager raised his glass. 'What's your first name?'

'Marianne.'

'Marianne,' he repeated, as if he were stretching a piece of elastic. A hand patted the bedclothes, another reached for my leg. 'Come on, girl, don't be prudish!'

310

I sprinted out of the room and back to the switchboard, hair flying. *Herr* Martin gave me a quizzical look, then breathed a sigh. 'That was a quick one! *Ja, Ja,* we've lost the war in more than one way!'

Next morning I found my employment terminated. No reason for my dismissal was given.

There were other jobs, off-beat, boring and often disagreeable. For some I applied in vain, and one did not last longer than two days. In their temporariness and idiosyncratic nature they all reflected the postwar and postmonetary reform era.

'What a profile! What an interesting hairline!' The local milliner and self-confessed former pillar of Hamburg's hat *haute couture* turned my face sideways and studied the shape of my head like an archaeologist a neolithic skull. American hit tunes were drowning the buzz of the town café where I was sharing a table with the lady and her companion – a young, smooth-looking beau.

Impeccably dressed and coiffured, the milliner was wearing one of her own creations. She looked curiously out of place in the provincial climate in which a hat was something made of felt and worn for church, weddings and funerals.

'Call me *Frau* Leonie,' she said, and introduced the young man at her side. 'Alexander is my photographer, hairdresser, cook, accountant, and *bel ami* – in short a genius!'

I shook a flabby hand.

'Would you like to model hats?' *Frau* Leonie asked. 'It would involve long hours in front of a mirror and cameras, to get your face and my hats into fashion magazines. I expect to be going back to Hamburg before long. Mark my words, hats will soon be *de rigueur* again for ladies. They'll do away with those ghastly wartime head-scarves and the utility hats of the Thirties!'

I smiled at the prospect of a job and *Frau* Leonie ordered another round of coffee and cakes for me before inviting me back to her flat and deciding on the first step that would launch me into my new career.

For an hour I sat patiently at a dressing table. Alexander manipulated my hair, plied it with curling tongs, rouged my cheeks and wielded a lipstick. He asked me to look arrogant or seductive or innocent, to suit the individual style of a hat, and when I went home I had five Deutschmarks in my pocket.

Next morning my hair was bleached. *Frau* Leonie explained that in her business one chose a face, a profile, a shape of head, and styled, dyed or peroxided a model's hair, in order to suit each *création*, not vice versa.

When the transformation was complete, I looked aghast at my flaxen-haired image. The hat artiste stayed ominously quiet.

'I'm sorry,' she said finally, raising her kimono-sleeved arms and looking like an exotic bat. 'Your skin tone, the colour of your eyes . . . they are totally at odds with your hair. The effect I had hoped to achieve just didn't come off. Perhaps we ought to try a reddish tint or dye it a deep . . .'

I reached for my coat and stormed outside, fuming, crying, furiously calculating how many weeks it would take for this yellow monstrosity to grow out.

The Labour Office sent me to see a British medical officer.

'Would you be free to take on the job of chaperone and interpreter?'

'Yes, sir!'

The doctor spent a week examining German girls and women who had applied for work as kitchen staff and waitresses in British army messes for signs of skin and venereal disease. For a week I wore a white coat and translated the doctor's instructions to each candidate.

'Please turn slowly around! Please stand with your legs wide apart! Thank you!'

For a week I felt their embarrassed respectability flood my face.

'Wanted: intelligent, English-speaking lady as assistant to Brunswick private investigator.'

I instantly replied to the advertisement. Not only was my rent due, but I was ready to accept any kind of work, especially – as the nature of the job implied – if it promised excitement and adventure not likely to be found within a small town's boundaries.

Herr Wendish, a balding, middle-aged man, representing a one-staff, one-room agency, studied my papers with forensic thoroughness.

'Have you any idea what the job involves?' he asked, and I described assignments worthy of Dr Watson.

Herr Wendish smiled indulgently. 'My dear girl, I am not playing Sherlock Holmes. I undertake discreet investigations into the lives of private individuals and report my findings to my clients. And I don't ask too many questions. After all, I have to make a living. If I were to take you on as an assistant, you'd have to be prepared to spend long hours hanging around a house or a barracks gate, or sitting in a café over too many cups of lousy coffee. Sometimes your work would take you to a dance hall where British soldiers meet German women, and sometimes you'd be required to find out how far . . . er, intimacy goes, I mean whether a couple is . . . or is not . . .'

'I understand,' I said.

'To be straight with you,' the man behind the desk continued, 'you'd be a kind of snooper, and you'd need a pretty thick skin for the job.'

I nodded.

Herr Wendish lit a Players. 'There's nearly always a woman involved, you see. After the war a lot of German women went for English soldiers like wasps for the jam pot. "The *Engländer* are so nice, so polite!" they say. A mess or dance hall is of course warm in winter, and drinks, real coffee, food and a bit of love are welcomed by many whose husbands were killed or who returned with a leg gone . . . Others used to do it for cigarettes and nylons, now they're doing it for Deutschmarks and – yes, some because they've fallen in love.' He flipped through a file. 'Here are some parents who are looking for their daughter – a pretty thing, just eighteen. She was last seen in town in one of those shady night-clubs that have lately mushroomed out of our ruins. For all I know she may now be a regular in some crummy Hamburg *Reeperbahn* joint, or walking the streets around Frankfurt or Hamburg Central. I hope you don't mind my speaking so frankly about such a subject, it's all part of the scene.'

'I don't,' I said. 'I am an adult.'

'So you are indeed!' *Herr* Wendish played with a smile and leaned back, arms crossed over his chest.

'You see, the war has thrown up so many people. Men and women, returning from where they got stranded in 1945, prisoners released from Russian camps and other lost souls with no family and no job to go back to. Many just started drifting.'

313

I remembered Hamburg's central station: ghostly figures in torn army coats, loitering, picking up discarded cigarette ends as if they were gold coins, shuffling from one cheap food stall to another in the hope of salvaging some edible scraps – men with grey, tired eyes who seemed to be waiting for a better future, for a train that would never come. And I remembered the children: dirty waifs in rags, roaming the concourse like stray dogs, some with outstretched hands, some sucking their thumbs. Nor would I ever forget the spivs, their oily hair, their inscrutable faces in which all that was alive were shifty eyes; or the women, some of them not long out of their teens, their hair bleached a tint too blonde, their lips painted a shade too crimson, their smiles as hollow as their rouged cheeks.

'I went through Hamburg Central last year,' I said.

Herr Wendish saw his next cue. '*Ja, ja*, the main railway stations – the magnets for many whom the war has jettisoned, the hunting grounds of black marketeers, procurers, touts, whores, the lot. Any services offered, anything sold for a quick mark. Positively Dantesque! But you're too young to know about the corrupting effects of a lost war!'

I stayed silent. There seemed no point in contradicting my interviewer.

'By the way,' he asked, 'what have you done to your hair?'

My eyes burned a hole into the carpet.

Herr Wendish reached into his wallet and handed me a five-mark note. 'Here, to cover your fare. Thank you for coming up. You'll be hearing from me. Excuse me if I don't show you out. My blessed leg – all wood!'

As I opened the door I saw my employment prospects flattening out. Indeed, I never heard from Brunswick's affable private eye again.

A telephonist's job came up at garrison headquarters on top of the Osterberg hill.

'Good morning, sir!', 'Please hold the line, sir.' I was back at a switchboard, handling calls as expertly and as smoothly as an operator in a grand hotel.

On my first morning on duty, junior officers, sergeants and corporals put their heads around the door to meet the German lady who was now manning the battalion's switchboard. Some came with offerings of tea and biscuits, others for a quick chat.

314

In the afternoon, a young sergeant turned up, whose dashing looks caught my breath.

'Hello, what have we got here?' he cried, straddling a chair. 'Word got round. It reached the sergeants' mess at the soup stage, and the officers' dining room by the time they were on to biscuits and cheese. I had to see for myself.' And – seeing my baffled face – 'Well, they say that we have not only got ourselves a German *Fräulein* who speaks and understands our lingo but, by gawd, she's got looks, too!'

'Haven't you people ever met a German girl before?' I asked.

'Some of the lads haven't, not one of real flesh and blood.' His smile was contagious. 'Would you like some chocolate? A cigarette?'

'I don't smoke.'

The sergeant did not lose any time. 'Would you like to come to the pictures or a dance with me sometime?'

Calls were coming in, and I busied myself with plugging and unplugging cords and taking a message from the *Herr Bürgermeister* to the *Herr* Commanding Officer. A hand lightly touched my shoulder, and the door clicked shut. Within the reach of my hand a bar of chocolate was winking at me.

Henceforth I spent more time in front of the mirror and even applied a touch of lipstick. At work, the daily visit of my knight without armour regularly sent me into a state of confusion, making me tangle up calls, or stammer to the voice at the other end of the line. Finally, not wanting to risk my reputation at the switchboard, and bowled over by Lancelot's blue eyes, I chose a quick and attractive remedy: I accompanied the sergeant to the next dance, and now woke up smiling in the mornings, stretching out my arms, welcoming another day.

But there was little time to delight in the new affairs of the heart: I was looking for new shores in my life. I had a paid job, a hot meal a day and plenty of sweet tea, and I was treated with respect and kindness by HQ staff, if not by some with an affection they might normally reserve for the unit's mascot. Yet I could not rid myself of a growing awareness that I had reached another turning point. The battalion would leave one day, another would take over the barracks complex and with it, like a piece of indented furniture, its switchboard operator – someone to take for granted just as I had come to take my job and its

315

fringe benefits for granted. Or was I rebelling against its monotony, against my mind not being stretched beyond simple operations and a set of stock phrases, a mere street organ grinding away at a fixed set of tunes? I want more! I kept telling myself. I want to study and see and do hundreds of things. And I long to go and see England through the eyes of the men who through poetry, or the powers of their descriptions, had planted haunting images in my mind.

As the days went by such cherished notions changed from compulsive daydreams into an obsession, until one morning I took my decisive step.

I replied to an advertisement inviting unmarried German girls up to the age of twenty-seven to apply for posts in England as student nurses or hospital domestics, and it was not long before I was short-listed and appeared before a selection committee made up of British ministry of labour officials. A spate of questions: 'What are your motives for wanting to go to England? Do you hope to marry an Englishman once you are over there? Do you object to a thorough medical examination? You know what we mean ... we have to be careful ... the postwar conditions ... many German women ...'

As soon as their interviewers had finished their verbal and visual scrutiny I saw my chance.

'I should like to go to Oxford,' I said.

'Why Oxford?'

'I have heard so much about it, and I'd like to study English language and literature in my spare time.'

Puzzled, the members of the panel looked at each other, and the lady who appeared to be in the chair, who wore a huge silver brooch on her prim blouse like a *Ritterkreuz*,[2] brusquely explained that there were no places for German student nurses at Oxford, only vacancies for domestics.

'I don't mind what kind of work I do,' I said.

She shrugged her shoulders. 'We automatically assumed you wanted to train as a nurse. A girl with your education and background!' She consulted a document. 'I think you'd be happier as a student nurse. The course would be equally demanding and involve a lot of study and sitting exams.'

[2] Knight's Cross.

316

'I should like to go to Oxford, please!' I persisted.

The panel remained silent. Hands flipped through papers, heads bent over typed lists. At last the chairlady's voice rose above whispered consultations.

'We could give you a domestic job at an Oxford teaching hospital. It would involve hard work: scrubbing and polishing floors, cleaning wards, doing shifts in the scullery . . .'

'I don't mind,' I said.

'. . . and you'd need a lot of elbow grease!'

'I beg your pardon?'

'You'd need to put a lot of elbow power behind your scrubbing brush.'

'Oh yes.'

'At the end of the day you'd be very tired,' someone else remarked. 'You'd be working with girls who are socially . . . who come from different backgrounds.'

'I don't mind,' I repeated, hoping I did not sound too much like a parrot, not dreading the challenge, but smiling inwardly at the prospect of kneeling on a floor, wielding a scrubbing brush with a 'greased elbow' while trying to memorise Hamlet's soliloquy or a romantic poem. I was not afraid of hard work: on the contrary, it would be an experience. Did the panel not realise that life in Germany since the end of the war had been anything but a bed of roses?

'Well, if you're sure that's what you want?' the chairlady inquired cautiously, like a barrister giving his client a last chance to retract a compromising statement.

'I'm sure!' I said, seeing myself sitting in an Oxford library, buried in a pile of books, gliding down the river Cherwell in a punt, soaking up all the enchantment, all the grace and grandeur of the colleges . . .

'Very well then!' she pronounced. 'It's Oxford for you! But remember, it's not language students they want back home, but girls ready to work hard, girls with a sense of duty, who will earn every penny of their salary and free return-fare. Remember, too, that each one of the girls we are choosing will become an ambassadress of her country. Life will not always be easy for you. Some men and women can't or won't forget. You may come across resentment, even hatred. British people have suffered, too, you know. So don't expect to be welcomed with open arms!'

'But it will be a beginning!' said an elderly man. His voice was laced with gentleness.

Two weeks later I joined a contingent of female labour and nursing recruits in a transit camp, to be registered, case-filed, chest x-rayed, weighed, examined for lice, boils, malnutrition, bad teeth and venereal disease ('Please stand with your legs wide apart, *Fräulein*! Thank you!'). I received vitamin pills and had an obligatory bath and shampoo. For three days, girls who came from cities or villages, who had *Abitur* or school-leaving certificates, and whose fathers were professors, farmers, tradesmen or war invalids, slept in bunk beds eight to a room, took their meals together and sorted each other out. By the time we left camp, those who spoke the same social language, and who were leaving their homeland not simply in pursuit of brighter lights, and better food, warmer rooms or an English husband, had formed a distinct group.

We arrived at the Dutch port in vicious November weather. At the sight of the boat waiting to ferry us across the Channel, many among us, inexperienced travellers and strangers to the sea as we were, started dragging our feet. In the steadily stiffening wind, the veteran coaster was lying restlessly at anchor, slapped hard by waves rolling in from a choppy, steel-grey sea over which darkness was falling fast. As I walked up the gangway, a huge breaker covered with dirty foam caused a sudden violent pitching of the vessel, and seemed to augur ill for the passage ahead. Like the rest of my travelling companions, I went straight below deck, into a hold crammed with two-tier bunks and reeking of troops, tobacco and vomit.

As soon as the boat had weighed anchor and reached the open sea, it became clear to us landlubbers that this was not going to be a journey for squeamish stomachs. By midnight, the wind had reached gale force, and the vessel was pitching and tossing, the sea pounding against its hull as if threatening to break it apart. The moaning and retching of the bunk occupants joined the groaning and creaking of the ship. Roller-coasting, big-wheeling, riding on a merry-go-round, I felt I was serving sentence for every crime I had ever committed. Finally, with the last shred of my evening meal gone, and racked with the unproductive contractions of my stomach, no longer caring whether I reached the safety of an English harbour or ended up at the bottom of the sea, I fell asleep.

When I woke, daylight was creeping through the portholes. The vessel's rolling movements had moderated, and I spotted a patch of blue sky over dull green, yet infinitely humbler breakers. I went up on deck and, turning my face into the fresh breeze, greedily soaked up the salty spray.

Harwich. We have arrived. Before me lies the English coastline, the Promised Land, the country of my romantic postwar dreams and aspirations. As the boat docks, a welcoming committee comes into view: sober-hatted matrons manning long tables laden with tea urns and sandwiches, men and women in uniform, faces, stern, officious, tense, unsure of smiles, sizing up the young Germans who are clutching the railing. I ask myself: aren't we bound to evoke in the minds of the people on shore thoughts of the German bogeyman, memories of some loved one who died from a German bullet, bomb or torpedo? Might not pictures of concentration camp horrors, stories of SS atrocities, superimpose themselves upon the faces of the arrivals? Suddenly I feel uncomfortably German, so much so that I would gladly suffer the rigours of another turbulent crossing not to have to go ashore. But as I walk down the gangway with wobbly knees, I feel my spirit of survival return with a vengeance, and it calls out defiantly, 'England, England, here I come!'

A gentle-faced lady smiles at me and hands me a cup of tea. 'Welcome to England, my dear!' she says, and her eyes do not accuse.

A SELECTED LIST OF BIOGRAPHIES
AVAILABLE FROM CORGI BOOKS

The prices shown below were correct at the time of going to press. However Transworld Publishers reserve the right to show new prices on covers which may differ from those previously advertised in the text or elsewhere.

CORGI BIOGRAPHY SERIES

☐	99315 8	NO TIME FOR ROMANCE	*Lucilla Andrews*	£3.95
☐	99065 5	THE PAST IS MYSELF	*Christabel Bielenberg*	£3.95
☐	99271 2	MY HAPPY DAYS IN HELL	*George Faludy*	£4.95
☐	99314 X	A VOYAGER OUT	*Katherine Frank*	£4.95
☐	12833 3	THE HOUSE BY THE DVINA	*Eugenie Fraser*	£3.95
☐	12863 5	THE LONG JOURNEY HOME	*Flora Leipman*	£3.95
☐	99247 X	THE FORD OF HEAVEN	*Brian Power*	£3.50
☐	99293 3	THE PUPPET EMPEROR	*Brian Power*	£3.95
☐	99305 0	HELEN OF BURMA	*Helen Rodriguez*	£4.50

ORDER FORM

All Corgi/Bantam Books are available at your bookshop or newsagent, or can be ordered direct from the following address:

Corgi/Bantam Books,
Cash Sales Department,
P.O. Box 11, Falmouth, Cornwall TR10 9EN.

Please send a cheque or postal order (no currency) and allow 60p for postage and packing for the first book plus 25p for the second book and 15p for each additional book ordered up to a maximum charge of £1.90 in UK.

B.F.P.O. customers please allow 60p for the first book, 25p for the second book plus 15p per copy for the next 7 books, thereafter 9p per book.

Overseas customers, including Eire, please allow £1.25 for postage and packing for the first book, 75p for the second book, and 28p for each subsequent title ordered.

NAME (Block Letters) ....

ADDRESS ....

....